AQA English and English Language

Higher Tier

Lindsay McNab

Imelda Pilgrim

Marian Slee

Series Editor

Imelda Pilgrim

Nelson Thornes

Published in 2010 by:
Nelson Thornes Ltd
Delta Place
27 Bath Road
CHELTENHAM
GL53 7TH
United Kingdom

10 11 12 13 14 / 10 9 8 7 6 5 4 3 2 1

A catalogue record for this book is available from the British Library
ISBN 978 1 4085 0595 3

Cover photograph: Heather Gunn Photography
Page make-up by Pantek Arts Ltd
Illustrations by Paul McCaffrey; additional illustrations by Pantek Arts Ltd

Printed and bound in Spain by GraphyCems

Acknowledgements

The authors and publisher would like to thank the following for permission to reproduce material.

Source texts: p2 Copyright Guardian News & Media Ltd 2009; p3 Courtesy of www.myvue.com, HarperCollins Publishers Ltd. © 1954 J.R.R.Tolkien, Thomas Cook Publishing; p5 Copyright Merrily Harpur/Fortean Times 2008; p6 Copyright Press Association; p12 Urban Concepts Don't Trigger Campaign; p21 Beyond Facebook extracted from iPod & iPhone User magazine. © IDG 2009; p24 Beyond Facebook extracted from iPod & iPhone User magazine. © IDG 2009; p27 From Pies and Prejudice by Stuart Maconie, published by Ebury. Reprinted by permission of The Random House Group Ltd; p33 'The Weapon' by Fredric Brown. Copyright © 1951, by Fredric Brown, copyright © 1978, by the Estate. Originally appeared in Astounding Science Fiction, April 1951 and reprinted by permission of the Estate and its Agent, Barry N. Malzberg; p37 www.adelaidenow.com.au (author Charles Miranda); p39 © Mark Carwardine, BBC zoologist, photographer and author; p42 Paola Cavalieri copyright Guardian News & Media Ltd 2007; p46 Is That It?, Bob Geldof, Pan Macmillan copyright © Geldof, 2005; p52 © Don McCullin courtesy of nbpictures.com; p54 The Road To Wigan Pier by George Orwell (Copyright © George Orwell, 1937), reprinted by permission of Bill Hamilton as the Literary Executor of the Estate of the Late Sonia Brownell Orwell and Secker & Warburg Ltd; p56 from Speak to the Earth: Wanderings and Reflections Among Elephants and Mountains by Vivienne de Watteville, published by W.W. Norton & Co. Inc., 1987. Reprinted by permission of The Random House Group Ltd; p58 Amnesty International; p59 reproduced with permission of Médecins Sans Frontières UK (MSF UK); p68 © The Times, 11 September 2007/nisyndication.com; p69 York Archaeological Trust; p70 The Boy With No Shoes copyright © 2004 by William Horwood reproduced by kind permission of William Horwood c/o Caroline Sheldon Literary Agency Limited; Norman McCaig, 'Below the Green Corrie' from The Poems of Norman MacCaig edited by Ewen MacCaig (Polygon, 2005), reproduced by Polygon, an imprint of Birlinn Ltd www.birlinn.co.uk; p82 Bill Gates, Business @ the Speed of Thought, 2000. Reproduced by permission of Penguin Books Ltd; p88 Copyright Guardian News & Media Ltd 2005; p89 © Telegraph Media Group Limited 2008/2009; p94 Microsoft Ltd for an extract from Matthew Plowright, 'The 10 things we hate on our holidays', MSN Money, 15 August 2006; p95 Solo Syndication Ltd for an extract from Sean Poulter and David Derbyshire, '13 billion ways YOU can help', Daily Mail, 27 February 2008; p102 If Nobody Speaks of Remarkable Things. Bloomsbury, 2002; p106 Extract from Student Grub by J. Arkless (Right Way, 1996) by kind permission of the publishers, Constable & Robinson Ltd, Text courtesy of VisitGuernsey; p108 CQ Transcripts; p109 Witch Child by Celia Rees courtesy of Bloomsbury; p113 Daily Mail article courtesy of Solo Syndication; p113 courtesy of the Belfast Telegraph; p115 © The Times, 9 May 2009/nisyndication.com; p119 HarperCollins Publishers Ltd. © 2003 John Walsh; p120 'Compass and Torch' © Elizabeth Baines, from Balancing on the Edge of the World (Salt, 2007); p122 'Voodoo', by Fredric Brown, copyright (c) 1954, by Fredric Brown, copyright (c) 1982, by the Estate. Originally appeared in Angels and Spaceships and reprinted by permission of the Estate and its Agent, Barry N. Malzberg; p123 'First Ice' translated by Stanley Kunitz from An Arrow in the Wall: Selected Poetry and Prose by Andrei Voznesensky edited by William Jay Smith and F. D. Reeve. English language translation copyright © 1987 by Henry Holt and Company. Reprinted by arrangement with Henry Holt and Company, LLC; p124 From Lion's Head, Four Happiness by Xiamei Martell, published by Vintage. Reprinted by permission of The Random House Group

Ltd; p125 Skcin; The Karen Clifford Skin Cancer Charity; p126 © The Times, 28 June 2009/nisyndication.com; p128 This article appeared in Sugar Ladmag, February 2009 issue; p129 Extract from 'A Child's Christmas in Wales' from Collected Stories (Orion) by Dylan Thomas, reprinted by permission of David Higham Associates; p131 Excerpt by Mervyn Peake from Titus Groans (© Mervyn Peake, 1992) is reproduced by permission of PFD (www.pfd.co.uk) on behalf of The Estate of Mervyn Peake; p132 Reproduced with permission from Paris City Guide 6th Edition © 2006 Lonely Planet; p132 The Long Goodbye by Raymond Chandler (Penguin Books, 1959), copyright 1953 by Raymond Chandler; p133 © Telegraph Media Group Limited 2009; p134 from Mist in the Mirror by Susan Hill, published by Sinclair-Stevenson. Reprinted by permission of The Random House Group Ltd; p135 John Steinbeck (Penguin, 2000). Copyright © John Steinbeck, 1937, 1965, Of Mice and Men first published in 1943 by Josef Weinberger Ltd (pka English Theatre Guild Ltd). Copyright © 1937 by John Steinbeck, copyright renewed 1964. Reprinted by permission of Josef Weinberger Ltd; p155 Gill Frances.Copyright Guardian News & Media Ltd. 2006; p168 ActionAid; p168 Publisher WWF-UK www.wwf.org.uk/adoption/tigerquick; p188 Article reprinted with the permission of eHow, Inc., www.ehow.com; p191 CQ Transcripts; p195 Provided by internet.com, a division of QuinStreet, Inc.; p196 From The New York Times, © 25 May 2009. The New York Times All rights reserved. Used by permission and protected by the Copyright Laws of the United States. The printing, copying, redistribution, or retransmission of the Material without express written permission is prohibited. **Photographs:** p1(a) Alamy/Golden Pixels LLC, (b) Alamy/Dave Porter, (c) Rex Features/Sipa Press; p2 Alamy/Dave Porter; p4 iStockphoto; p6 iStockphoto; p8 Crimestoppers Trust; p13 Getty/Samir Hussein; p16(a) Bloomsbury, (b) Alamy/Photos 12; p18 Bloomsbury; p20 (a) Bloomsbury, (b) Penguin, (c) Bloomsbury; p23 Alamy/Heymo Vehse; p25 Alamy/The London Art Archive; p27 Alamy/nagelestock.com; p28 Getty/Michael McQueen; p30 Corbis/ Hulton-Deutsch Collection; p37 Getty/AFP; p39 Science Photo Library/Pat and Tom Leeson; p40 Photolibrary/Ian Mcallister; p42 Science Photo Library/Lawrence Migdale; p44 Fotolia; p46 Getty/Redferns/Mike Cameron; p48 Getty/Time Life Pictures; p52 Getty/Central Press; p55 Getty/Bob Thomas; p61 VII Network/Donald Weber; p68 Getty/John William Banagan; p76 Education Photos/John Walmsley; p81 Education Photos/John Walmsley; p84 Fotolia; p88 Getty Images; p95 © P. Wallerstein; p97 iStockphoto; p99 Photolibrary/Sodapix; p102 Getty/Charles Bowman; p104 Alamy/Paul White; p105 Fotolia; p106 Visit Guernsey Images/Chris George; p107 Getty/Clive Nichols; p108 Getty/Spencer Platt; p109 Fotolia; p120 Getty/Todd Warnock; p121 Photolibrary/Caroline Penn; p124 Random House; p125 L'Oreal; p126 Reuters/Nigel Roddis; p134 Dennis Gay; p135 Ronald Grant Archive; p136 Arenapal/Nigel Norrington; p147 Alamy/Pictorial Press; p148 Fotolia; p150 Alamy/Pictorial Press; p152 (a) Fotolia, (b) iStockphoto, (c) Getty/Spencer Platt,(d) Getty/Mark Allan; p155 Alamy/blickwinkel; p161 Ronald Grant Archive; p165 Rex Features/Paramount/Everett; p167 Photolibrary/Jon Feingersh; p168 (a) Action Aid/Liba Taylor, (b) Photolibrary/Anup Shah; p169 Barnardo's, BBH and Kiran Master for their advertisement; p178 Hat Trick Productions Limited; p184 (a) Heather Gunn Photography, (b) Getty/AFP; p188 Photofusion/Paul Doyle; p189 Getty/Stuart Franklin; p194 Alamy/Oote Boe Photography 2; p197 Photolibrary/Boutet Jean-Pierre.

Every effort has been made to contact the copyright holders and we apologise if any have been overlooked. Should copyright have been unwittingly infringed in this book, the owners should contact the publishers, who will make the corrections at reprint.

Contents

Section A — Reading

Section B — Writing

AQA GCSE English and GCSE English Language

Nelson Thornes and AQA

Nelson Thornes has worked in partnership with AQA to ensure that the student book and the accompanying online resources offer you the best support possible for your GCSE course. The print and online resources together **unlock blended learning**; this means that the links between the activities in the book and the activities online blend together to maximise your understanding of a topic and help you to achieve your potential.

All AQA-endorsed resources undergo a thorough quality assurance process to ensure that their contents closely match the AQA specification. You can be confident that the content of materials branded with AQA's 'Exclusively Endorsed' logo have been written, checked and approved by AQA senior examiners, in order to achieve AQA's exclusive endorsement.

About your course

This book has been written to guide you through your GCSE English or GCSE English Language. It will help you to develop skills you need to succeed, not only in your exams and assessments, but in whatever you decide to do afterwards.

You will either be studying for a GCSE in English or English Language. If you are studying GCSE English, you will be doing literature as part of this course. If you are studying GCSE English Language, you will also be taking GCSE English Literature.

Parts of this book are designed to develop your skills in reading, writing and communicating about a range of texts: non-fiction, literature, media and transcripts. So, whichever route through your GCSE you take, you will be well prepared.

How to use this book

The first three sections of the book each cover a key English skill:
- Reading
- Writing
- Speaking and listening

You will be assessed on each of these skills either by an exam or through a controlled assessment. After you've worked through each section, you are shown how to use these skills effectively when being assessed in the 'Making your skills count' chapters.

The fourth section of the book covers spoken language, which is tested only in GCSE English Language.

The final section of the book covers the basic rules of punctuation and spelling. Remember, you will gain marks for being able to spell and punctuate your work accurately.

The features in this book include:

Objectives

At the beginning of each chapter you will find a list of learning objectives that contain targets linked to the requirements of the specification.

Activity

Activities to develop and reinforce the skills focus for the lesson.

Check your learning

A list of points at the end of the chapter that summarise what you have covered.

Some (but not all) chapters feature:

Biography   Background

Biographies and backgrounds provide you with additional information about a writer or a text.

Key terms

Key term: term that you will find it useful to be able to define and understand. The definitions also appear in the glossary at the end of the student book.

Make a note

Useful points for you to keep a note of.

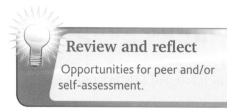

Review and reflect

Opportunities for peer and/or self-assessment.

Speaking and listening

Specific activities testing speaking and listening skills.

Stretch yourself

Extension activities to take the work in a chapter further.

 Top tip

Guidance from the examiners or moderators on how to avoid common pitfalls and mistakes, and how to achieve the best marks in the exam or controlled assessment.

Online resources

These online resources are available on **kerboodle!** which can be accessed via the internet at **www.kerboodle.com/live**, anytime, anywhere.

If your school or college subscribes to **kerboodle!** you will be provided with your own personal login details. Once logged in, access your course and locate the required activity.

Throughout the book you will see this icon whenever there is a relevant interactive activity available in **kerboodle!**.

Please visit **kerboodle.helpserve.com** if you would like more information and help on how to use **kerboodle!**.

Weblinks for this book

Because Nelson Thornes is not responsible for third party content online, there may be some changes to this material that are beyond our control. In order for us to ensure that the links referred to are as up-to-date and stable as possible, please let us know at webadmin@nelsonthornes.com if you find a link that doesn't work and we will do our best to redirect these, or to list an alternative site.

R eading plays a part in almost every area of our lives.

We read to:

- learn new things
- find out about the world we live in
- work out how to make things
- access essential information
- catch up on our friends and family
- experience pleasure and enjoyment.

As you have progressed through school you have developed your skills in reading. At first you learned to recognise a range of words and to understand their meanings. You have come a long way since then. You read frequently and often work out meaning without having to think too hard.

This section of the book will help you to further develop your skills in reading. You will focus on selecting information for purpose, exploring meaning and thinking about context, using inference and deduction, and analysing the writer's techniques and their effects on the reader.

The chapters in this section are designed to help you meet the Assessment Objectives that underpin your GCSE course. These are written for teachers but you might like to read them in full (they're explained in more detail on pages 66 and 77).

Candidates should demonstrate the ability to:

- Read and understand texts, selecting material appropriate to purpose, collating from different sources and making comparisons and cross-references as appropriate.
- Develop and sustain interpretations of writers' ideas and perspectives.
- Explain and evaluate how writers use linguistic, grammatical, structural and presentational features to achieve effects and engage and influence the reader.
- Understand texts in their social, cultural and historical contexts (GCSE English only).

By the end of this section you will have covered all of the skills outlined in the Assessment Objectives. By the end of your GCSE course you will have used these skills to help you write your controlled assessments and to complete Section A of your GCSE English or GCSE English Language exam.

But it doesn't stop there. You don't stop reading once your GCSEs are over. The writers of this book have chosen texts that they hope will interest you and that will make the experience of reading an enjoyable one so that, whatever you decide to do with your life after GCSE, you will continue to use and develop your reading skills.

1

Objectives

In this chapter you will:

read texts and show your understanding of them

select appropriate material to answer questions

explain how writers use words to affect the reader.

Top tip

Reading plays an important part in developing your skills in English. Aim to increase and vary your reading throughout your GCSE course.

Finding the answer

Reasons for reading

People read in different ways, depending on what they are reading and why they are reading it. Each of Texts A to E have distinguishing features to do with the ways in which they are organised and the presence or absence of visual prompts.

Activities

1 For Texts A to E, describe:
- what each text is
- the distinguishing features that helped you to identify each one.

2 For Texts A to E, explain:
- why you might be reading each one
- whether you would read the whole text or parts of it and the reasons for this.

3 a Make a chart like the one below listing all the different things you might read in a normal day and your reasons for reading them. Don't forget to include text read on screen.

Things I might read	Reason

b Compare your list with that of two or three other students to discover whether you read:
- less than average
- the average amount
- more than average.

4 Choose one of the things you might read in a normal day. Describe its distinguishing features in a way that would help another student to recognise what it is without seeing it. Test out your description on another student.

Rest of radio

Radio 1 97.6–99.8 MHz
6.30 The Chris Moyles Show **10.0** Annie Mac **12.45** Newsbeat **1.0** Fearne Cotton **4.0** Scott Mills **7.0** Zane Lowe **9.0** In New Music We Trust **10.0** Colin Murray **12.0** BBC Introducing **2.0** Ras Kwame **4.0** Max from 1Xtra

Radio 2 88–91 MHz
6.0 Sarah Kennedy **7.30** Terry Wogan **9.30** Richard Allinson **12.0** Jeremy Vine **2.0** Steve Wright **5.0** Chris Evans **7.0** Mike Harding **8.0** Mark Radcliffe **10.0** Trevor Nelson **11.0** Steve Lamacq

Radio Five Live 693, 909 KHz
6.0 Breakfast **9.0** Victoria Derbyshire **12.0** Midday News **1.0** Simon Mayo **4.0** Drive **7.0** 5 Live Sport **10.0** 6-0-6 **11.0** Richard Bacon **1.0** Up All Night **5.0** Morning Reports **5.30** Wake Up To Money

Xfm 104.9 MHz
6.0 Alex Zane **9.0** Ricky Shaw **1.0** Jo Good **4.0** Dave Berry **7.0** Music: Response With Steve Harris **10.0** X-Posure With John Kennedy **1.0** Overnights

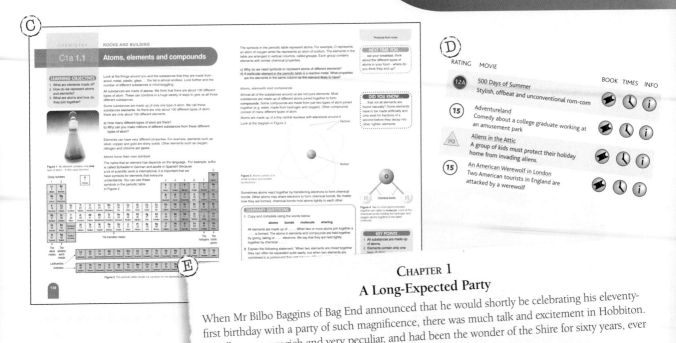

CHAPTER 1
A Long-Expected Party

When Mr Bilbo Baggins of Bag End announced that he would shortly be celebrating his eleventy-first birthday with a party of such magnificence, there was much talk and excitement in Hobbiton. Bilbo was very rich and very peculiar, and had been the wonder of the Shire for sixty years, ever since his remarkable disappearance and unexpected return …

J.R.R. Tolkien, *Lord of the Rings*, 1954

Reading for information

A common reason given for reading is to 'find out things'. In order to 'find out things' the reader needs to:

- read with understanding
- locate the information they need.

In some texts information is clearly 'signposted' to help the reader find the relevant details quickly, as in Text F, an extract from a travel guide about transport in New York City. Test your skills in locating the information you need by answering the questions that follow.

Arrival

By air

International flights arrive at **John F Kennedy (JFK)** Airport in Queens or **Newark** in New Jersey. From JFK, the quickest way into Manhattan is to take a taxi for a set rate plus bridge and tunnel tolls and a tip. Uniformed dispatchers will guide you towards the taxi stand and issue a leaflet outlining costs and regulations. Always take a licensed New York City taxi, painted yellow.

Both JFK and Newark are huge international airports, with several terminals spread out over a wide area. When leaving New York, if travelling by public transport, it is important to leave enough time for your bus to reach the right terminal. To be on the safe side, allow 30 minutes.

Getting around

MetroCards

Most people get around the city by **bus** or **subway** at $2 a ride, regardless of distance. In Manhattan, the most important thing to remember is whether you are going **uptown** (Bronx-bound) or **downtown** (Brooklyn-bound). Almost all lines travel up and downtown; to switch between east and west, take the 42nd Street shuttle between Grand Central and Times Square.

You must purchase a Metropolitan Transit Authority (MTA) **MetroCard** to ride the subway or buses. MetroCard vending machines are located in subway stations and accept cash and credit cards. Unlimited ride MetroCards permit hop-on, hop-off travel and, if you're in New York for a week and plan to use the

[continued overleaf]

subway regularly, offer better value. The MetroCard includes some museum discounts too.

Subway rides are fast; buses are handy for short trips and good for sightseeing, but they can be slow in traffic. One advantage of buses over the subway is that there are more cross-town routes – though, as Manhattan is only two miles wide, it may be quicker to walk. Bus maps are available from subway stations and the Visitors' Bureau in Columbus Square.

Taxis

Licensed taxis are metered, with the fare varying according to the distance travelled and time spent in traffic. Drivers will expect a tip of at least ten per cent – though you are in no way obliged to tip – and if you are going outside Manhattan you are also responsible for paying any bridge and tunnel tolls that you incur.

Yellow metered taxis (also called 'cabs') are everywhere and can be hailed from the street. Available taxis travel with a roof-top number lit, but they won't stop for customers if the sign's 'Off Duty' portion is lit.

Licensed taxis, which are yellow, have a medallion number on the roof and a driver's licence number on the dashboard.

Walking

Unlike other American cities, Manhattan seems designed for walking. From 14th Street to Central Park, the streets are laid out in a **grid system** with 'streets' running from east to west and 'avenues' from north to south. The only major exception is Broadway, an old Indian trail which refuses to conform.

Adapted from WHS, *Destination: New York*, 2005

Activities

5

a   In which direction is the downtown subway bound?

b   What are laid out in a grid system?

c   Name the two main airports serving New York City.

d   What is the best Metrocard to buy if you are in New York for a week?

e   How do you know if a taxi driver is off duty?

f   Where can you get bus maps?

g   Which main street does not conform to the grid system?

h   When taking a taxi, what must you pay for if going outside Manhattan?

i   Why should you allow an extra 30 minutes if travelling by public transport to JFK or Newark airport?

j   What advantage do buses have over the subway?

6   Check your answers with another student. Together, identify and list the **presentational features** or 'signposts' that are used in the 'New York City' text to help the reader find the relevant information quickly.

Finding the right details

Information in texts is not always so clearly signposted. Many texts are written in continuous prose. The reader has to scan the surface of the text to find specific details. This is a very useful skill to develop, particularly for research purposes.

Activity

7
You have to compile a record of 'Big Cat' sightings in the UK. Copy the following table and complete it using details from the article that follows (Text G).

Date	Time	Place	Eye-witnesses	Distinctive features
23 July 2008		Close to Soham		
	Evening			Taller and longer than German Shepherd dog Muscular Jet black Big paws Curled tail Large cat head Little pointed ears Loud growl
		Road between Easton and Weston, Portland Bill, Dorset	Martin O'Neill (prison officer)	

Review and reflect

Compare your chart with another student's. Where your answers differ, look again at the texts to find out which of you has selected the correct details.

(G)

Alien Big Cat Diary

Merrily Harpur of the Dorset Big Cat Register and Big Cats in Britain presents her bimonthly column of all the Alien Big Cat sightings fit to print with a round-up of activity during June and July 2008.

June – July 2008

It hadn't been spotted for quite a while, but on 23 July there were numerous reports of the sun having come out – and, along with it, emerged a representative sample of Britain's ABCs.

Alan Cleve was driving his freight train towards Ely in Cambridgeshire at 7.50 on that beautiful morning, when he had what he described as 'a WOW! moment'. He had just left Soham and was going at only about 65 km/h when an 'inky black' ABC crossed the track in front of him.

'It got up from one side of the track and walked across in a purposeful but leisurely way, glancing at me but not stopping. I had closed the distance to about 37 m before it disappeared into the undergrowth on the other side of the track. Its size was obvious as the track was a standard gauge 1.4 m wide, and it spanned the distance between the rails.'

On the same day, near Shrewsbury, Shropshire, Lorraine Fletcher and her daughter Chloë, out for an evening stroll by their local fishing pool near Mousecroft Lane in Radbrook, had the fright of their lives.

'We were first struck by the number of rabbits around,' reported Lorraine, 'and they were behaving quite erratically. Then we noticed a little black-and-white cat on the other side of the pool, about two houses width away from us, fleeing away very fast.' She added: 'We then saw emerge from the bushes – a massive, black, shiny panther. It was a bit taller than a German Shepherd dog and longer, more muscular. It was jet black, with big paws, a long curled tail, large cat head and little pointed ears. It growled very loudly – a deep roar turning into a high-pitched snarl, before padding off into the undergrowth. We just looked at each other as if to say "let's get out of here" and ran.'

The muscular, German Shepherd-sized, inky black ABCs that Alan, Lorraine and Chloë described are typical of about 80–85 per cent of ABCs reported. The remaining 20 per cent of animals described are often puma-like or lynx-like, but many display a confusing mixture of big cat characteristics. The third sighting of the day was of just such an animal: as closely and accurately observed as the other two.

On 23 July, on Portland Bill in Dorset, Martin O'Neill, a prison officer, was cycling home from work at 5.20 pm on the road between Easton and Weston. He was passing one of the area's famous stone quarries when an animal he at first assumed to be a dog came out from the quarry side through the hedgerow.

'I thought I was going to run it over as I was going quite fast and it had stopped to look at me when I was about 30 yards away. I stopped the bike to look at it, as I was taken aback. It was a cat about the size of an Alsatian or slightly smaller; fair in colour – tan with what I thought were stripes on its back. Its mouth was open as if it were panting with the heat. It had a cat's face, and cat's ears – pointed and quite large – and huge eyes. It then continued to amble across the road into the hedgerow on the right-hand side of the road. What struck me was its tail: it was as long as its body and really scraggly with 2–3 inch-long fur, and tapered. It was exciting – I feel lucky to have seen it.'

Adapted from *Fortean Times*, September 2008

Working out the meaning

Writers often imply certain things through what they say and how they say it. They do this to influence the reader. To become a good reader it is necessary to be alert to the implications and subtleties of a text. To do this, the reader needs to:

- question the content of what they are reading
- be aware of how writers use words to influence them.

Activity

8 Read Text H, the opening of a newspaper story about big cat sightings, and then answer the questions which focus on the implied rather than the stated meaning in the highlighted areas.

1 Why is 'reliable' in inverted commas? What might it be suggesting about other reports?

2 What is suggested by the use of the word 'revealed'?

3 What does this suggest about this information?

4 What is the writer emphasising by using this phrase?

5 Why do you think the writer has included this detail about the rangers?

6 What possibly relevant piece of information is not given to the reader?

H

1 '**Reliable**' big cat sightings **revealed** **2**

Two big cats were caught on camera by rangers who were filming a deer survey, the Forestry Commission revealed today.

3 Under a Freedom of Information Act request, the government agency confirmed that two 'reliable' sightings of large cats have taken place in the last seven years. Experts monitoring deer using thermal imaging cameras spotted the animals on two separate occasions in different parts **4** of the Forest of Dean, Gloucestershire.

Commission spokesman Stuart Burgess said the sights had been confirmed by 'very experienced' rangers unlikely to mistake deer **5** for big cats.

He said today: 'Both were observed in low light, using heat-activated vision equipment while they were carrying out a deer census. The colour of the animals couldn't be made out, but these are very experienced guys and they know what is and what isn't a deer. One **6** definitely believed that what he saw was some sort of large cat.'

James Woodward, *The Independent*, 6 January 2009

Activity

9 Using your answers to Activity 8 to help you, what do you think the writer wants the reader to think about these big cat sightings? Give evidence to support your answer.

Identifying bias

When someone is prejudiced for or against a thing or a point of view, we say they are **biased**. Bias can be identified through:

- what the writer says and doesn't say
- the way the writer says it.

Activities

10 Read Text I, the opening paragraph from one writer's letter to a newspaper. For each highlighted word or phrase, explain:

- what is implied by it
- why the writer has chosen it.

I read with interest that police in Scotland are wasting a great deal of energy in their attempts to establish the veracity of accounts of so-called 'big cat sightings'. Pumas, lynx and even leopards, we are told, are taking over our countryside and the police are using expensive resources in order to prove this. Helicopters have been deployed following alleged sightings, samples collected and sent for analysis, and data suitably collated and delivered obediently to the hands of the almighty Big Cats in Britain group.

11 Write a paragraph in which you explain how the writer's choice of words suggests bias.

Check your learning

In this chapter you have:

- identified distinguishing features of texts
- located information in a text
- selected material for a specific purpose
- considered how writers use words to influence the reader.

2

Grand designs

Objectives

In this chapter you will:

investigate how two texts are organised

consider the ways presentational features are used for effect.

Purpose and audience

A media text such as the Crimestoppers poster that follows would be produced by both a writer and a designer. In deciding how to structure and present the text they would first consider their intended **purpose** and their intended **audience**.

A text can have more than one intended purpose and more than one intended audience.

Key terms

Purpose: the intended purpose of a text is the reason for which it is being produced.

Audience: the intended audience of a text is the reader for whom the text is written.

A

IMAGINE THIS WAS YOUR MATE

YOU KNOW WHO DID IT

WHAT WOULD YOU DO...?

CRIMESTOPPERS
0800 555 111
Call anonymously wih information about crime

Activities

1 Look at Text A carefully. The following are all possible intended purposes. Rank them in order, placing the one you think is the main purpose first. Give reasons for your choice.

   a To make people think about personal responsibility.

   b To attract attention.

   c To reassure people that action is being taken to stop knife crime.

   d To encourage witnesses of knife crime to call Crimestoppers.

   e To persuade people to call Crimestoppers if they know someone who has committed a knife crime.

   f To raise awareness about knife crime.

2 Compare your order with that of another student. Discuss the reasons for any differences you have.

3 Which of the following do you think is the main intended audience of the poster?

   ● the general public?

   ● school children?

   ● victims of knife crime?

   ● teenage boys?

   ● teenage girls?

   Give reasons for your choice, based on evidence in the poster.

Content

As well as considering purpose and audience, the writer and designer also need to consider the **format** the text will take. This has a significant effect on what they put in it. In this case it is a poster. Posters are often pinned on walls. People don't usually spend a long time reading them. The message needs to be conveyed quickly, clearly and with maximum impact. They first need to consider:

● what **words** to use

● what **images** to use.

> **Key terms**
>
> **Format:** the way a text is arranged or presented, e.g. as a leaflet, letter, poster. Sometimes also referred to as form.

Activities

4 The writer uses three simple sentences:

   ● Imagine this was your mate.

   ● You know who did it.

   ● What would you do …?

   How are the highlighted words in these sentences used to target intended purpose and audience?

5 The images are used to tell a story: they give the words meaning. Explain what story is told in the images.

6 a Explain the link between the three simple sentences and the images.

   b Explain the link between the Crimestoppers logo and details, and the contents of the poster.

Structure

Once the words and the images have been chosen, the designer needs to consider how to position them on the page to achieve maximum impact. This poster could have looked very different …

In this sketch the eye is drawn immediately to the victim lying in the street, making the victim the focus point. The designer of the poster on page 8 has chosen not to do this.

Activity

7 With another student consider the following questions to help you work out things about the way Text A is structured and the reasons for this.

a What is the background scene for this poster?

b To whom do you think the words 'Imagine this was your mate' refer – the boy hiding behind the wall, the victim of knife crime or the perpetrator of knife crime? At what point of looking at Text A do you realise this?

c How is the story of what has happened revealed to you?

d The face of the witness is shown three times. What is different about the ways the three faces are shown to you?

e Which person is the main focus point of Text A – the victim, the perpetrator or the witness? How is this linked with the main purpose of the poster?

f What is significant about the placing of the question 'What would you do …?' to the left of the Crimestoppers logo? Why do you think this question is in a larger font than the previous sentences?

Presentational features

Once the content and structure of the poster had been decided, the designer needed to consider finer points of presentation. One of the main decisions to be made would have been what colours to use. There are many factors that might influence the choice of colours. On the right are just a few of the questions a designer might need to ask and answer before deciding which colours to use.

Should colours reflect a particular mood or idea?

Do they stand out enough?

What do I want the audience to think?

Activities

8 Examine the use of colour in Text A.
Comment on the uses and effects of:

- black and red
- yellow
- white.

9 Look closely at the poster. What other points could you make about the way the content, both the words and the images, is presented to you?

The designer would also have needed to make decisions about font type and size, and the type of images – photos, detailed drawing, sketches – used.

Writing about features

So far, features of language, structure and presentation have been identified. The next step is to make relevant comments on these which explain how the features are used and the likely effect on the reader. It is the comments on the features that will show your understanding of:

- **how** they have been used
- **why** they been used in this way.

Text B shows the first paragraph of one student's writing about the Crimestoppers poster. The parts of the writing that describe the features are highlighted in blue and the comments are highlighted in pink.

B The first thing that strikes you about this poster is its colours. The striking red and black background, with its connotations of night and danger, and the bold white font immediately attract attention. There is very little actual writing on this poster. The writing addresses the reader directly using 'your' and 'you'. This is intended to make the poster personal and directly relevant to the reader and to encourage them to find out what this poster is about. The first sentence is a command: 'Imagine this was your mate.' The use of the word 'mate' makes it sound less formal and perhaps less threatening – a mate is someone you would want to help. The words, printed in white capitalised font, stand out clearly against the red and black background but they don't really make sense without the pictures. It's the pictures that give the words their meaning.

Activity

10 Read and copy Text C, the second paragraph of the same student's writing about the poster. Use highlighters to separate the parts that describe features from the parts that comment on them.

C At first glance it's not clear who you are meant to imagine as 'your mate'. There is a boy hiding behind a wall but it's only when you look closely at the framed pictures that you realise 'your mate' relates to the actual victim of the knife crime. By imagining him as 'your mate', you are being encouraged to put yourself in the position of witness to a knife crime. It is the witness, rather than the victim, who forms the visual focal point of the poster. That's because its purpose is to get you to think about what you should do if you witness a knife crime. The image of the boy is repeated three times. Each image is an enlarged copy of the previous one with the final image showing in detail the scene reflected in the dark glasses worn by the witness. In this way the story of what has happened is gradually revealed and forces the reader to focus on what it feels like to witness such a scene.

11 Below are four sentences that describe other features of the Crimestoppers poster on page 8. For each sentence write a comment that shows your understanding of how the feature has been used and why it has been used in this way.

- The boy is wearing a hooded jacket and dark glasses.
- The colour white is used for the writing, the picture framing and the background to the Crimestoppers logo.
- The colour yellow is used to highlight the boy's glasses and what is reflected in them.
- The Crimestoppers logo lies to the right of the question, 'What would you do …?'

More about purpose and audience

As you have seen, texts can have more than one intended purpose and more than one intended audience. Writers and designers use content, structure and presentational features to target these. They also need to closely consider the form of their text and how this will affect the features they use. Text A was a poster. Text D, 'The Hip-Hop Opera Premiere', is a flyer – a single-page advertisement – which is usually handed out to the general public on the streets for them to read as they walk along or when they have a spare moment.

Activities

12 Writers and designers want to have maximum impact on their readers. List three ways in which the differences between a poster and a flyer might affect their ideas about:

- the detail they should include
- how to structure the material
- the presentational features they should use.

13 Look at Text D and copy and complete the following chart. In the first column list the different intended audiences and purposes of 'The Hip-Hop Opera Premiere flyer'. In the second column list your reasons for thinking this. Share your ideas with another student and together agree the main purpose and the main intended audience.

Intended purposes and audiences	Reasons for thinking this
Purposes:	
Audiences:	

14 Work in a pair and, using what you have learned in this chapter to help you, make notes on:

- the content of the flyer
- how this content has been organised on the page
- the presentational features used.

15 Compare your notes with those of another pair. Add any further points that you think are relevant to the way the flyer is presented.

16 Spend a few minutes preparing your ideas and then, still in groups of four, take it in turns to talk about how effective each of you thinks this flyer is. Remember there is no single correct viewpoint. You might find all of it effective, some of it or none of it. The important thing is that you can support your viewpoint with reference to details in the flyer. If you want to, you can make comparisons with the Crimestoppers poster.

Stretch yourself

1 Write your own commentary on the 'Hip-Hop Opera Premiere' flyer. Re-read the opening paragraphs of the student's writing on pages 11–12 to remind yourself how to describe and comment on features of structure and presentation.

2 Produce your own poster alerting students of your own age to the potential dangers of one of the following:

- binge drinking
- internet chat rooms
- extreme dieting.

Check your learning

In this chapter you have:

- considered the importance of purpose and audience
- examined the content, structure and presentation of two texts
- practised developing comments on features of a text
- considered the effectiveness of a text.

3

Objectives

In this chapter you will:

examine some of the techniques used by writers in the openings of novels and the effect these have on the readers.

Story openings

Starting to write

You have probably written many short stories during your years studying English. Some of you might even have written a full-length novel. If you have, you will know just how long it takes to plan, write and edit your work. You will also know how many hours go into simply working out how to start your story.

Activity

1

Imagine you are a writer writing the opening paragraphs of a novel for which you have already spent several months researching and planning. What might you be hoping to achieve in those opening paragraphs? How might you try to achieve those things? Share your ideas with one or two other students and collate a list.

Perspective and character

Text A is taken from the opening of *The Kite Runner* by Khaled Hosseini. The story is told in the **first person** from the **perspective** of one of the characters in it. A first-person narrative is indicated by the use of 'I' (first-person singular) or 'we' (first-person plural). Use of the first-person narrative allows the reader to see and experience events through the narrator's senses and feelings. The narrator is a fictional character, just as are all the other characters in the story, and cannot give the thoughts and opinions of other characters unless clearly told about them. It is important for the reader to work out as much as possible about the character of the narrator in order to decide what 'really' happens.

Activity

2

Read Text A closely. What do you learn about:

- The narrator's past life?
- How the narrator feels about his past life?
- The narrator's present life and how he seems to feel about it?

Following clues

Writers often give readers clues about their story in the opening paragraphs. For example, the first sentence of Text A refers to something significant that happened in the narrator's life on a day in the winter of 1975, creating an expectation in the reader that the story will reveal what did happen that day.

Activity

3

What other clues are you given in the opening paragraphs connected to:

- The people who will play a part in the story?
- Where the story will be set?
- The outcome of the story?

I became what I am today at the age of twelve, on a frigid overcast day in the winter of 1975. I remember the precise moment, crouching behind a crumbling mud wall, peeking into the alley near the frozen creek. That was a long time ago, but it's wrong what they say about the past, I've learned, about how you can bury it. Because the past claws its way out. Looking back now, I realize I have been peeking into that deserted alley for the last twenty-six years.

One day last summer, my friend Rahim Khan called from Pakistan. He asked me to come see him. Standing in the kitchen with the receiver to my ear, I knew it wasn't just Rahim Khan on the line. It was my past of unatoned sins. After I hung up, I went for a walk along Spreckels Lake on the northern edge of Golden Gate Park. The early-afternoon sun sparkled on the water where dozens of miniature boats sailed, propelled by a crisp breeze. Then I glanced up and saw a pair of kites, red with long blue tails soaring in the sky. They danced high above the trees on the west end of the park, over the windmills, floating side by side like a pair of eyes looking down on San Francisco, the city I now call home. And suddenly Hassan's voice whispered in my head: *For you, a thousand times over*. Hassan the harelipped kite runner.

I sat on a park bench near a willow tree. I thought about something Rahim Khan said just before he hung up, almost as an afterthought. *There is a way to be good again*. I looked up at those twin kites. I thought about Hassan. Thought about Baba. Ali. Kabul. I thought of the life I had lived until the winter of 1975 came along and changed everything. And made me what I am today.

Khaled Hosseini, *The Kite Runner*, 2004

Using language to convey meaning 🅺!

A writer's tools are words. Writers choose them consciously and deliberately to convey meaning to the reader as explained below.

I became what I am today at the age of twelve, on a frigid overcast day in the winter of 1975.

Before we know anything at all about what happened on this day the writer uses words to influence us and guide our expectations. The day is described as being **frigid** and **overcast**. The writer could have used the word **cold** or **freezing** but instead chose the word **frigid** which has connotations of a lack of affection and human warmth. Similarly the day is **overcast**. The writer could have used **grey** or **dull** but instead chose the word **overcast**. This has connotations of things being covered over or obscured, perhaps just as what happened that day had been. Through the use of these words, the writer guides the reader to predict that something bad happened on that day.

4 Think about the highlighted words in the following sentences. Consider the possible alternatives the writer could have chosen and then copy and complete the table below. The first two rows have been completed using the examples from the previous page.

> I remember the precise moment, crouching behind a crumbling mud wall, peeking into the alley near the frozen creek. That was a long time ago, but it's wrong what they say about the past, I've learned, about how you can bury it. Because the past claws its way out.

Word chosen	Alternative word choices	What the chosen word suggests or implies
frigid	• cold • freezing	lack of affection and human warmth
overcast	• grey • dull	things being covered over or obscured
crouching		
peeking		
claws		

5 Now look at the following sentences that describe the kites in the park. Identify words that you think the writer has used to create a different mood to that of the opening paragraph and explain why you think they've been chosen.

> Then I glanced up and saw a pair of kites, red with long blue tails soaring in the sky. They danced high above the trees on the west end of the park, over the windmills, floating side by side like a pair of eyes looking down on San Francisco, the city I now call home.

Unforgettable extraordinary... it is so powerful that for a long time after everything I read seemed bland
ISABEL ALLENDE

Shattering devastating and inspiring
OBSERVER

The Kite Runner
KHALED HOSSEINI

Character revealed through speech

Writers sometimes tell their story from the point of view of someone outside it. This is called a **third-person** narrative. Characters in the story are identified as 'she' or 'he' (third person singular) or 'they' (third-person plural). As the narrator is not a character, he or she is able to have an overview of everything that occurs and is thought and felt.

In the opening to *Pride and Prejudice* the writer, Jane Austen, presents two characters, allowing the reader to discover things about them from what they say and how they say it. Read Text B closely before answering the questions.

(B)

It is a truth universally acknowledged, that a single man in possession of a good fortune must be in want of a wife.

However little known the feelings or views of such a man may be on his first entering a neighbourhood, this truth is so well fixed in the minds of the surrounding families, that he is considered as the rightful property of some one or other of their daughters.

'My dear Mr Bennet,' said his lady to him one day, 'have you heard that Netherfield Park is let at last?'

Mr Bennet replied that he had not.

'But it is,' returned she; 'for Mrs Long has just been here, and she told me all about it.'

Mr Bennet made no answer.

'Do not you want to know who has taken it?' cried his wife impatiently.

'You want to tell me, and I have no objection to hearing it.'

This was invitation enough.

'Why, my dear, you must know, Mrs Long says that Netherfield is taken by a young man of large fortune from the north of England; that he came down on Monday in a chaise and four to see the place, and was so much delighted with it that he agreed with Mr Morris immediately; that he is to take possession before Michaelmas, and some of his servants are to be in the house by the end of next week.'

'What is his name?'

'Bingley.'

'Is he married or single?'

'Oh! Single, my dear, to be sure! A single man of large fortune; four or five thousand a year. What a fine thing for our girls!'

'How so? How can it affect them?'

'My dear Mr Bennet,' replied his wife, 'how can you be so tiresome! You must know that I am thinking of his marrying one of them.'

'Is that his design in settling here?'

'Design! Nonsense, how can you talk so! But it is very likely that he may fall in love with one of them, and therefore you must visit him as soon as he comes.'

Jane Austen, *Pride and Prejudice*, 1813

Activities

6   Using evidence from Text B, what can you discover about:
- Mrs Bennet's views on marriage?
- The way Mrs Bennet talks to her husband?

7   Using evidence from the text, what can you discover about:
- Mr Bennet's views on marriage?
- The way Mr Bennet talks to his wife?

8   Using what you have discovered from your answers to Activities 6 and 7, what have you learned about the relationship between Mr and Mrs Bennet?

Writer's viewpoint

By careful deduction and closely following clues in the text, it is sometimes possible to work out the writer's viewpoint.

Re-read the opening sentence: 'It is a truth universally acknowledged, that a single man in possession of a good fortune must be in want of a wife.'

Here the narrator presents an **opinion** as an absolute **fact**.

The question is: does the writer want us to accept this statement as fact or to question it? To help you answer that question you must think about the conversation between Mr and Mrs Bennet that follows it.

When a writer uses words to say one thing, but then shows that they believe something else to be true then they are using **irony**. When a writer uses irony you say that they are being ironic or ironical.

Activities

9
  a Which of the two characters, Mr or Mrs Bennet, appears to agree with the opening statement? Give evidence to support your answer.

  b Which of the two characters, Mr or Mrs Bennet, is presented more favourably? Give evidence to support your answer.

  c Using your answers to a and b to guide you, what do you think is the writer's view on the opening statement?

10 Look again at the opening of *Pride and Prejudice*. Find two examples of irony and explain why you think they are ironic.

Identifying tone

One route to identifying the writer's viewpoint is through identification of **tone**. Tone is the mood or feeling the writer creates. Read Text C: the opening of *Holes* by Louis Sachar. Think about the tone the writer creates before working through the tasks that follow.

Key terms

Tone: the mood or atmosphere created.

(C)
There is no lake at Camp Green Lake. There was once a very large lake here, the largest lake in Texas. That was over a hundred years ago. Now it is just a dry, flat wasteland.

There used to be a town of Green Lake as well. The town shrivelled and dried up along with the lake, and the people who lived there.

During the summer the daytime temperature hovers around ninety-five degrees in the shade – if you can find any shade. There's not much shade in a big dry lake.

The only trees are two old oaks on the eastern edge of the 'lake'. A hammock is stretched between the two trees and a log cabin stands behind that.

The campers are forbidden to lie in the hammock. It belongs to the Warden. The Warden owns the shade.

'Unmistakably powerful'
Philip Pullman, The Guardian

Out on the lake, rattlesnakes and scorpions find shade under rocks and in the holes dug by the campers.

Here's a good rule to remember about rattlesnakes and scorpions: if you don't bother them, they won't bother you.

Usually.

Being bitten by a scorpion or even a rattlesnake is not the worst thing that can happen to you. You won't die.

Usually.

Sometimes a camper will try to be bitten by a scorpion, or even a rattlesnake. Then he will get to spend a day or two recovering in his tent, instead of having to dig a hole out on the lake.

But you don't want to be bitten by a yellow-spotted lizard. That's the worst thing that can happen to you. You will die a slow and painful death.

Always.

If you get bitten by a yellow-spotted lizard, you might as well go into the shade of the oak trees and lie in the hammock.

There is nothing anyone can do to you anymore.

Louis Sachar, *Holes*, 2000

Activities

11 Louis Sachar creates tone by using a number of techniques as shown in the following passage. Read through the annotations below before matching them to the appropriate places in the extract.

During the summer the daytime temperature hovers ❶ around ninety-five degrees in the shade – if you ❷ can find any shade. There's not much shade in a big dry ❸ lake. ❹

❺ The only trees are two old oaks on the eastern edge of the 'lake'. A hammock is stretched between the two trees and a log cabin stands behind that.

The campers are forbidden to lie in the hammock. It belongs to the Warden. The Warden owns the shade. ❻ ❼

ⓐ Uses sarcasm to emphasise the obvious.

ⓑ Writes in the present tense to create a sense of immediacy.

ⓒ Uses simple sentence structures to emphasise each point.

ⓓ Addresses the reader directly to place you there and help you picture what it is like.

ⓔ Uses short paragraphs to punctuate the detail for emphasis and to make it sound very matter of fact.

ⓕ Uses simple adjectives sparsely to create a sense of a barren environment.

ⓖ Uses sarcasm to show that something is ridiculous.

12 Find and write down two further examples of each of the following techniques in the rest of the passage:

- use of sarcasm
- addressing the reader directly
- short paragraphs to punctuate the detail for emphasis
- short sentences to emphasise each point.

13 Using what you have learnt from Activities 11 and 12, what do you think the writer thinks and feels about Camp Green Lake? Explain why you think this.

Examining the three openings together

Speaking and listening

In this activity you are going to review all three novel openings in the light of what you have learned in this chapter. Work in pairs or small groups and keep notes on your discussion. Focus your discussion on the following prompts:

- The benefits and drawbacks of
  - a third-person narrative
  - a first-person narrative.
- The clues each writer gives about what is to follow.
- The ways each writer has used words to affect and influence their readers.
- The ways each writer has focused on characters.
- The tone of each opening.

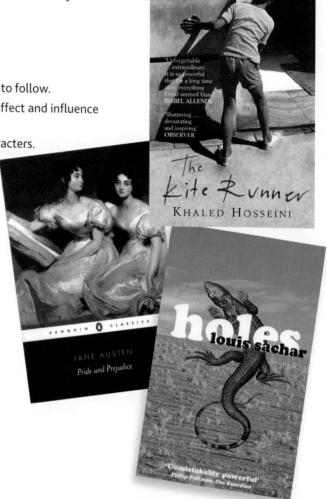

Activity

14

Once you have discussed the three openings, decide which one you think has the most effect on the reader. Either:

a Write two or three paragraphs explaining your choice.

b Give a short presentation explaining your choice.

Make a note

Remember to refer to the techniques the writer uses as well as the content in your explanation.

Stretch yourself

Examine and write about the techniques used by a writer in the opening paragraphs of a novel of your choice.

Check your learning

In this chapter you have:

- considered the role of the narrator
- detected clues in a text
- examined writers' use of words for effect
- thought about the writer's viewpoint
- explored how writers present characters and create tone.

4

Judging the evidence

What does evaluate mean?

There are three main stages in the process of **evaluating** a text for English.

Stage 1

The first step is to study significant features of the text and work out its intended purpose(s) and audience(s).

> **Key terms**
>
> **Evaluate:** when you evaluate something you make a series of judgements on it based on evidence.

Stage 2

The next stage is to consider the likely effects of the features that have been identified and how successful they are likely to be in:

- achieving the intended purpose(s)
- interesting the intended audience(s).

There is no single correct answer. Just as people will have different views on an album, a magazine or a TV programme, you might think all or none of the page is successful or that some parts are and some parts aren't. The important thing is that you can give clear reasons for your judgements and support them with close reference to details of the text. Remember you are evaluating the text, not what it is writing about. Your personal opinions about Facebook are not relevant to your judgements on the text.

Beyond Facebook

The internet could have been invented especially for social networking – and for iPhone or touch owners, keeping up with friends on the go has never been easier

By Andy Penfold

Everyone's on an online social network these days – in the past four years such sites have become the new way to socialise. Since the inception of Facebook in 2004, the idea of catching up with mates online has gone way beyond the sending of a simple email or even using web features, such as live messenger services. Now you can exchange photographs with your nearest and dearest, seek out your best buddies from days of yore, embark on gaming tournaments with strangers, or even share your creative musings with the world and go job-hunting in a mere matter of mouse clicks.

It was inevitable that this technology would soon be taken to the next level, and made available to the iPhone and iPod touch. Free apps such as MySpace, Facebook, Twitter, and others bring these networks to your favourite gadgets, letting you to take your networking away from the desktop and onto the road. We look at how each app works, and give you the skinny on all your social iPhone options.

Activities

1   In pairs or small groups, study Text A, which is the opening page of a magazine article on social networking. Make notes on the following areas:

Structure	Presentational features	Language
• How the page is organised • What is placed where	• Images • Colours • Fonts	• How the reader is addressed • Tone • Specific examples of language use

2   Use what you have learned from Activity 1 to help you identify:

- the intended purpose(s) of the page
- the intended audience(s) of the page.

Remember to use specific examples from the extract to back up any points you make.

Activity

3 Copy the following table. In the first column describe four separate features of structure, presentation or language that you have identified. Complete the second column by writing a comment on the effect(s) and/or assessing its likely impact on the intended reader. An example has been done for you.

Feature of structure, presentation or language	Comment on effects
The background photographs of the teenagers separated by different blocks of colour.	The teenagers in the background all look sad, which seems to suggest to the reader that they would be happier if they were on an online social network. The separate blocks of colour are effective in adding to the impression of them being isolated and alone.

Stage 3

Once you have considered carefully the effects of the features of a text, you are ready to write. You need to show that there are different ways of viewing things and that you can make judgements based on considered evidence.

Activity

4 Read Text B, the opening paragraphs of a student's answer to the question:

To what extent is the opening page of the article 'Beyond Facebook' likely to achieve its purpose and interest its intended audience?

The main features of the answer are annotated for you.

Supports point with detail from the text

Makes a judgement

Supports judgement with reasons

Identifies feature of presentation

Makes a judgement

Comments on feature and effect

Offers alternative view

Supports alternative view with reference to text

This page is intended mainly for young people as suggested by the photographs it displays which are all of teenagers. Its main purpose is to introduce the subject of social networking for iPhone or iPod touch owners and to encourage readers to read on.

The page would almost certainly attract readers' attention as it is colourful and offers a range of features to look at. The background colours are varied and slightly muted, as are the background images of young people, perhaps to suggest a range of moods and feelings. This would link directly with the blocked words 'Friend status and mood'. However, all the faces are vaguely sad looking which doesn't really give you a sense that online social networking is an enjoyable experience. This does, however, contrast with the faces on the iPhone which are all happy and smiling so perhaps this is deliberately done to suggest that, no matter what your mood, social networking is for you. Alternatively, it could be suggesting that you are sad and isolated and cut off from other people unless you network. This interpretation would explain the separate blocks of colours which form distinct barriers between the teenagers in the background.

Identifies intended audience

Identifies two intended purposes

Comments on feature

Identifies feature of structure

Uses discursive marker to link ideas

Uses discursive marker to link ideas

Identifies feature of structure and presentation

Uses discursive marker to link ideas

Activity

5 Now read the next two paragraphs of the same student's answer (Text C). Identify and note one example of each of the following features:

a links text to intended purpose

b links text to intended audience

c identifies features of structure, presentation and use of words

d comments on features

e supports comments with details from the text

f makes a judgement

g supports judgement with reasons

h offers alternative view

i supports alternative view with reference to the text

j uses discursive marker to link ideas.

You could record your notes in a table like the one below:

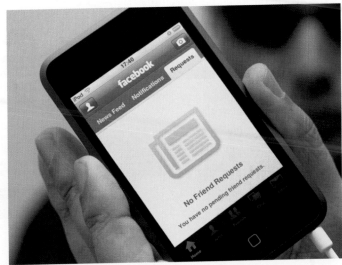

Feature	Example from student's writing
Links text to intended purpose	

© The writer uses language to persuade the reader. Exaggerated phrases such as 'has never been easier' and 'Everyone's on an online social network these days' are there to make the reader think they could try it too. The words address the reader directly with phrases such as 'Now you can exchange ...'. This method would probably be successful in that it would encourage the reader to have a go. Informal language is used to target the teenage reader directly with phrases such as 'best buddies' and 'give you the skinny'. These might make the reader more interested, though some people might prefer a less chatty and more practical approach. It's only at the end of the two paragraphs that you find out what the article that follows is going to be about, probably because the writer wants to hook you in first, though, personally, I think this should have come earlier. Some people might have stopped reading before they get to this bit.

Overall, the text works well with the images enhancing the message of the writing that life is better if you social network. I like the way moody colours are used for the background faces and the way the sad expressions contrast with the happy faces on the iPhone. However, I think this would have been more effective if they'd used the same teenagers for both sets of pictures, suggesting that now they are networking they are much happier. This would have helped to make the meaning clearer and consequently had more effect on the reader.

Writing your own evaluation

You are now going to use what you have learned so far in this chapter to help you write an evaluation. Text D is the next page of the article on social networking.

Top tip

Remember: evaluation is about making judgements based on evidence.

Activities

6 Work through a to c to help you make notes for your writing.

a Study Text D closely. Make notes on:
- structure
- presentational features
- language.

b Identify:
- the intended purpose(s) of the page
- the intended audience(s) of the page.

c Think about and make notes on the likely effects of the features you have identified and how successful the writer and designer have been in:
- achieving the intended purpose(s)
- interesting the intended audience(s).

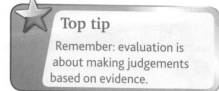

Facebook

Everyone's favourite network offers one of the finest apps out there...

Facebook started out as a Harvard student's tool for keeping in touch with other students. From this humble beginning in 2004, it has grown into a massive social network. It's no longer restricted to just students – anyone over the age of 13 can join – and the site now has more than 120 million active users.

It seems everyone is on Facebook, and the iPhone application lets you take this network on the go, chatting with friends in real time, keeping up to date with events and status updates, and viewing your friends' photos on the move. The iPhone 3G takes this to a new level – if you can get 3G coverage, you'll have this information at all times. Here's the lowdown on the App Store's most popular social networking widget.

Facebook secret...
Shake to update adds fun to iPhone Facebook...

Find your way around Facebook...

7 You are now ready to answer the question: To what extent is the second page of the article 'Beyond Facebook' likely to achieve its purpose and interest its intended audience?

Before starting to write, remind yourself of the features of a written evaluation by looking back at Activity 5. You might find it useful to organise your writing in the following way:

- Paragraph 1: Explain what you think is the main purpose and who you think is the intended audience of this page.
- Paragraph 2: Write about how the page is organised, commenting on and evaluating the effects of this.
- Paragraph 3: Write about the main presentational features, commenting on and evaluating the effects of these.
- Paragraph 4: Write about the main features of language use, commenting on and evaluating the effects of these.
- Paragraph 5: Briefly summarise the effectiveness of the page as a whole, perhaps adding an additional feature for your reader to consider.

8 When you have completed your writing, highlight and annotate examples of where you have:
- made a judgement
- supported your judgement with reasons based on the text.

Check your learning

In this chapter you have:
- applied what you have learned about structure, presentation and language to two texts
- studied features of a written evaluation
- written your own evaluation of a text.

Texts in contexts

Background

When someone first reads a text it is often without knowing anything of the background of the writer or the time or place about which it is written. In this chapter you will discover how finding out more about the background can help the reader develop a better understanding of a text.

Texts in time

When someone reads a text, they need to consider the time in which it was written. All languages change over time, in the words that are used, the spellings of words and the order in which the words are written or spoken. At first, the language might seem unfamiliar to the reader and require extra effort to understand it. Similarly, a text might deal with unfamiliar ideas, things that would have been understood by the readers of the time in which it was written.

Activity

Read Text A, an extract from 'The Knight's Tale' by Geoffrey Chaucer and Text B, the poem 'Quickdraw' by Carol Ann Duffy. They are separated in time by more than 600 years.

a In pairs, try to work out the general meaning of Text A. Use your knowledge of modern English to help you.

b What problems do you think Chaucer might have had in understanding Text B? What things would have seemed strange and unfamiliar to him? List them and explain why you think he would have had problems with them.

(A)

The Knight's Tale

Whilom, as olde stories tellen us,
Ther was a duc that highte Theseus;
Of Atthenes he was lord and governour,
And in his tyme swich a conquerour,
That gretter was ther noon under the sonne.
Ful many a riche contree hadde he wonne,
What with his wysdom and his chivalrie...

Geoffrey Chaucer, 'The Knight's Tale', 14th century

(B)

Quickdraw

I wear the two, the mobile and the landline phones,
like guns, slung from the pockets on my hips. I'm all
alone. You ring, quickdraw, your voice a pellet
in my ear, and hear me groan.

You've wounded me.
Next time, you speak after the tone, I twirl the phone,
then squeeze the trigger of my tongue, wide of the mark.
You choose your spot, then blast me

through the heart.
And this is love, high noon, calamity, hard liquor
in the old Last Chance saloon. I show the mobile
to the Sheriff: in my boot, another one's

concealed. You text them both at once. I reel.
Down on my knees, I fumble for the phone,
read the silver bullets of your kiss. Take this ...
and this ... and this ... and this ... and this ...

Carol Ann Duffy, 'Quickdraw', 2005

Texts in dialect

Both Texts A and B are written in **Standard English**. The standard form of any language is the one most often used in print. It is widely understood by the people of that time, though only a few people use it when they talk. Many people across the world speak a variety of regional English, depending on where they come from. This is called **dialect**.

Activity

2

With a partner:

- try to identify where these dialectic forms might be spoken:

  g'day mate   he's a reet scalley   nowt taken owt   why aye hinney   have a butcher's at this

- identify when and where dialectic forms are used in the media, particularly on television and radio

- identify and write down examples of dialect used in your own area and their meaning in Standard English.

Some writers choose to write in dialect. Texts C and D are extracts from two poems written in different centuries and in different dialects. The first one might be familiar to you.

Auld Lang Syne

Should auld acquaintance be forgot,
And never brought to mind?
Should auld acquaintance be forgot,
And auld lang syne?

For auld lang syne, my dear,
For auld lang syne,
We'll tak a cup of kindness yet,
For auld lang syne!

Robbie Burns, 'Auld Lang Syne', 1788

Bans a Killin

So yuh a de man me hear bout!
Ah yuh dem seh dah teck
Whole heap a English oat seh dat
yuh gwine kill dialec!

Meck me get it straight, mas Charlie,
For me no quite understand –
Yuh gwine kill all English dialec
Or jus Jamaica one?

Ef yuh dah equal up wid English
Language, den wha meck
Yuh gwine go feel inferior when
It come to dialec?

Louise Bennett, 'Bans a Killin', 1996

Activity

3

a With a partner:

- identify the dialects used in each poem
- work out the meaning of the verses.

b Suggest three reasons that would explain why some writers choose to write in dialect.

Texts and culture

As you have seen, some writers choose to write in dialect and, in doing so, associate themselves with a particular culture. But the word 'culture' has many other connotations beyond dialect. It's a broad term for the ideas, knowledge and beliefs that are shared by the people of an area, a country, a race or a social group. Writers often assume that their readers will understand the references they make.

Activity

4 Read Text E, from the opening of *Pies and Prejudice* by Stuart Maconie. It contains many cultural references that would be understood by readers in this country but not necessarily by readers in another country. Read the passage and then, with a partner:

● check how many of the highlighted cultural references you understand

● talk about how these references might present difficulties to a reader from another country.

This book, then, is an attempt to rediscover both the north itself and my own inner northerner. Does the north still exist? Are the hand-wringing cultural theorists right when they talk of a Britain of identikit prefab towns each with a Body Shop, Costa Coffee and Waterstone's? Or is the north still more likely to rejoice in a flagship Cash Converters than a flagship Harvey Nicks, whatever the fashionistas of Leeds might think?

The north. What is it? Where is it? Where does it begin and end, what does it mean to be northern and why, in a country that you could drop and easily lose in one of the American Great Lakes, does that two and a half hour journey from London to Manchester or Leeds still feel like crossing time zones, political borders and linguistic and cultural frontiers?

When we say the north, what do we really mean? It's something both powerful (like Newcastle Brown) and attractively vague (like most Oasis lyrics). The north means the lake poets and Lindisfarne Island and at the same time sink estates, ASBOs and the Aids capital of Britain (Doncaster, if you're interested). The north is big and complicated. Square metres of it are crowded, square miles of it are almost deserted. Surprisingly for an area so well covered by CCTV, it still says 'Here Be Dragons' on the *Daily Telegraph* and Radio 4's map of Britain.

And so, by supersaver and service station, by West Coast Main Line and M6, I began the journey back home. 'Home is the place,' wrote Robert Frost, 'where, when you have to go there, they have to take you in.' But would it still feel like home? Would they have to take me back? Would I want them to?

Stuart Maconie, *Pies and Prejudice*, 2007

Activity

5

In his final paragraph, Maconie questions whether the north would 'still feel like home'. This suggests that he believes there are certain things about the north that make it different to other places.

Think about where you live. In pairs, make a list of the things that you think make it 'different'. You might like to think about:

- the way people talk
- popular foods
- how people dress
- local customs and traditions.

Share your ideas with another pair and add to your list if appropriate.

Write a paragraph introducing a stranger to the culture of your home area to a stranger.

Context

The context of a text relates to when and where it was written, and by whom. It is not essential to know the context of a text to read and understand it. However, knowing the context can, sometimes, greatly enhance the reader's understanding and appreciation of a text.

Activity

6

Work with another student. Read Text F to carefully a few times before thinking about and answering the questions below. Base your answers on evidence given in the poem.

a What do you learn about the past of the person they are moving 'into the sun'?

b How do you know he has just died?

c What is the tone of the first stanza?

d In your own words, explain the questions the poet asks.

e What is the tone of the second stanza?

f How does the poet feel about this death?

g How does the content of the poem link with its title?

h What does the poem make you think about and how does it make you feel?

Futility

Move him into the sun –
Gently its touch awoke him once,
At home, whispering of fields unsown.
Always it woke him, even in France,
Until this morning and this snow.
If anything might rouse him now
The kind old sun will know.

Think how it wakes the seeds, –
Woke, once, the clays of a cold star.
Are limbs, so dear-achieved, are sides,
Full-nerved – still warm – too hard to stir?
Was it for this the clay grew tall?
– O what made fatuous sunbeams toil
To break earth's sleep at all?

Wilfred Owen, 'Futility', 1918

Now that you have read and thought about the poem, you are going to learn more about its context. Read the following information:

- **Historical context**: 'Futility' was written in 1918. It is about a young man who was a soldier and who died fighting for his country, Britain, in the First World War (1914–18). The First World War, also known as the Great War and the War to End all Wars, was a global military war in which more than 70 million military personnel were mobilised and more than 15 million people were killed.

- **Social context**: At the start of the war people in Britain were very optimistic. They loved the tales of heroism that filtered back and the belief that it was a great honour to fight and die for your country was widely held. As time progressed, however, and they learnt more about the terrible conditions under which the soldiers lived and the horrific experiences they faced, attitudes started to change.

- **The writer**: Wilfred Owen (1893–1918) is regarded by many as one of the leading poets of the First World War. He enlisted at the age of 22 and started the war as a cheerful and optimistic man but soon changed his view after traumatic experiences. These included being blown high into the air by a trench mortar and landing in the remains of a fellow officer. He was sent home to recover from shell shock but chose to return to the front. He was killed in action at the Battle of the Sambre just a week before the war ended and was posthumously awarded the Military Cross. Of his poetry, he once said: 'My subject is war, and the pity of war.'

Activities

7 Re-read 'Futility'. Using what you have learned about the context, what more can you now say about:
- the man who has died and how he has died?
- the tone of the first and second stanzas and the reasons for the differences in tone?
- how the poet feels about the man's death?
- how the poet feels about war?
- why the poet chose the title 'Futility'?

8 Rewrite your answer to the question: What does the poem make you think about and how does it make you feel?

9 Look again at Picture G that accompanies the poem. Do you think it is an appropriate reflection of the poem? If you could change it, how would you? Give your reasons.

More about context

Thinking about texts alongside others that have been written at the same time can help to develop understanding and appreciation. You have learnt from reading the social context that, early in the war, many believed it was an honour to die for your country. Such a view was promoted in the following poem by Rupert Brooke, written in 1914 at the start of the First World War. Brooke also joined the Forces but died in 1915 before taking part in active service.

Activities

10 Read Text H closely a few times. With a partner, talk about its meaning, and the attitude to death through war that is promoted in it, before answering the questions that follow.

   a For whom do you think the poem is written?

   b What main points does Brooke make?

   c How would you describe the tone of this poem? Refer to the poem to support your answer.

   d How might this poem make readers in England at that time feel?

11 Think again about 'Futility' on page 28. Explain how Owen challenges the ideas set out in 'The Soldier' through his poem.

The Soldier

If I should die, think only this of me:
That there's some corner of a foreign field
That is for ever England. There shall be
In that rich earth a richer dust concealed;
A dust whom England bore, shaped, made aware,
Gave, once, her flowers to love, her ways to roam,
A body of England's, breathing English air,
Washed by the rivers, blest by suns of home.

And think, this heart, all evil shed away,
A pulse in the eternal mind, no less
Gives somewhere back the thoughts by England given;
Her sights and sounds; dreams happy as her day;
And laughter, learnt of friends; and gentleness,
In hearts at peace, under an English heaven.

Rupert Brooke, 'The Soldier', 1914

Stretch yourself

Choose a subject that has featured in the news lately. It could be a war, a disaster, a crime or something else. Write a poem or a short story that reflects or is linked to your choice of subject.

Check your learning

In this chapter you have:
- considered how language changes over time
- examined the use of dialect in two extracts
- learned about the cultural, social and historical contexts of texts.

A twist in the tale

Objectives

In this chapter you will:

consider how stories are structured to achieve particular effects

examine how writers manipulate readers

think about how a character is created

develop your ideas beyond a text.

Using a dictionary

A dictionary is a very useful tool. As well as giving the meaning(s) of a word, it will explain how to pronounce the word, the word type (for example, verb, noun, adjective), how to use the word and the origins of the word.

Activity

1 Read Text A, a dictionary entry for the word 'narrate', and answer the following questions:

a Which part of the word 'narrate' should you emphasise when pronouncing it?

b What is the main meaning of 'narrative'?

c What is the name given to someone who tells a story?

d From which language is the word 'narrate' derived?

The desire to tell stories is strong, whether orally, through verse or through prose. The story told in a narrative can be fiction, non-fiction or a mixture of the two.

A reader's expectations

Most stories have an opening (that sets the scene), development (the main action of the story which generally presents a conflict of some kind) and a resolution (which may be expected or unexpected). One way of developing understanding of how a story is constructed is to stop at regular stages and consider how the writer is building up the reader's expectations.

narrate (*say* na-**rate**) *verb*
    to tell the story of an event, experience, etc.
narrative (*say* **narra**-tiv) *noun*
1. a recounting of events, experiences, etc.
2. the subject matter of a narrative.
Word Family: **narrator**, *noun*; **narration**, *noun*, a) a narrative, b) the act or process of narrating.
(Latin *narrare* to make known)

Heinemann English Dictionary, 1995

Background

Fables, short stories in prose which carry a moral message, date back to Aesop, a slave and storyteller, who lived in Ancient Greece (620–560 BC) being one of the most famous of ancient storytellers.

Activity

2 Read Text B (page 32), a fable attributed to Aesop, in short stages, stopping to answer each of the questions on the left before continuing.

The Bear and the Travellers

Two men were travelling together, when a Bear suddenly met them on their path. **❶** One of them, who happened to be in front, climbed up quickly into a tree and concealed himself in the branches. **❷** The other, seeing that he must be attacked, fell flat on the ground, and when the Bear came up and felt him with his snout, and smelt him all over, he held his breath, and feigned the appearance of death as much as he could. The Bear soon left him, for it is said he will not touch a dead body. **❸** When he was quite gone, the other Traveller descended from the tree, and laughingly inquired of his friend what it was the Bear had whispered in his ear. **❹** 'He gave me this advice,' his companion replied. **❺** 'Never travel with a friend who deserts you at the approach of danger.' **❻**

Misfortune tests the sincerity of friends. **❼**

Aesop, 'The Bear and the Travellers'

❶ What do you think will happen next? Why do you think this?

❷ Do you think the first man acted wisely? What do you think will happen to the second man?

❸ Why, according to the story, does the bear not attack the man?

❹ What is the mood of the man who descended from the tree? What word shows you this?

❺ What do you think the advice is?

❻ How does this provide a 'twist' to the tale?

❼ Use your own words to explain the moral of the story.

As you will have discovered, Aesop draws on the reader's common knowledge (for example, that bears and men don't generally mix well) and on their expectations (for example, that the second man will be attacked) to give more impact to the moral of the story.

Narrative structure

'The Bear and the Travellers' is narrated in **chronological order**; Text C, 'The Weapon', is also told in chronological order.

Activity

3 Read Text C closely. Below are key points from the story but not in the order in which they occur. Make a list of the points in the correct chronological order.

a Niemand declines a second drink.

b The doorbell rings.

c A stranger, Mr Niemand, asks to come in.

d Niemand starts to talk about Graham's work.

e Harry enters the room and asks Graham to read him a story.

f Dr Graham is sitting alone in an unlighted room.

g Niemand leaves, telling Graham he has left a gift with Harry.

h Graham thinks Niemand a fool to give a loaded revolver to Harry.

i Harry goes back to his room.

j Graham makes it clear to Niemand that he will not give up his work.

k Niemand accepts Graham's offer of a drink.

l Graham introduces his son to Niemand.

m Niemand goes into Harry's room.

Check your order with a partner before moving on to the next task.

The Weapon

The room was quiet in the dimness of early evening. Dr James Graham, key scientist of a very important project, sat in his favourite chair, thinking. It was so still that he could hear the turning of pages in the next room as his son leafed through a picture book.

Often Graham did his best work, his most creative thinking under these circumstances, sitting alone
5 in an unlighted room in his own apartment after the day's regular work. But tonight his mind would not work constructively. Mostly he thought about his mentally arrested son – his only son – in the next room. The thoughts were loving thoughts, not the bitter anguish he had felt years ago when he had first learned of the boy's condition. The boy was happy; wasn't that the main thing? And to how many men is given a child who will always be a child, who will not grow up to leave him? Certainly that was
10 rationalization, but what is wrong with rationalization when – The doorbell rang.

Graham rose and turned on lights in the almost-dark room before he went through the hallway to the door. He was not annoyed; tonight, at this moment, almost any interruption to his thoughts was welcome.

He opened the door. A stranger stood there; he said, 'Dr Graham? My name is Niemand; I'd like to talk
15 to you. May I come in a moment?'

Graham looked at him. He was a small man, nondescript, obviously harmless – possibly a reporter or an insurance agent.

But it didn't matter what he was. Graham found himself saying, 'Of course. Come in, Mr Niemand.'
A few minutes of conversation, he justified himself thinking, might divert his thoughts and clear his
20 mind.

'Sit down,' he said, in the living room. 'Care for a drink?'

Niemand said, 'No, thank you.' He sat in the chair; Graham sat on the sofa.

The small man interlocked his fingers; he leaned forward. He said, 'Dr Graham, you are the man whose scientific work is more likely than that of any other man to end the human race's chance for survival.'

25 A crackpot, Graham thought. Too late now he realized that he should have asked the man's business before admitting him. It would be an embarrassing interview; he disliked being rude, yet only rudeness was effective.

'Dr Graham, the weapon on which you are working –'

The visitor stopped and turned his head as the door that led to a bedroom opened and a boy of fifteen
30 came in. The boy didn't notice Niemand; he ran to Graham.

'Daddy, will you read to me now?' The boy of fifteen laughed the sweet laughter of a child of four.

Graham put an arm around the boy. He looked at his visitor, wondering whether he had known about the boy. From the lack of surprise on Niemand's face, Graham felt sure he had known.

'Harry' – Graham's voice was warm with affection – 'Daddy's busy. Just for a little while. Go back to
35 your room; I'll come and read to you soon.'

'"Chicken Little"? You'll read me "Chicken Little"?'

'If you wish. Now run along. Wait. Harry, this is Mr Niemand.'

The boy smiled bashfully at the visitor. Niemand said, 'Hi, Harry' and smiled back at him, holding out his hand. Graham, watching, was sure now that Niemand had known; the smile and the gesture were
40 for the boy's mental age, not his physical one.

The boy took Niemand's hand. For a moment it seemed that he was going to climb into Niemand's lap, and Graham pulled him back gently. He said, 'Go to your room now, Harry.'

The boy skipped back into his bedroom, not closing the door.

Niemand's eyes met Graham's and he said, 'I like him,' with obvious sincerity. He added, 'I hope that
45 what you're going to read to him will always be true.'

Graham didn't understand. Niemand said, '"Chicken Little", I mean. It's a fine story – but may "Chicken Little" always be wrong about the sky falling down.'

Graham suddenly had liked Niemand when Niemand had shown liking for the boy. Now he remembered that he must close the interview quickly. He rose, in dismissal. He said, 'I fear you're
50 wasting your time and mine, Mr Niemand. I know all the arguments, everything you can say I've heard a thousand times. Possibly there is truth in what you believe, but it does not concern me. I'm a scientist, and only a scientist. Yes, it is public knowledge that I am working on a weapon, a rather ultimate one. But, for me personally, that is only a by-product of the fact that I am advancing science. I have thought it through, and I have found that that is my only concern.'

55 'But, Dr Graham, is humanity ready for an ultimate weapon?'

Graham frowned. 'I have told you my point of view Mr Niemand.'

Niemand rose slowly from the chair. He said, 'Very well, if you do not choose to discuss it, I'll say no more.' He passed a hand across his forehead. 'I'll leave, Dr Graham. I wonder, though … may I change my mind about the drink you offered me?'

60 Graham's irritation faded. He said, 'Certainly. Will whisky and water do?'

'Admirably.'

Graham excused himself and went into the kitchen. He got the decanter of whisky, another of water, ice cubes, glasses.

When he returned to the living room, Niemand was just leaving the boy's bedroom. He heard
65 Niemand's 'Good night, Harry,' and Harry's happy 'Night, Mr Niemand.'

Graham made drinks. A little later, Niemand declined a second one and started to leave.

Niemand said, 'I took the liberty of bringing a small gift to your son, doctor. I gave it to him while you were getting the drinks for us. I hope you'll forgive me.'

'Of course. Thank you. Good night.'

70 Graham closed the door; he walked through the living room into Harry's room. He said, 'All right, Harry. Now I'll read to –'

There was sudden sweat on his forehead, but he forced his face and his voice to be calm as he stepped to the side of the bed. 'May I see that, Harry?' When he had it safely, his hands shook as he examined it.

He thought, only a madman would give a loaded revolver to an idiot.

Fredric Brown, 'The Weapon', from the collection of short stories *From These Ashes*, 2001

Manipulating the reader's expectations

When someone reads a story they use their own ideas to **interpret** what they are reading. They **infer** and **deduce** things based on the details in the story and the things they associate with these details. A skilful writer manipulates the reader's expectations by setting clues and, sometimes, deliberately misleading the reader with regard to what will happen. The following activity will help you to identify how and when the writer does this in 'The Weapon'.

Activities

4 Answer the following questions, referring to details in the text to support your answers where appropriate.

a What mood or atmosphere is created in these lines?

> Lines 1–10 'The room … when –'

b How does the writer lead the reader to think that something bad could happen to the son?

c What is the effect of this three-word sentence?

> Line 10 'The doorbell rang.'

d What first impression is given of Niemand? How does this influence the reader's expectations?

> Lines 16–17 'Graham looked at him … agent.'

e What impression did you have of Graham before these lines? How do these lines change or develop that impression?

> Lines 23–28 'The small man … on which you are working –''

f How does the writer lead the reader away from the expectation that something bad could happen to the son?

> Lines 32–44 'Graham put an arm … with obvious sincerity.'

g How does the writer seek to turn the reader against Graham in these lines?

> Lines 49–56 'He said … point of view Mr Niemand.'

h Why is this scene not described for the reader?

> Line 64 'When he returned … boy's bedroom.'

i How does the writer build up tension in these lines?

> Lines 67–73 'Niemand said … examined it.'

j What conclusions does the writer intend the reader to draw from the final line of the story?

> Line 74 'He thought … to an idiot.'

5 Compare your answers to Activity 4 with another student's answer. Add to them if you have missed something important or changed your mind.

6 Using what you have learned from your analysis of the story, write a developed answer to this question: How does the writer guide and manipulate the reader's expectations in 'The Weapon'?

Examining a character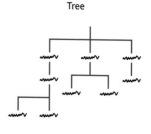

Most narratives contain characters. These are developed by the writer as the story progresses. In order to study a character the reader needs to take note of:

- **What the writer tells them directly about the character**: this is the literal detail and will often include a description of physical characteristics, such as appearance and voice.
- **What they can learn from what the character says**: examine their words and the implications of what they say.
- **What they can learn from what the character does**: examine their actions and the implications of these.
- **Any inconsistencies between the character's physical appearance, their words and their actions**: for example, is Niemand as harmless as he looks? Are his kind words towards Harry matched by his actions?

Activity

7

Make notes on the character Niemand. Include details on his appearance, his words, his actions and any inconsistencies between these. Your notes can be presented in any form you choose.

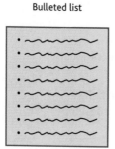

Spider   Bulleted list   Table   Tree

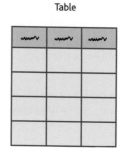

Developing your response to a character

To develop interpretation of a character, the reader needs to ask some wider questions such as:

- What is his or her role within the story?
- Does he or she have a wider relevance?
  (Did you know that *niemand* is the German word for 'no one'?)
- Can they, as a reader, identify with the character?
- Is there evidence to suggest the writer agrees or disagrees with the character?

Activity

8

a Use the questions above as a starting point for extending your notes on the character of Niemand.

b Share your ideas with another student, or work in small groups, and add any further good ideas to the notes you have made.

Developing and sustaining interpretation

Reading helps to develop thinking. It is often possible to apply ideas from a story to other relevant areas. Aesop's short story acts as a starting point from which to question the whole idea of friendship and to consider what really makes a good friend. Similarly, Frederic Brown's short story can help us to develop our own ideas about areas of history and modern life.

Read Texts D and E which relate to the use and testing of nuclear weapons.

On August 6, 1945, the USA, by order of President Harry S. Truman, dropped the nuclear weapon 'Little Boy' on the Japanese city of Hiroshima. Three days later a further nuclear weapon was detonated over Nagasaki.

By the end of 1945 the bombs had killed as many as 140,000 people in Hiroshima and 80,000 in Nagasaki. Roughly half of these were killed on the days of the bombings and the others died from injuries or illnesses attributed to radiation poisoning. In both cities, the overwhelming majority of the dead were civilians.

These are, to date, the only attacks with nuclear weapons in the history of warfare.

Court says nuclear test soldiers can sue Britain

THE British High Court has concluded thousands of Australian servicemen and their families were treated as nuclear 'guinea pigs', giving them the right to sue the British Government.

The bombshell decision found the British Ministry of Defence did have a case to answer that it unfairly exposed servicemen from Australia, Britain, New Zealand and Fiji to atomic fallout during the series of tests in South Australia, Western Australia and off the eastern coast on atolls in the Pacific during the 1950s.

The military men were promised 'the greatest show on Earth' but instead were exposed to serious levels of radiation that years later would kill many from a series of illnesses; many close to the drop zone also saw their children and their children's children suffer genetic defects.

Tests on their bodies later showed they had been exposed to dangerous levels of radiation but the effects were not known or at least understood.

Adapted from Charles Miranda, *Adelaide Now*, 5 June 2009

Speaking and listening

Brown wrote 'The Weapon' in 1951. Working in groups of three, talk about, and record your views on, the following questions:

- How does the knowledge of what happened in Hiroshima and Nagasaki in 1945 and in the Pacific tests of the 1950s further your understanding or interpretation of Brown's story?
- How does this knowledge add to your understanding and interpretation of the last line of the story?
- Does 'The Weapon' have any relevance for current scientific developments such as cloning and genetic engineering?

Stretch yourself

In both 'The Bear and the Travellers' and 'The Weapon' the narrative was used to develop a story that had a moral message. Write your own fable for modern times.

Check your learning

In this chapter you have:

- examined the structure of a fable
- traced the chronological order in a short story
- examined how a writer manipulates a reader's expectations
- studied how a writer creates a character
- used ideas in a text to inform your own thinking beyond it.

7

Objectives

In this chapter you will:

trace the development of a writer's ideas

understand and explain the ideas expressed by writers

make appropriate references to texts

examine how writers use language to influence their readers.

Analysing argument

Identifying key points

Following an argument means understanding, explaining and interpreting the writer's ideas. In order to do this it is necessary to identify the key points in the argument.

Activity

1   Read Text A, an article in which the writer expresses his point of view about an environmental issue. As you read it, sort out the key points below into the order in which they appear in the text.

a   The Great Bear Rainforest is a wonderful place to visit.

b   A wider area of the Great Bear Rainforest should be saved.

c   Plans to protect the Great Bear Rainforest might not be a cause for celebration.

d   Many conservationists are not setting high enough targets for saving the environment.

e   It is rare that plans to save an area of environmental importance are actually carried through.

Ⓐ

Wild Thoughts

The Great Bear Rainforest has been saved. Normally when I hear news like that I sigh in disbelief. It's hardly ever true. 'Saved' usually means 'given temporary reprieve' or 'merely on the agenda'.

This time, however, I can't decide if I should be sighing or singing. The Canadian province of British Columbia has announced plans to protect a huge swathe of Pacific Coast rainforest – the largest tract of intact temperate rainforest left on Earth – and the newly brokered deal will save about a third of this vast area specially for wildlife.

I was in this wilderness of ancient trees, glacial waterfalls, rocky headlands, coves, inlets and bays just a few months ago. Stretching seamlessly from Vancouver all the way to Alaska, it is home to everything from bald eagles and beavers to wolves and whales. The highlight of my trip was an hour crouching almost within touching distance of a spirit bear, a rare white form of the American black bear and one of the region's most famous inhabitants. It's an exhilarating place.

[continued overleaf]

Conservation groups and First Nation communities have been fighting to protect the Great Bear Rainforest – which covers an area about twice the size of Belgium – since the late 1980s. After several premiers, umpteen ministers of the environment and countless meetings, books, reports, protests, blockades and arrests, the recent announcement is undeniably welcome news. Most conservation groups have been tripping over themselves to sing the government's praises. But is protection of a third enough?

What we're saying is that two-thirds of one of the world's most important wildlife regions on the planet is up for grabs. The agreement does specify that any logging and mining in the area must be sustainable, but anyone who believes that must be kidding themselves. Canada's logging industry has an appalling track record. The sad fact is that we've become used to losing environmental battles. Our expectations are now so low that we are thankful for progress of any kind. I'm not saying that every last tree needs to be saved, but perhaps we should revert to the days when we aimed a little higher.

www.markcarwardine.com, May 2006

How writers influence their readers

When presenting an argument writers often use facts to support their point of view. Sometimes they use facts to manipulate their readers into sharing their point of view. Here are some of the reasons why writers use facts:

- to give emphasis to a particular point
- to reinforce a particular point
- to convince the reader
- to inform the reader
- to persuade the reader
- to make the reader question further.

Activity

2

When you are following an argument you need to identify the reasons why the writer is using a particular fact and what they are hoping to achieve by this.

Copy and complete this table to help you work out why and how the writer is using facts in 'Wild Thoughts'.

Fact	Reason for use	Desired effect
The Canadian Province of British Columbia has announced plans to protect a huge swathe of Pacific Coast rainforest	To inform the reader	To make the reader aware there is a rainforest in Canada and that it is to be protected
It is home to everything from bald eagles and beavers to wolves and whales		
The rainforest covers an area twice the size of Belgium		
The agreement does specify that any logging and mining in the area must be sustainable		

Writers also use opinions to influence their readers when presenting an argument. Sometimes they state opinions as if they were facts, for example:

> The sad fact is that we've become used to losing environmental battles.

This is not a fact, it is the writer's opinion. Why do you think he has presented his own point of view as a fact? How might the word 'sad' influence the reader?

Activity

3 Copy and complete the table below to show how and why opinions are used in 'Wild Thoughts'. Use the list of reasons in Activity 2 to help you.

Opinion	Reason for use	Desired effect
It's an exhilarating place.		
Anyone who believes that must be kidding themselves.		
Our expectations are now so low that we are thankful for progress of any kind.		

Referring to details in the text

When you write an explanation of an argument you need to make references to the text. To answer the question below you would have to refer to the text to write your explanation.

- What is Mark Carwardine's response to the news that the Great Bear Rainforest is to be saved?

There are several ways in which you can make references to texts.

- **By using quotations taken directly from the text.**
  For example: When he heard the news Mark Carwardine's first thought was 'Normally when I hear news like that I sigh in disbelief.' He goes on to say 'I can't decide if I should be sighing or singing.'
- **By referring to the text without using the exact words and phrase used by the writer.**
  For example: On hearing the news his first reaction was that he should sigh in disbelief as news like that is hardly ever true. Then he continues to say he couldn't decide whether to sigh or sing.
- **By paraphrasing the writer's words.**
  This means using your own words to express the writer's ideas. For example: On hearing the news he wasn't sure whether it was a cause for celebration or not. He knows from experience that conservation news of this kind does not actually mean that an area for conservation will be permanently saved.

Activity

4 What conclusion does Mark Carwardine reach about the decision to save the Great Bear Rainforest?

Answer this question using one or more of the methods of making references to texts. When you have finished show your answer to a partner and compare the methods you have used.

In addition to using fact and opinion to influence their readers, writers use a range of other techniques.

You are now going to examine some of them in Text B, an article in which the writer raises and answers the question of whether chimpanzees deserve the same rights as humans.

(B)

The Murder of Johnny

He may have been a bit of a thug, but he was shot down simply for being a non-human ape

Johnny was shot dead on Saturday, in the green meadows of Whipsnade. Here, north of London, he lived with his friend Koko and five other companions. Johnny, in his 40s, was 'a bit of a thug', according to some. Was this a reason to kill him? He wasn't attacking anyone, and had no gun. Surely whoever pulled the trigger was arrested, and the shooting investigated?

Not so. For Johnny was a chimpanzee, not a human. He was not a member of the privileged club that enjoys basic moral rights. In fact he was an object, an item of property under the law. That's why he could be deprived so lightly of his life. That's why he had been for decades deprived of his freedom. The wildlife park was his prison; and when he did what any of us would have done in his place – he escaped – he was shot dead.

Why this radical difference in treatment? Is it because chimpanzees are not members of our biological group?

Chimpanzees, gorillas and orang-utans are our closest relatives, sharing 98–99% of our DNA. Shouldn't we suppose that Johnny and his fellow beings are quite similar to us?

And so they are. The gestures with which they communicate are similar to ours; they are capable of complex coordination and social manipulation.

People have the right to life, freedom and welfare. That is what Johnny deserved. True that 'bit of a thug' couldn't be easily convinced to return to his prison. But he should never have been kept prisoner in the first place.

We would not shoot dead a human escapee. But there will come a time when this killing will be seen for what it is – murder.

Adapted from Paola Cavilieri, www.guardian.co.uk, 5 October 2007

Rhetorical questions

Rhetorical questions are used by writers to emphasise or draw attention to their ideas and to provoke the reader's thoughts. They are also used to influence the reader's opinion. For example, in the first paragraph the writer asks the question 'Was this a reason to kill him?' The writer intends to make readers question whether it was fair to shoot Johnny. By asking this question the writer is manipulating readers into thinking that Johnny did not deserve to be shot.

> **Key terms**
>
> **Rhetorical question:** a question that is asked to draw attention to a particular point.

Activity

a Find and write down two more examples of rhetorical questions in Text B.

b For each example explain how and why the writer is attempting to influence the reader by the question she has asked.

Emotive use of language

Writers **use language emotively** to persuade readers to share their opinions. For example, when the writer says 'he had been for decades deprived so lightly of his freedom' she is presenting the reader with the fact that the chimpanzee had been kept in a zoo. By using the word 'deprived' she is appealing to the reader's sympathy by making them feel that the chimpanzee has not been allowed what should be his by right, namely, his freedom.

> **Key terms**
>
> **Emotive use of language:** this is used to make the reader react in a particular way (e.g. feel surprised or shocked).

Activity

Look at the following examples of emotive use of language taken from the text and explain what feelings you think the writer intended to invoke when she used them:

> The wildlife park was his prison …

> People have the right to life, freedom and welfare. That is what Johnny deserved.

> … he was an object, an item of property …

Identifying bias

You have just seen how writers can use language emotively to influence readers. The presence of emotive language can be an indicator of bias. Bias is seen in an argument when the writer's personal beliefs and feelings are used to influence the reader's judgement. What are the writer's feelings about chimpanzees in the article?

Biased arguments are often one-sided, and this can be detected in the language used by the writer. At the beginning of the article the writer uses language that tricks the reader into believing Johnny is a human being. For example, the word murder, for most people, implies the deliberate killing of a human being. In this text murder is used to denote the killing of a chimpanzee. It is used to influence readers into sharing the writer's belief that chimpanzees should be regarded in the same way as humans.

7 The title of Text B is 'The Murder of Johnny'. Write an unbiased title for the article.

8 Look at the examples below where the writer deliberately uses language to influence the reader.

> … he lived with his friend Koko and five other companions.

> … he did what any of us would have done …

> … he should never have been kept prisoner in the first place.

For each one:

- explain what the writer intends readers to think
- rewrite the phrase so that the bias is removed.

Bringing the learning together

To revise the techniques you have learned for tracing the development of a writer's ideas and explaining the points of view in a text, read Text C, an article about travel.

C

Travel doesn't need to cost the earth

What is the worst part of the day for you? I'm willing to bet most of you would say it's your journey to work or to school. For many of us it's become an ever increasing nightmare. It's a hassle, it's exhausting and time consuming and worst of all it's expensive! The problem of course is the traffic slowing everything down and creating pollution. Traffic on Britain's roads has more than doubled in the past 25 years and nowhere is this more evident than in our towns and cities during the rush hour. A recent report shows that hundreds of local authorities in Britain break EU regulations on the emission of nitrogen dioxide which has been linked with asthma, stunted lung growth in children and even premature death.

There has to be a solution to this early morning misery. One town in Belgium appears to have found it. Hasselt, the fourth-largest town in Belgium, had the largest congestion problem. However this was rapidly eliminated when the town introduced free public transport for all. Unlike British towns the priority was not traffic, but people – a philosophy which we should certainly try to emulate. If one town in Belgium can do it, then why can't we?

At present public transport is unreliable and often infrequent which is why many avoid it, using cars instead. Free, reliable and very frequent bus and train services would remove our ridiculous dependence on the car. Free public transport would guarantee every person's undeniable right to mobility – from schoolchildren to workers, the disabled and the unemployed, families and young people. There would be a decrease in risks to health and surely much welcomed improvements for businesses as more people shop in traffic- and congestion-free streets. Traffic chaos would be eliminated once and for all and that fume-spewing monster, the car, would be banished from the streets of our towns. The result of free public transport would be a dramatic increase in cutting vehicle emissions and global warming.

All it would take is a little bit of nerve for town councils across the land to say 'No more cars in our town.' So why don't they do it now?

Activities

9   Now re-read Text C and make notes on answers to the following questions:

a   What are the main points of the writer's argument?

b   Find examples of places where the writer uses **facts** and **opinions** to influence the reader.

   i   Find two examples of language used emotively.

   ii   Find two examples of rhetorical questions.

c   How are these used to influence the reader?

d   Could you detect any bias in your examples? If so, explain how and why it is used.

10   Now use your notes to answer this question:

How does the writer present his argument in 'Travel doesn't need to cost the earth'?

Follow this structure:

● Explain how the writer's argument develops throughout the text by referring to the key points.

● Show how fact and opinion are used to influence the reader.

● Explain how rhetorical questions and emotive use of language are used to persuade the reader to share the writer's opinion.

● Show where bias is evident in the text. Explain how the bias is intended to influence readers.

● Remember to make references to the text to support the points you make.

Check your learning 🄚!

In this chapter you have:

● identified the key points in an argument

● learned how writers use fact and opinion to influence their readers

● used a range of methods to refer to texts

● recognised a range of techniques used by writers to influence readers

● learned how to recognise bias in a text.

The writer's point of view

Reading between the lines

In this chapter you are going to develop your skills in using inference and deduction to read a text and to work out the writer's point of view. Using the skill of inference means that you work out your own ideas about a text, based on what you read. This is sometimes known as reading between the lines.

After someone has read a text for the first time they will have formed an impression of what the writer is saying to their readers.

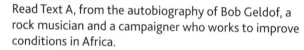

Activity

1 Read Text A, from the autobiography of Bob Geldof, a rock musician and a campaigner who works to improve conditions in Africa.

When you have finished reading think about your response to the following questions:

● What is the text about?

● Why did the writer write it?

● How did it make you feel?

Then compare your answers with those of a partner. Your answers might not be the same, as different people can have different opinions about texts.

All day I had been on the phone trying to promote a single from the album. I went home in a state of blank resignation and switched on the television. But there I saw something that completely changed my perspective.

The news report was of famine in Ethiopia. From the first seconds it was clear that this was a horror on a monumental scale. The pictures were of people who were so shrunken by starvation that they looked like beings from another planet. Their arms and legs were as thin as sticks, their bodies spindly. Swollen veins and huge, blankly staring eyes protruded from their swollen heads. The camera wandered among them like a mesmerized observer, occasionally dwelling on one person so that he looked directly at me, sitting comfortably in my living room. And there were children, their bodies as fragile and vulnerable as premature babies but with the consciousness of what is happening to them gleaming dully from their eyes. All around was the murmur of death like a hoarse whisper, or the buzzing of flies.

From the first few seconds it was clear that this was a tragedy which the world had somehow contrived not to notice until it had reached a scale which constituted an international scandal. You could hear that in the tones of BBC reporter Michael Buerk. It was the voice of a man who was registering despair, grief and disgust at what he was seeing. At the end the newscaster remained silent. Paula* burst into tears and then rushed upstairs to check on our baby Fifi, who was sleeping peacefully in her cot.

The images played and replayed in my mind. What could I do? Did not the sheer scale of the thing call for something more? A horror like this could not occur today without our consent. We had allowed this to happen. I would send money. But that was not enough. I had to withdraw my consent. What else could I do? I was only a pop singer – and by now not a very successful pop singer. All I could do was make records no one bought. But I would do that, I would give the profits of the next Rats** record to Oxfam.

What good would that do? It would be a pitiful amount. And I would withdraw my consent.

Yet that was not enough.

*Paula Yates – his partner at the time
** The Boomtown Rats – Geldof's band

Bob Geldof, *Is That It?*, 1986

In order to fully understand the meaning of a text you have to read it more closely. Answer these questions to help you work out how the writer's ideas develop from the start to the end of the text.

Activity

2

a   What thoughts are preoccupying the writer in the opening paragraph of Text A?

b   Why has his point of view changed in paragraph 2?

c   What is the significance of Paula's reaction?

d   What different thoughts and feelings are going through the writer's mind in the penultimate paragraph?

e   Write down three words which you think best describe Bob Geldof's reaction to the news broadcast.

f   Look at the final sentence. How have the writer's thoughts changed from the first paragraph?

Making inferences

When you read a text you make inferences or deductions based on what the writer says. You work out your own interpretation based on the evidence in the text.

Activity

3 Copy this table and complete it using your own ideas about what the words and phrases suggest to you, the reader.

Evidence from the text	Interpretation
There was horror on a monumental scale.	This makes me think something terrible had happened. It suggests Geldof was extremely shocked by what he saw. The word 'monumental' emphasises his reaction, implying the horror was on a scale not seen before.
People so shrunken by starvation they looked like people from another planet.	
The camera … occasionally dwelling on one person so that he looked directly at me, sitting comfortably in my living room.	
All around was the murmur of death like a hoarse whisper, or the buzzing of flies.	
A tragedy the world had contrived not to notice …	

Understanding the writer's perspective

Before reading an unfamiliar text it can be useful to know something of the background to help you understand the writer's perspective. Before you read Text B, the poem 'The Charge of the Light Brigade', study this information:

Background

- The poem was written to commemorate a charge by British cavalry forces (soldiers on horseback) during the Battle of Balaclava in 1854.
- Tennyson wrote the poem after reading a report of the battle in *The Times*.
- A serious mistake by the officers in charge led to the cavalry bearing only light arms to ride towards the heavily armed Russian infantry and artillery (soldiers with guns and cannons) who greatly outnumbered them.
- 673 soldiers took part in the charge, 113 were killed, 247 were wounded, only 195 returned fit for active service and 475 horses were lost.
- There was public outrage at what was felt to be unnecessary loss of life.

Activity

 Now talk briefly with a partner about this background information. Think about:

- which facts stand out particularly for you and why
- the approach the poet might have taken – for example, do you think he might have focussed on the officers' mistake?

As you read Text B, make notes recording your first impressions. These might be connected with:

- the events in the poem
- the way the poem is written
- the way the poem makes you feel.

Once you have read the poem share your first impressions with another student.

(B)

'The Charge of the Light Brigade'

Half a league, half a league,
Half a league onward,
All in the valley of Death
Rode the six hundred.
'Forward, the Light Brigade!
Charge for the guns!' he said:
Into the valley of Death
Rode the six hundred.

'Forward, the Light Brigade!'
Was there a man dismay'd?
Not tho' the soldier knew
Some one had blunder'd:
Theirs not to make reply,
Theirs not to reason why,
Theirs but to do and die:
Into the valley of Death
Rode the six hundred.

Cannon to right of them,
Cannon to left of them,
Cannon in front of them
Volley'd and thunder'd;
Storm'd at with shot and shell,
Boldly they rode and well,
Into the jaws of Death,
Into the mouth of Hell
Rode the six hundred.

Flash'd all their sabres bare,
Flash'd as they turn'd in air
Sabring the gunners there,
Charging an army, while
All the world wonder'd:
Plunged in the battery-smoke
Right thro' the line they broke;
Cossack and Russian
Reel'd from the sabre-stroke
Shatter'd and sunder'd.
Then they rode back, but not
Not the six hundred.

Cannon to right of them,
Cannon to left of them,
Cannon behind them
Volley'd and thunder'd;
Storm'd at with shot and shell,
While horse and hero fell,
They that had fought so well
Came thro' the jaws of Death,
Back from the mouth of Hell,
All that was left of them,
Left of six hundred.

When can their glory fade?
O the wild charge they made!
All the world wonder'd.
Honour the charge they made!
Honour the Light Brigade,
Noble six hundred!

Alfred, Lord Tennyson, 'The Charge of the Light Brigade', 1854

Developing an interpretation

When you interpret a text you put forward your own ideas about the text and the writer's point of view. An interpretation is based on what the evidence in the text suggests to you. For this reason your interpretation may differ from that of another student because interpretations reflect your own thinking.

Activity

5 Here are some interpretations of 'The Charge of the Light Brigade'.

> This is a poem that glorifies war.

> This is a poem that sympathises with the plight of ordinary soldiers.

> This poem could be viewed as an anti-war poem.

Decide which statement you agree with most and share your ideas with another student. Explain the reasons for your decision.

To develop your interpretation you need to select evidence from the text and explain what it suggests to you. For example, the words 'Honour the Light Brigade' could suggest that Tennyson wanted to glorify war and the soldiers' deeds in his poem. The word 'honour' suggests that heroic deeds have been performed.

Developing and sustaining an interpretation

When you develop an interpretation of a writer's ideas you need to extend your comments in detail based on evidence from the text. Sustaining an interpretation means that you continue to develop your points by looking very closely at the text and continuing to explain your own point of view about it.

Activity

6   Copy the table below. Make your own comments and interpretations for each of the quotations, explaining what the words suggest about the writer's point of view.

Evidence from the text	Interpretation
Boldly they rode and well	
They that had fought so well	
Noble six hundred!	

Activity

7   **a** Read Text C, a student's response to 'The Charge of the Light Brigade'. It has been annotated to show how the answer has been developed.

    b Now read Text D, a more developed response. Identify where the student has:

- identified the poet's point of view
- referred to the text
- developed and sustained comments
- made connections between different parts of the text.

Explains writer's viewpoint briefly

Uses supporting evidence from text

C

Tennyson admires the bravery of the soldiers. He writes 'boldly they rode and well'. This suggests that they were not afraid to go into battle. Later in the poem he writes 'plunged in the battery-smoke, right thro' the line they broke.' This tells the reader that they surged forward into the enemy with great courage.

Makes one simple comment on evidence

Makes simple comment on this evidence

Uses further evidence from the text

D

When Tennyson writes 'boldly they fought and well' it is clear that he admires the bravery of the soldiers. The word 'boldly' suggests that they were fearless in battle. The positive tone in the word 'well' indicates that he is praising the soldiers. The use of the two words in one line is to convince readers of his admiration for the soldiers. Their courage is again emphasised in the lines 'plunged in the battery-smoke, right thro' the line they broke.' Here the word 'plunged' emphasises their bravery implying they threw themselves into the battle almost recklessly without any thought for their own safety. As they broke right through the enemy line it could be assumed that they had been successful. Through his choice of vocabulary Tennyson encourages his readers to share his admiration for the soldiers' daring and selfless behaviour on the battlefield.

When you develop and sustain an interpretation of the writer's meaning you gather evidence from a range of areas in the text to compile an overall view of the writer's meaning. You have already examined the bravery of the soldiers and the conditions of battle. Next you are going to examine the writer's attitude to those who sent them into battle, and the way in which the soldiers are made to seem like victims.

Activity

8 Text D modelled an interpretation of Tennyson's portrayal of the soldiers' bravery. Now you are going to focus on the way in which Tennyson makes the conditions of the battle seem horrific. Select two or three quotations to show what the battle was like for the soldiers and develop your interpretation of them.

● Comment on individual words and phrases from your selected quotations.

● Explain how these words express or emphasise the writer's point of view.

● Explain what they suggest to the reader.

Compare your interpretations with those of another student.

Activity

9

a In the second stanza Tennyson uses the word 'blunder'd'. What does his choice of vocabulary tell you about his opinion of the battle commanders?

b Look again at the following lines 'Theirs not to … do and die'. What is suggested about the soldiers' response to the commanders' instructions?

Why do you think the writer has chosen to use repetition at this point?

c Dramatic imagery is used by the writer in the lines 'Into the jaws of Death, into the mouth of Hell'. What impact do these images have on the reader? How do they help to emphasise the writer's attitude to the plight of the soldiers?

Review and reflect

Using your answers from the previous tasks to help you, write about 8 to 10 lines to answer the question:

How does Tennyson express his feelings about war and the conduct of the soldiers in 'The Charge of the Light Brigade'?

In your answer you should:

■ refer to the methods used by the writer

■ select quotations from the text

■ write extended comments to explain your interpretation of the writer's meaning.

Stretch yourself

Work with a partner to prepare an imaginary interview with the writer of 'The Charge of the Light Brigade'. Plan the questions together for a role play of this interview. One of you should play the part of the interviewer and the other Tennyson.

Your questions and answers should cover the following areas:

● why the poem was written

● opinions on the behaviour of the soldiers and their commanders

● some of the techniques used in the poem.

Check your learning

In this chapter you have:

● selected a range of details from texts

● interpreted the writers' meaning based on evidence in the text

● developed your comments in detail.

Alternative interpretations

Objectives

In this chapter you will:

extend your skills in interpreting the writers' ideas and perspectives in texts

express your own opinions on texts

offer alternative interpretations of texts.

Interpreting the writer's ideas

In order to interpret the writer's ideas it is necessary to think carefully about what they are saying. In Text A, Don McCullin – a famous war photographer – writes about his work. Answer the questions in Activity 1 after reading the article closely.

(A)

Sitting here in a cottage in Somerset, I should perhaps be enjoying the birdsong and the soft rolling hills. I'm not, because I live on a military flight path, and instead of the birds I hear the engine noise of dive-bombing aircraft flown by pilots who are readying themselves for a war in Iraq. C-130 transport planes are streaming into the air force base at Brize Norton, and the flapping sound of Chinook helicopters keeps putting me back in Vietnam.

If you are a decent human being, war is going to offend you because it has no purpose other than to satisfy someone's desire for power and profit. And it is the little people who suffer. At the first whiff of trouble, the rich and the informed get into their Mercedes-Benzes and off-road vehicles and leave. The poor people, the very last of the dregs of society, can't escape. They get the bill.

I got into war photography because I felt I could approach it in a more dignified way than other people. I felt compassion for the victims of war, and I believed I would never do anything to betray that compassion. I remember visiting a hospital when they brought in a boy who had been hit by one of Saddam's helicopter bombs. This boy was burnt from head to toe; his whole body was bleeding. I remember thinking, then, that I should give this profession up.

Of course, it is the photographer's job to show some of that horror, to say: this is the real war, this is what it's like on the ground, this is what war does to you.

I have only ever considered myself a photographer – nothing more, nothing less. I went to war and thought of people and pain, not exhibitions and awards. I looked into people's eyes and they would look back and there would be something like a meeting of guilt. As a war photographer, you cannot escape guilt, particularly when the man in front of you who is just about to be shot appeals to you to help him.

Photography is not just about photographs: it's about communication. It's not about you. It's not about art. You are there just to record. Sometimes, all too rarely, what you record is acts of human decency, of kindness and compassion – I have seen men cradling dying comrades and weeping. But that's the only side of war you will see that's beautiful.

Adapted from www.guardian.co.uk, 14 February 2003

War orphans photographed by Don McCullin

Activity

1

a   Why do you think the writer chose to begin his account with a reference to the English countryside?

b   What is the effect of his addressing the reader directly at the start of the second paragraph?

c   Suggest possible meanings for the sentence 'They get the bill.'

d   What different feelings does McCullin appear to have towards his job?

e   What does the final sentence suggest about McCullin's attitude to war?

Exploring alternative interpretations

In Activity 1 you started to develop your interpretation of the writer's thoughts and feelings. As it is not possible to be certain about what the writer thinks, it can be useful to offer alternative interpretations based on what you have read.

Activities

2

Discuss each of the quotations below with a partner to produce two (or more) interpretations for each. An example has been given for the first quotation. The highlighted words indicate that the student is exploring meanings and suggesting alternatives.

❝Photography is not just about photographs; it's about communication.❞

This *suggests* that McCullin feels a photographer has an important message to put across to people who see his photographs. *Perhaps* he is implying that people will continue to think about the meaning behind the photographs for some time after they have viewed them. This *may* give readers a different perspective on the role of the photographer. They *may* see him as a teacher or even a preacher.

❝I looked into people's eyes and they would look back and there would be something like a meeting of guilt.❞

❝Sometimes, all too rarely, what you record is acts of human decency, kindness and compassion.❞

❝At the first whiff of trouble, the rich and the informed get into their Mercedes-Benzes and off-road vehicles and leave.❞

When you have discussed possible interpretations with a partner, compare your ideas with those of another pair of students. How different or similar were your interpretations?

3

Now use your answers to Activity 1 and Activity 2 to help you write a fuller response to this question:

What impressions have you formed about Don McCullin's attitude to war and to his job as a war photographer?

In your answer you should write about:

● what Don McCullin appears to think about war

● why you think he became a war photographer

● what seem to be the challenges of his job.

Remember to offer alternative interpretations to some of your points.

Analysing the writer's perspective and use of language

A writer's perspective can be detected in the language they use to present their ideas to readers. When you write an interpretation of a text you need to look closely and in detail at the language used by the writer to make an impact on readers. Read Text B, where George Orwell shares with readers his opinion of industrial landscapes in the north of England.

I remember a dreadful afternoon in the environs of Wigan. All round there was the lunar landscape of slag* heaps, and to the north, through the passes as it were, between the mountains of slag, you could see the factory chimneys sending out their plumes of smoke. The canal path was a mixture of cinders and frozen mud, crisscrossed by the imprints of innumerable clogs**, and all around and, as far as the slag heaps in the distance, stretched the 'flashes' – pools of stagnant water that had seeped into the hollows caused by the subsidence of ancient pits. It was horribly cold. It seemed a world from which vegetation had been banished: nothing existed except smoke, shale, ice, mud, ashes and foul water.

But even Wigan is beautiful compared with Sheffield. Sheffield I suppose could justly claim to be the ugliest town in the Old World.

One scene especially lingers in my mind. A frightful patch of waste ground (somehow, up there, a patch of waste ground attains a squalor that would be impossible even in London) trampled bare of grass and littered with newspapers and old saucepans. To the right an isolated row of gaunt four roomed houses, dark red, blackened by smoke.

To the left an interminable vista of factory chimneys, chimney beyond chimney, fading away into a dim blackish haze.

*slag: waste material from coal mining
**clogs: heavy wooden-soled shoes worn by workers

George Orwell, *The Road to Wigan Pier*, 1937

Activity

4 When you analyse a writer's use of language you focus on individual words and phrases and the effect they have on the reader. You can comment on the mood or tone that is created, as well as associations that are formed in the mind of the reader. Copy and complete the following table with your own response to the examples in note form.

Example	Impact on reader
The canal path was a mixture of cinders and mud, crisscrossed by the imprint of innumerable clogs…	• portrays an unattractive image of the place • frozen mud creates cold, unwelcoming tone • imprints of innumerable clogs suggests many unpleasant journeys have been made along canal
I remember a dreadful afternoon in the environs of Wigan.	
It was horribly cold.	

Now that you have looked more closely at the writer's use of language, you are going to extend your ideas and write your own interpretation of Text B. Begin by looking at Text C, an interpretation by a student in response to this question: How does Orwell reveal his opinions of the industrial landscape of the north of England?

Ⓒ

Useful phrase for considering effect on the reader

Includes brief details from the text to develop point of view/ considers impact on readers

George Orwell begins his description in a very negative way. When he says 'I remember a dreadful afternoon' the word 'dreadful' makes me think he does not have happy memories of the place he is about to describe. This is confirmed when he begins to write in detail about his visit to Wigan. The landscape described is almost alien – 'a lunar landscape' from which 'vegetation has been banished'. He selects unpleasant details such as 'mountains of slag' and pools of 'stagnant water' to encourage readers to share his opinion. He seems surprised by the ugliness of the landscape and yet at the same time the detail in which he writes about it possibly suggests that he is also fascinated by it. Perhaps he has not seen an industrial landscape before. I wondered why he went on to visit Sheffield which he describes as the 'ugliest town in the Old World'.

Offers alternative interpretations of writer's feelings

Useful words to introduce interpretation

Student expresses own opinion about George Orwell's perspective

Activity

5 Continue the above answer, focusing on Orwell's writing about Sheffield.

In your answer you should:

- show how the opening lines relate to the rest of the text
- refer briefly to details from the text
- explain the effect on the reader, of particular words and phrases
- use appropriate vocabulary to make your points and to introduce your interpretation
- consider alternative interpretations where possible.

Reviewing your learning

Activity

6 Read Text D which was written during the 1930s by Vivienne de Watteville after she arrived in Kenya 'to go into the wilds unarmed and win friendship with the animals'. With a partner, discuss the answers to the questions that surround it.

Key terms

Simile: a direct comparison of one thing with another.

(D)

What mood is the writer in as she approaches the rhino?

The wind had risen to a tearing gale, and nosing straight into it I approached the rhino somewhat downhill. There was no chance of this steady blow jumping round to betray me, and it was strong enough to carry away any sound of my footsteps. Precaution was therefore unnecessary, and I walked boldly up to them. Just how close I was, it is hard to say: but I felt that I could have flipped a pebble at them, and I noted subconsciously that the eye of the one nearest me was not dark brown as I had imagined it, but the colour of sherry.

Why does she include the detail about the colour of his eye?

And the experience has left me in some doubt whether a rhino has such poor sight as is commonly believed. Perhaps they heard the clicking of the cinema camera. This may have given the nearer one my direction, and then my coat or the brim of my hat flapping in the wind possibly caught his eye. At any rate, his ears pricked up, his champing jaws were held in suspense, and that little pale eye was definitely focused on me.

How does the continued focus on the rhino's eye help to change the mood of the account?

He lifted his head, trying to catch the wind. It told him nothing, but now he came deliberately towards me, nose to the ground and horn foremost, full of suspicion. I pressed the button and tried to keep a steady hand. This was not easy, for a rhino seen through the finder of a small camera looks remote, and it is only when you take the camera down to make sure, that you are horribly startled to see how near he really is. In the finder I saw his tail go up, and knew that he was on the point of charging. Though it was the impression of a fraction of a second, it was unforgettable. He was standing squarely on a flat boulder that raised him like a pedestal, and he seemed to tower up rugged and clear-cut as a monument against the clouds.

What impact does the writer's use of the second person 'you' have on the reader's view of events?

What is the effect of the simile in the final line?

Vivienne de Watteville, *Speak to the Earth: Wanderings and Reflections Among Elephants and Mountains*, 1935

Activity

7 Using the techniques you have practised so far, write a paragraph in answer to each of the following questions:

a What impressions have you formed about Vivienne de Watteville's character and motives and her attitude to wildlife? Remember to offer alternative interpretations and to refer to the text to support your points.

b How does the writer create an image of the rhino? Remember to analyse the writer's use of language in your response.

Swap your answer with another student. Check that they have:

● offered more than one interpretation of de Watteville's character and motives

● referred to details from the text and commented on the effect of language features on the reader

● given his or her opinion about the text.

Stretch yourself

Find a piece of travel writing and work out what the writer's thoughts and feelings are about the place, events or people they are describing. How does the writer's use of language help to reveal their feelings?

Check your learning

In this chapter you have:

● read texts closely

● formed your own ideas about meanings in texts

● developed an understanding of writers' perspectives

● made a detailed analysis of language and its impact on the reader.

10

Objectives

In this chapter you will:

study two texts, thinking about and making notes on audience and purpose, use of presentational features, and use of language

study the features of a written comparison and write your own comparison.

Making comparisons

Purpose and audience

The first step in preparing to compare two texts is to identify their purpose(s) and audience(s). Texts often have more than one purpose and audience.

Texts A and B were both produced by charities. Read them both carefully. Text A is part of a leaflet produced by Amnesty International, a campaigning organisation that aims to protect people wherever justice, fairness, freedom and truth are denied.

IF YOU DON'T CARE ABOUT HUMAN RIGHTS YOU'VE PROBABLY NEVER HAD THEM TAKEN AWAY

A

IF YOU WANT TO KNOW THE VALUE OF HUMAN RIGHTS IMAGINE LIVING WITHOUT THEM

Imagine you weren't entirely happy with your government. So you wrote them a letter saying why. And imagine a few days later the police came to your home and took you from your family and put you in a mental asylum. And left you there for two years.

Or that you were at home playing with your children. And three soldiers broke in and raped you. And you went to their commanding officer to complain. But he did nothing. And the next day the soldiers came back to your house and tied you up. And beat you. And stabbed you with a bayonet.

Or imagine you were on holiday. And you were arrested at the airport, but not told why. Instead you were flown secretly to another country where you were tortured before being sent to a prison camp. And that six years later you were still there.

Or suppose you were attending a regular church meeting. Just a low-key affair with a few friends. And then one day you were arrested and locked inside a shipping container and left there for months. And you were told you would not be set free unless you signed a form renouncing your beliefs.

All of these things really happened. To real people. One of them lives in Turkmenistan under a highly repressive regime. Another is a UK resident. And yet all four have shared one hard and bitter lesson. They have all learnt the true value of 'human rights'.

For them, human rights are not some lofty concept – some distant set of irrelevant laws. For these men and women – and for millions of others like them – human rights are the single most important thing in the world. Because they know that where there are no human rights, there is no safety, no protection, no shelter, no hope and – all too often – no life.

And they know something else too. They know that what is true for them, is true for us all. For you, for me, and for every human being on the planet.

Because the truth is, our basic human rights are the only thing that stand between us and torture, poverty, hunger, disease, disappearance, execution… What could possibly be of greater value than that? And what could be more important to protect?

FREEPOST RRRR-RHUC-HTZK
Amnesty International UK
3 Chapel Road
Redhill
RH1 1QD

**AMNESTY INTERNATIONAL
PROTECT THE HUMAN**

Text B is a page from a magazine produced by Médecins Sans Frontières (MSF), an independent humanitarian medical aid organisation. MSF is also known as Doctors without Borders. The quotation in the headline is part of the Hippocratic Oath, traditionally taken by doctors to observe a code of medical ethics.

(B)

"I WILL REMEMBER THAT THERE IS ART TO MEDICINE AS WELL AS SCIENCE"

MEDECINS SANS FRONTIERES

Name:
Solveig Hamilton

Role: Doctor

Nationality: British

Country: Chechnya

"When their mother became ill, Magomed and his brother looked after her – not realising that she had TB, and that they were in danger of contracting the illness from her. Soon Magomed started feeling weak, and developed a terrible cough.

Improved standards of living and healthcare mean that tuberculosis (TB) is incredibly rare in the UK and western Europe. But in the aftermath of war, it is a deadly problem for people in Chechnya.

People here endure woeful, cramped, unsanitary living conditions. Four years after the worst of the fighting stopped many still live in ruined buildings with no electricity or mains water supply. The perfect conditions for TB to flourish.

Magomed only realised he might have TB after watching a MSF public information film. He visited a MSF clinic and as soon as he'd been diagnosed we began treatment.

Fortunately, Magomed's TB was diagnosed early enough for it to still be treatable, and he soon started to look better and gain weight. But then there was a major setback. Local security forces arrested Magomed, suspecting him of previous involvement with a criminal group (a claim which was never proved). In detention, Magomed could no longer come to our clinic – but we couldn't give up on him, especially as it's very dangerous to interrupt a course of TB treatment. So we treated him by 'remote control', sending him drugs and written advice by post. While the method was unusual, it cured him completely.

TB is a massive problem here, but there are only five functioning TB clinics in the whole of Chechnya, serving one million people. Four of these clinics are supported by MSF, with volunteers training doctors and diagnostic teams, supplying essential drugs, and treating patients directly.

11

MSF's international volunteers like me get outstanding support from our Chechen colleagues, who guide and advise patients through the treatment process, and run public information campaigns about TB. With their continued support MSF will continue the long battle to combat TB in Chechnya.

Reviewing X-rays in a MSF-supported TB diagnostic centre in Shelkovskoy village.

© Misha Galustov/agency.photographer.ru

Activity

1

a Copy and complete the following table by identifying the intended purpose(s) and audience(s) for Texts A and B on the previous pages. In the second and fourth columns of the chart give your reasons for thinking this.

Text A	Reasons for thinking this	Text B	Reasons for thinking this
Purpose ● ●		Purpose ● ●	
Audience ● ●		Audience ● ●	

b Check your table with another student's. Are there any purposes and/or audiences that you missed? If so, add them to your table.

c Highlight or underline any purposes/audiences that are common to both texts.

Presentational features

You are now going to think about the presentational features that appear in these two extracts. The identification of these features is only the first step. The next step is to work out how and why each feature is used within the text. The final step is to assess its effectiveness. In order to do the second and third steps, you need to consider the connection between the feature and the intended purpose and/or audience.

Activity

2

a Identify the presentational features that are used in Texts A and B. Explain how and why each feature is used and comment on its effectiveness. Recording your ideas in two simple tables like the one below (one for Text A and one for Text B) helps to ensure that you cover all three steps.

Text A: Feature	How/why the feature is used	Opinion on effectiveness
Use of colour		

b Check your table with another student's. Are there any significant presentational features that you missed? If so, add them to your table.

c Think and talk about any differences in opinion about the effectiveness of the features. Develop and/or change your view if appropriate.

d Place an asterisk (*) beside any presentational features that are common to both texts.

Developing your comments

When writing about presentational features you need to show that you understand the part they play in the text as a whole. Text C is a student response written about the use of illustrations in Text B. The annotations show you how the comment has been constructed.

(C)

Identification of illustrations

There are three distinct pictures in Text B, a photograph of the doctor, a map showing Chechnya's geographical position and a photograph of workers in a TB diagnostic centre in Chechnya supported by MSF. The illustrations are used to break up the text and make it look more interesting as, without them, it would simply contain the heading and a continuous block of type-print. The photograph of the doctor, placed alongside her details, gives the reader a stronger sense of who the writer is and makes the text more personal. The fact that she is smiling reinforces the written text's message that the work she does is rewarding. As she is looking directly at the reader, it suggests that she is honest and someone who can be trusted. The map is designed to show the geographical location of Chechnya though it could be argued that it's not that helpful. Many readers might need a wider perspective in order to work out where Chechnya is. The photograph taken in the clinic demonstrates the work that is done and so illustrates the written text, though this particular clinic is not specified in the text. The text as a whole is designed to inform the reader and the illustrations, when taken together, enhance this purpose, giving visual images of the written text; they are functional rather than thought-provoking.

Comment on purpose of illustrations

Analyses and evaluates image

Evaluates effectiveness of image

Links to written text

Evaluates effectiveness

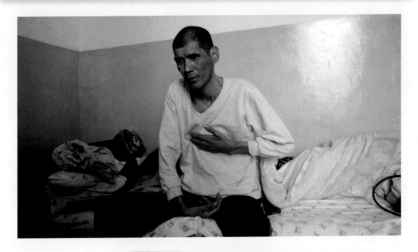

Illustrations can sometimes be more abstract than functional. They can be designed to provoke thought as well as to reflect the written text.

Activity

3

a With a partner, examine the image at the bottom left of Text A. Make notes on it using the following prompts:
- What does it appear to be?
- What does it make you think of?
- How does it reflect the written text?
- What is the link between it and the Amnesty logo that can be seen at the top right of Text A?
- How effective is it?

b Using your notes to help you, write a detailed comment on the use of this image.

Developing comments on language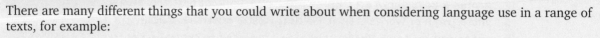

There are many different things that you could write about when considering language use in a range of texts, for example:

simplicity/complexity of vocabulary · discourse markers · rhetorical questions · directives · adjectives · exaggeration · type/variety of sentence structures · tenses · emotive language · repetition · lists · pronouns

Activity

4 Using the list above to help you, identify, with examples, different features of the use of language in both Text A and Text B.

As with presentational features, the identification of features of language use is only the first step. The next step is to work out how and why the feature is used within the text. The final step is to assess its effectiveness. To do this well you need to develop your skills in examination and analysis. Text D is a student response written about the use of the word 'imagine' in Text A. The annotations show you how the comment has been constructed.

(D)

Identifies usage → The word 'imagine' is clearly important. It is used in the main heading, at the start of the first paragraph and twice more in the body of the text. When we

Explores meaning → 'imagine' something, we form a mental picture of it. Often we use our imagination to take us to worlds and places we know little of. The writer is both inviting and directing the reader to 'imagine' the experiences of others. It makes the assumption that these experiences are not our own and subtly suggests that they are made up and unreal, perhaps to emphasise just how awful and unbelievable they are. The word 'Imagine' at the start of the first paragraph is followed by the word 'or' at the start of the next three paragraphs. Clearly the reader is being directed to 'Imagine this or this or this or this' with each paragraph describing a different situation. The word 'imagine' is the word that provides the link between the four paragraphs. The pattern is only broken by the opening of the first paragraph in the second column where the emphasis is shifted. Now we find the words 'really' and 'real', emphasising that these situations, the one the reader has been asked to imagine, are not made up. The writer has effectively held the reader in suspense, forcing them to put themselves in the place of these 'imaginary' victims, before finally revealing, for maximum impact, that they are the real-life experiences of real people.

Considers word in immediate context

Interprets

Considers word in broader context

Analyses and evaluates

Clearly you could not write in such detail about every feature of language use. You should aim to select three or four of the more significant features in the text. Examine the features closely, work out a range of things about them and then develop your comment. In this way you start to develop the ability to examine, analyse and write well about language use.

Activities

5 **a** Work with a partner and make notes on the use of each of the following features of language selected from Texts A and B. Remember, where appropriate, to think about:

- the feature itself
- the feature within its immediate context
- the feature within the text as a whole
- intended purpose and audience.

Text A

- the use of the past and present tenses
- the unusual sentence structures that start with conjunctions – for example, 'And', 'Or', 'But' and 'Because'
- the use of repetition – for example, 'human rights', 'no'.

Text B

- the use of the past and present tenses
- the use of complex sentence structures
- the use of emotive language – for example, 'deadly problem', 'the long battle to combat TB'.

b Join another pair and share your ideas on each feature of language. Add to your notes.

6 Choose one of the features of language that you examined closely In Activity 5. Using your notes to help you, write a developed comment about the use of that language feature.

Writing a comparison

When you compare two texts you focus on the similarities and/or differences between them. You need to connect the point made about one text with the point made about the other and develop your comment on them both. You do not need to compare everything; your comparison should be based on the focus of the question. This may be the use of language and/or presentational features – for example:

- Compare the ways in which presentational features and language are used for effect in Text A and Text B.

This question can be broken down to highlight the different things you need to do:

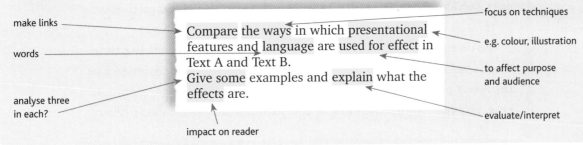

make links

words

analyse three in each?

Compare the ways in which presentational features and language are used for effect in Text A and Text B. Give some examples and explain what the effects are.

focus on techniques

e.g. colour, illustration

to affect purpose and audience

evaluate/interpret

impact on reader

A quick plan for the answer to this question might look something like this:

Text A
- Purpose: engage, interest, raise empathy, inform, gain support.
- Audience: teenagers? adults? potential supporters.
- Presentation: colour/image – barbed wire/heading/framed/balanced/logo.
- Language: imagine, sentence structures, repetition, tenses.

Text B
- Purpose: inform, interest, explain, gain support.
- Audience: adults – current supporters of MSF – people wanting to know more about MSF's work.
- Presentation: map and photos/heading/colour?
- Language: tenses, complex vocab and sentence structures, emotive lang.

Read the following paragraphs that are the opening of one student's answer to this question. Study the annotations that show the skills demonstrated by the student. The words highlighted in yellow show you where and how the student has made comparisons between the texts.

Both Text A and Text B are produced by charities, which presumably are both aiming to raise awareness and gain more supporters. Text A seems to be focused on directly engaging the reader in an attempt to make them empathise with the victims of torture whilst Text B is more of an informative text, perhaps partly designed for current supporters who want an update on the work of MSF. Both texts use presentational and language features for different reasons and with different effects.

Shows understanding that presentation and language are directly linked to intended purpose and audience

Text A, the Amnesty International leaflet, has the more striking presentation. The presentation is deceptively simple with the two sides seeming to frame and balance the typed text and being visually linked by the use of colour and the image of the barbed wire. In contrast, Text B is busier with three distinct images separating out the print, presumably to add interest and illustrate some of the content of the written text. Interestingly, contrasting colours are used in the headings of both texts. The contrasting colour (pink in Text A and red in Text B) marks a shift in the text and puts emphasis on the words 'imagine' and 'remember' respectively, as though forcefully directing the reader to do these things.

Evaluates

Evaluates

Interprets

The image of the barbed wire in Text A is a more abstract one than those used in Text B, designed to prompt all kinds of associations in the mind of the reader. It looks as though it is a destroyed telegraph pole, perhaps suggesting lack of communication and things being

Interprets

kept quiet. The destruction of the pole suggests war and violence and the barbed wire has connotations of pain and secrecy, barbed wire being used both to keep people in and to keep people out. Furthermore, *— Analyses and interprets* the barbed wire image is reflected in the AI logo where it surrounds the candle which effectively suggests that this charity offers light *Analyses and interprets —►* and hope. All these ideas are echoes of the content of the written *— Links to content of written text* text – the person held in a mental asylum for two years, the person stabbed with a bayonet.

While the images in Text B are less interesting, they do, generally, serve their purpose of illustrating the text. The picture *Evaluates —►* of the doctor adds a personal touch; the fact that she is looking *Analyses —►* directly at the reader and smiling implies that she is honest and suggests her work is rewarding and worthwhile. The second photograph illustrates the text's reference to the clinics supported by *— Links to content of written text* MSF, perhaps to aid the reader's understanding of the type of work that takes place there. The map is designed to inform the reader as to the geographical location of Chechnya, though it is debatable *◄— Evaluates and links to content* how useful this is. Unless the reader is already familiar with the geography of the area, it would do little to further understanding.

Activity

7 Now write the part of this answer that focuses on the use of language in both texts. You can use the student's notes or make your own. Aim to show that you can:

- analyse uses of language
- make perceptive and interpretative comments on the effect of language use
- evaluate effectiveness
- make intelligent and relevant comparisons.

Stretch yourself

Using what you have learned in this chapter, write a clear revision guide for students on how to write a good comparison.

Check your learning

In this chapter you have:
- considered the purposes and audiences of two texts
- explored uses of presentational features in two texts
- examined the uses of language in two texts
- compared the uses of presentation and language features for effect in two texts.

Making your reading skills count in the exam

About the exam

There is one exam paper in GCSE English and GCSE English Language. Its focus is:

- Understanding and producing non-fiction texts.

The paper is divided into two sections:

- **Section A:** Reading (one hour, worth 20% of your final marks)
- **Section B:** Writing (one hour, worth 20% of your final marks)

In this chapter we will deal with Section A. You will find out more about Section B in Chapter 22, which follows the Writing chapters.

In Section A, you will be asked to read three non-fiction items and answer four questions. There will be one question on each item. The fourth question will name one item and will ask you to choose a second one. It will ask you to compare the treatment of a specific feature, such as use of language, in the two items.

What you need to know

You have one hour to demonstrate the reading skills summarised in the Assessment Objectives. They are printed below. The annotations help explain their meaning in more detail.

Show skills such as inference, deduction, exploration and interpretation

Select detail in order to answer it

Read and understand texts, selecting material appropriate to purpose, collating from different sources and making comparisons and cross-references as appropriate.

Select and use material from two different texts in order to answer the question

Point out similarities and differences between two texts, and make relevant connections between them

Make judgements on the effectiveness of the features used in the text

Focus in detail on the techniques of the writers and designers

Examine and analyse the words and the order in which they are placed, the way the text is organised and the use of presentational features

Explain and evaluate how writers use linguistic, grammatical, structural and presentational features to achieve effects and engage and influence the reader, supporting their comments with detailed textual references.

Consider how the writer/designer is trying to manipulate the intended reader

Refer to the text in detail to support the points you make

Sample questions

The questions in the exam are based on the Assessment Objectives.

Here are four example questions. The marks awarded for each answer are given.

---

1   Read Item A, the online article *The First Emperor at the British Museum*.
    What do you learn about the writer's views of the exhibition at the British
    Museum from reading this article?   *(8 marks)*

Here you are being asked to:
- read and understand a text
- select material appropriate to purpose.

---

2   Now read Item B, an extract from the Jorvik Viking Centre leaflet.
    How do the colours and the images add to the effectiveness of the text?   *(8 marks)*

Here you are being asked to:
- explain and evaluate how writers use structural and presentational features
  to achieve effects and engage and influence the reader
- support your comments with detailed textual references.

---

3   Now read Item C, *Finding Treasure*, which is an extract from a non-fiction book.
    What are some of the thoughts and feelings the writer recalls in his account of
    his search for hidden treasure?   *(8 marks)*

Here you are being asked to:
- read and understand a text
- select material appropriate to purpose.

Now you need to refer to Item C, *Finding Treasure*, and either Item A or Item B.

4   Compare the ways in which language is used for effect in the two texts.
    Give some examples and explain what the effects are.   *(16 marks)*

Here you are being asked to:
- collate from different sources and make comparisons and cross-
  references as appropriate
- explain and evaluate how writers use linguistic and grammatical
  features to achieve effects and engage and influence the reader
- support your comments with detailed textual references.

The texts referred to in this sample paper are printed on the
following pages. Read them closely.

Activity

1   With a partner, or on
your own, make notes on
the answers you would
give to each of the above
questions.

The First Emperor at the British Museum

A platoon of China's terracotta warriors has landed in the British Museum

The First Emperor, which opens this week at the British Museum, is our chance to catch up with the most momentous archaeological discovery of the 20th century. Finally, visitors will come face to face with the near-legendary warriors of China's terracotta army.

Advance ticket sales are already breaking box-office records. Soon the queues will be running round the block. But will it be worth it? Must you join the crush? The answer – though it may not be apparent at first glance – must emphatically be yes.

The outcome of years of diplomacy and planning, this exhibition represents the biggest display of terracotta warriors yet to be lent outside China. But when you tot them all up – including the charioteer's stocky clay horses – only 20 figures are actually included. That's hardly an army. It's not even a platoon. This show can hardly recreate the overwhelming wonder that the visitor to China must surely feel as he first comes face to face with phalanx after phalanx marching out of eternity.

At first glance the emperor's companions might appear rather shabby. As patched and repaired as old teddy bears, they have lost all but a few faded traces of the brightly coloured pigments that once gave them dazzling presence. The archer's bow has disintegrated. The acrobat's spinning plate has broken and the strongman's weights have dropped. Exhibition designers and curators have to work hard to create a sense of spectacle. But they succeed brilliantly.

What actually confronts the visitor is a display that takes as its primary focus the terracotta figures. These are what you will stand and stare at. Look carefully and you will be spellbound.

At first you pick out the different headdresses, haircuts, styles of armour or shoe of the various divisions and ranks. But it is only as you confront them face to face, that you start to feel the full force of this extraordinary achievement. Figures that start out remote, turn into people that we recognise and know.

You can see the spread of cultures which this empire must have incorporated in faces that range from delicate Turkic features to broad Mongolian heads. But there is something more universal even than that in this show. It lies in the expressions of the faces, in the shapes of the eyes and the set of the lips. You can pick each one out like the character of a person that you know. You can feel a profound sense of relation.

In the end, it is not the achievements of an emperor that this show celebrates, but the lives of these individuals, upon whom his empire was founded.

Adapted from Rachel Campbell-Johnston, 'The First Emperor at the British Museum',
The Times, 11 September 2007

(B)

TRAVEL BACK 1000 YEARS...

...on board your time machine through the backyards and houses to the bustling streets of Jorvik. Everything here is based on facts – from the layout of the houses, the working craftsmen, the language of the gossiping neighbours, to the smells of cooking and the cesspit!

As you travel through the busy market place, you will experience a blast of smoke as you pass the blacksmith's furnace, smell the fish on the riverside and visit the hearth scene inside the Viking home.

You are in JORVIK!

GET FACE TO FACE WITH THE VIKINGS

Be one of over 15 million visitors who have met the world famous JORVIK Vikings and learn about their life in our three exciting exhibitions that delve more into York's Viking past.

Are you a Viking?
Using this unique exhibition you can discover how the Vikings have influenced your life and see if you could in fact be a Viking!

Artefacts Alive
Our four holographic Viking ghosts will introduce you to 800 Viking Age finds and explain how some of these items were used in everyday life.

Unearthed
Stories of Viking Age life, death, battle and disease can all be revealed through the examination of 10-11th century bones. See a real life skeleton of a Viking killed in battle and discover what secrets he might tell. Talks by archaeologists throughout the day.

Finding Treasure

The search for treasure is the journey of life, but its pursuit puts you in the way of risk and danger, and brings death to some along the way.

I stared down at the sandy shingle at my feet and it was like seeing the pink skin beneath the fur of an animal. The waves in the night had stripped the beach bare of its normal shingle cover and what was left behind were hard deposits of mud and sand into which old pebbles and bits of glass and corroded metal had set. It was somewhere in there that I'd seen the treasure.

As the waves pulled back and gave me moments of safety, I bent forward for a better view of the shingle-sand to try to catch again a glimpse of that magical silver and green treasure.

The sea crashed to my right and a wall of water began to surge towards me. The wind roared at my back and chilled my neck, the sound of the grating shingle mounted in my ears, but all I could do was search at my feet, my eyes racing to find … to find …

The only thing I saw was a spike of metal, black-red, which when I pushed at it with my boot turned out to be no more than a shred of old copper wire. Yet I bent to pick it up, something being better than nothing to the treasure hunter. Straightening up with the wall of water almost on me, I ran. And ran.

But it came roaring up the beach so fast it caught my legs and feet and made me fall, my hands plunging through its green-white depth to the shingle beneath, water forcing its way up my sleeves. I pushed myself upright and the water paused, turned and suddenly began to drag me back in the opposite direction, this time so powerful at my legs that it nearly toppled me backwards into the path of the next wave. It was in my boots, up my legs, pulling, pulling like a thousand watery hands, and its roar in my ears was the beginning of a vast silence I would hear for ever if I gave up.

I stumbled again, fell back into the water, heaved myself up as it tried to drag me back down, and blindly staggered up the shingle until bang! I hit the sea wall and there was blood on my hand from a graze on my forehead.

The steps were too far away to reach had another great wave come. But instead the water weakened below me and retreated. It petered out into yellow foam that died down into the shingle below where I stood. The next wave was nowhere near as powerful as the last, nor was the one after it, and sopping and sodden though I was, my eyes soon returned to their search of the shingle, as my greed for treasure took over.

I ventured back down the beach to where I had been, one eye on the waves, watching for another big one, the other unable to let the shingle go. That was when I saw again the crescent of green and silver I had first glimpsed, the fallen moon of a coin peeking from the shingle-sand that had long since accepted and held on to it, until the day came when it was uncovered for eyes to see if, in that rage of water, they dared to go and look.

I bent down as yet another great wave mounted up behind me and I picked up my first treasure of the sea.

Adapted from William Horwood, *The Boy With No Shoes*, 2005

Sample answers

You have one hour in which to read three texts and answer four questions. You need to give focused answers. The following activities will help you do this.

Activity

2

Remind yourself of Question 1 out of 8 (page 67). Read Texts D and E, which are two students' answers to this question. The first, Student A, was awarded 5 marks. The second, Student B, was awarded 8 marks.

a In pairs, identify which of the following skills each student demonstrates:

- offers evidence that the text is understood
- engages with the text as an article
- considers the impact of the text on the reader
- develops comments
- offers relevant and appropriate quotations
- interprets information
- makes perceptive comments
- adopts an overview.

b What advice would you offer Student A to help him or her achieve the higher mark of Student B?

Ⓓ Student A

The writer seems to be quite excited about the exhibition at first because she talks about it being 'momentous'. She also says it is 'near-legendary' which means that these warriors have been around for a long time. But then, even though she says people should definitely go and see it, she points out all the things that are wrong with it like there are only 20 figures and some bits of them are missing like the archer's bow. That might make people less likely to go but if they read on they will still want to because she seems to say that it doesn't matter that it's not a full army. She thinks the exhibition designers have done a brilliant job because you get to see the figures as real people: 'people that we recognise and know'. At the end of the article she says these figures will keep you 'spellbound' as though you'll never want to stop looking at them and that the exhibition is really about them and not the Emperor at all even though it talks about the Emperor in the headline.

Ⓔ Student B

The writer moves from excitement, through scepticism to finally arrive at enchantment. She offers a fair and honest analysis for the reader acknowledging the potential hazards of 'the crush', the initial disappointments of the 'rather shabby' figures, but then capturing our imagination with her account of how it feels to 'stand and stare' at each individual figure. This is not about an army, or even a platoon, as the article's sub-heading suggests. This is about the individual – the person behind the figure, both its creator and its model. In these figures she perceives the range of ethnic origins and, more significantly, the individual characters – the characters we meet in our everyday modern lives, the characters to whom we are directly related. It is this 'sense of relation' that causes her ultimately to so strongly recommend the exhibition and to refer to its designers as having 'succeeded so brilliantly'. The temptation to stand 'spellbound' in front of these figures would be difficult for any reader to resist.

Activities

3 Remind yourself of Question 2 (page 67).

a Read Text F, a response by a student who achieved a mark of 5 out of 8. The annotations show you the skills demonstrated by the student.

> The pictures show you how you will travel and some of the things you will see at the Viking museum. There are people of different ages in the transporter so it makes you think it would be a place where all the family could go. The girl looks as though she is going to have a helmet put on her head so it shows that you can do different things while you're there as well as look. The three people at the bottom are all wearing Viking costumes and they are all looking straight at the reader. The background is dark so that the white print can stand out against it and the pictures are lit up as though a light is shining on them to draw your attention to what you will see and do if you go there. The picture of the transporter and the village scene is set above the writing that tells you all about this and when you see the picture of the girl, just below it the writing says 'Be one of over 15 million visitors' so she is one of the visitors. The paragraph just above the three Vikings is about stories of 'Viking Age' so, again, the picture links to the writing. The orange colour on the first section is like a curtain so it's as though the curtain is going to be opened and you're going to go into the darker section where you'll see everything.

▢ describes what is seen

▢ links the picture content to the content of the text

▢ explains and starts to interpret

b In order to gain higher marks the student would need to show he or she could:

- analyse the images in more detail
- make perceptive comments when linking the images to written content
- comment on the impact of the pictures collectively as well as individually
- show closer consideration of intended purpose(s) and audience(s).

List additional points this student could have made to achieve a higher mark.

4 Remind yourself of Question 3 (page 67). You are going to practise writing comments that could be included in this answer.

a Start with an overview of the mixture of thoughts and feelings that the writer recalls in the passage. Identify these and write two or three sentences showing you understand that a range of thoughts and feelings were experienced.

b Show that you can write about the thoughts and feelings in a perceptive way. Use quotations to support your points. Write one paragraph about the boy's feelings of hope and one paragraph about the boy's feelings of fear.

c Remember this is a non-fiction text. The writer is writing about his own memories. Write one paragraph explaining how the writer captures the thoughts of a young boy in the passage.

Activity

5 Remind yourself of Question 4 (page 67).

You must refer to Item C, *Finding Treasure* and can choose either Item A or Item B.

You are advised to choose **some** examples. It is much better to analyse two or three good examples from each text than to write about ten examples in a superficial way.

a Compare Texts G and H, taken from two different students' answers. Identify why the comments in Text G are worth more marks than those in Text H.

(G) Student A

He uses colour when he writes about the 'crescent of green and silver'. This helps the reader to imagine what the coin looks like and to understand why the boy wanted to find it. He says it's a 'fallen moon' which shows that it is something of value and worth looking for.

The writer of Text B also uses language to help create a picture. He directs the reader to 'Travel back' and 'Get face to face with ...' almost as though it's an order and the reader must do these things. He uses lists to show you all the different things you can see there and writes about the 'bustling streets' to suggest that there are lots of things happening and that you need to go and see them.

(H) Student B

Colour is used throughout the passage as a means of description. We have the 'black-red' copper wire, the 'green-white' depth of the water and the 'yellow foam'. But it is at its most effective when incorporated in the description of the coin, 'the crescent of green and silver'. This image reveals just how little of the coin is visible, a reality echoed in the words 'glimpsed' and 'peeking'. The word 'silver' suggests value and 'green' has connotations of desire and envy, both words helping to explain the lengths the boy has gone to in his attempt to find the 'treasure'. The image is sustained in the metaphor of the 'fallen moon', the 'crescent' being the only visible part, reinforcing the impression that this is something extraordinary and rare.

Text B is very different in its intended purpose and this is reflected in the language used. There is very little use of imagery and only the occasional adjective such as 'bustling'. The emphasis is supposed to be on facts and the writer uses lists and groups of three to convey to the reader the different things he will see at Jorvik. However, it is the verbs that are of most interest. Verbs such as 'travel', 'delve', 'discover' and 'revealed' help to suggest a journey of discovery to a place where things can be gradually uncovered, strangely much like the boy in Text C finally uncovers the coin. There is a sense of mystery created as you 'travel' in your transporter, not simply around the centre but back through time.

b Write your own response to Question 4. Aim to show that you can:

- closely analyse the use of language and its effects
- comment perceptively on how meaning is revealed through language choice
- make relevant points of comparison throughout your response.

c In pairs, read and assess your answers to Question 4. Decide which one is the best and agree the reasons for your choice.

Check your learning

In this chapter you have:

- studied how the Assessment Objective for Reading is tested in the exam
- examined texts and questions in a sample paper
- considered how to achieve the highest marks you can in your exam.

12

Making your reading skills count in the controlled assessment

Objectives

In this chapter you will:

learn more about how your reading skills are tested in the controlled assessment

explore the different choices available to you

consider how to achieve high marks in your controlled assessment.

What is controlled assessment?

During your GCSE course, the reading skills that you have developed during the first ten chapters of this section of the book will be tested by controlled assessment. What this will involve depends on whether you are studying GCSE English or GCSE English Language.

GCSE English

Controlled assessment title
Understanding creative texts

Mark value
20% = 40 marks

Texts you will have to study
- a play by Shakespeare
- a prose text from either a different culture or the English Literary heritage
- a poetry text from either a different culture or the English Literary heritage

If you chose to study prose for your English literary heritage text then you will have to study a poetry text for your different culture text. You will produce **three** pieces of writing.

Choice of task
One of:
- themes and ideas
- characterisation and voice

Planning and preparation
You are allowed to spend time discussing the texts and task, and you may make brief notes which can be taken into the controlled assessment.

Time for writing
Up to 4 hours

Expected length
About 1600 words

GCSE English Language

Controlled assessment title
Understanding written texts (extended reading)

Mark value
15% = 30 marks

Texts you will have to study
One extended text from any genre, including non-fiction – for example:
- a novel
- a collection of short stories
- a play
- a collection of poems
- a literary non-fiction text

You will produce **one** piece of writing.

Choice of task
One of:
- themes and ideas
- characterisation and voice

Planning and preparation
You are allowed to spend time discussing the texts and task, and you may make brief notes which can be taken into the controlled assessment.

Time for writing
Up to 4 hours

Expected length
About 1200 words

You are allowed to take brief notes into the controlled assessment and to use a clean copy of the text. You are not allowed:

- **annotated versions of the texts**: copies of texts need to be 'clean'
- **pre-prepared drafts**: you must not write out a 'rough' version of your response and either seek advice about it or take it into the controlled assessment
- to take your writing out of the controlled assessment room between sessions.

Your preparation may be based on discussion with other students of the text and task. You must spend time thinking about:

- key points you will make and the order you will make them in
- sections of the text you will focus on to make and develop your key points.

Identifying key sections of the text is an important part of your preparation. The best writing is always focused on important parts of the text. When you focus on sections you are more likely to comment on details of the writer's language. In your planning, therefore, you could make a note of the key sections of the text you wish to explore so that you do not waste time in the controlled assessment searching for appropriate passages.

In planning your response you are allowed to spend time reading, re-reading and discussing the texts. One of the best ways to approach any literary text is to discuss it with others but it is important to develop your personal response. In the higher assessment bands the descriptor used is 'confident, assured'. You are more likely to exhibit confidence and assurance if you are exploring your own ideas rather than trying to make sense of someone else's.

Introducing the tasks

There are two options for the controlled assessment task:

- **Themes and ideas**: this means you will need to write an essay in which you focus on one of the main ideas explored by the writer. For example, in *Romeo and Juliet* Shakespeare dramatises ideas about love and hate – you might be asked to develop your understanding of what the play shows about love and hate.
- **Characterisation and voice**: you might be asked to concentrate on how the writer presents one character or the relationship between characters in a text.

One of the most important differences between exams and controlled assessments is that you have quite a lot of time to prepare for the controlled assessment task. You will know the task – unlike those in the exam – and you will be able to discuss and research the task in lessons before the controlled assessment.

To do well in the controlled assessment task you will need a good understanding of the Assessment Objectives for Reading. You will find a detailed breakdown of two of the objectives in Chapter 11, which focus on the reading part of the exam. However, there are another two Assessment Objectives for Reading which only apply to controlled assessment.

GCSE English

Understand texts in their social, cultural and historical contexts.

- Develop and sustain interpretations of writers' ideas and perspectives.

You need to be able to build up and extend your understanding of writers' ideas. This shows how controlled assessment is different from examination. In examination there is less time to answer questions whereas in controlled assessment you have quite a lot of planning time and time to extend your ideas.

- Understand texts in their social, cultural and historical contexts.

'Contexts' refers to the kind of times and society in which the texts were written. For example, in the 17th century Shakespeare wrote a play called *The Merchant of Venice*, which features a central character who is Jewish. If you have some understanding of what life was like for Jewish people in Shakespeare's time, you will have a better grasp of the different ideas explored in the play.

GCSE English Language

- Develop and sustain interpretations of writers' ideas and perspectives.

You need to be able to build up and extend your understanding of writers' ideas. This shows how controlled assessment is different from examination. In examination there is less time to answer questions whereas in controlled assessment you have quite a lot of planning time and time to extend your ideas.

Sample tasks and sample answers

GCSE English

You have to write about three texts and have up to four hours in which to do so. This means each response will take little longer than one hour. When you plan you must take this into consideration. If you write at great length about two texts and only briefly about the third, you may lose marks. You will be expected to:

- make an appropriate number of points for the time allowed
- select points and supporting evidence
- plan to finish your response in about one hour.

GCSE English Language

You have up to four hours to complete your task but you only have to write about one text. This means that you have the time to explore a single text in more depth and detail than in GCSE English. It is important to break your task down into separate stages. For example, if you are responding to a play or novel you might decide to explore three or four separate sections of the text in detail and spend an hour on each section.

Here is a sample task based on the Themes and ideas topic area.

> 1 Explore the ways people's relationships with nature are developed in a text from the English Literary Heritage.

Explore the ways means that you need to spend time identifying, explaining and evaluating:

- the writer's ideas
- some of the techniques used by the writer to develop their ideas.

In your response you need to show that you can select material appropriate to the task and use material from different parts of the text(s).

A text from the English Literary Heritage is a text written by an important writer who is no longer alive.

Activity

a Read Text A and look at the annotations, which draw attention to some of the ideas and techniques used.

b Copy out and annotate Text B in a similar way, keeping in mind that the task is asking you to comment on the writer's relationship with nature.

(A)

Below the Green Corrie

The mountains gathered round me
like bandits. Their leader
swaggered up close in the dark light,
full of threats, full of thunders.

But it was they who stood and delivered,
They gave me their money and their lives,
They filled me with mountains and thunders.

My life was enriched
with an infusion of theirs.
I clambered downhill through the ugly weather.
And when I turned to look goodbye
to those marvellous prowlers
a sunshaft had pierced the clouds
and their leader,
that swashbuckling mountain,
was wearing
a bandolier of light.

Norman MacCaig, 'Below the Green Corrie'

'But' introduces a change of idea developed in the rest of this line and the following two. 'Stood and delivered' is a reference to the old-fashioned phrase 'Stand and deliver' used by highwaymen when they were demanding money and valuables from their victims

An 'infusion' is the process of extracting certain active properties – the writer sees mountains as living things able to exert a force on people

The 'dark' and 'thunders' and 'ugly weather' of the early part of the poem are now replaced with light – again this reflects the change of idea in the poem

A simile is used to convey an impression of danger to the reader

The repetition adds to the sense of threat

The change in idea – that nature, rather than being threatening is actually life-enhancing is developed through the use of a precise word

This is an oxymoron – it is surprising to see things as usually unpleasant as 'prowlers' called 'marvellous'. This helps unite the two main ideas of the poem so far – that mountains are threatening but also wonderful

These two words return us to the idea of 'bandits' but a word like 'swashbuckling', rather than being threatening is romantic and glamorous. A 'bandolier' – an ammunition belt usually worn across one shoulder is also associated with the stereotypically romanticised view of bandits and pirates

(B)

Storm in the Black Forest

Now it is almost night, from the bronzey soft sky
jugfull after jugfull of pure white liquid fire, bright white
tipples over and spills down,
and is gone
and gold-bronze flutters bent through the thick upper air.

And as the electric liquid pours out, sometimes
a still brighter white snake wriggles among it, spilled
and tumbling wriggling down the sky:
and then the heavens cackle with uncouth sounds.

And the rain won't come, the rain refuses to come!

This is the electricity that man is supposed to have mastered
chained, subjugated to his use!
supposed to!

D.H. Lawrence, 'Storm in the Black Forest'

You should plan to answer the question in the task using the amount of evidence reasonable for allowed time. For example, here is how one student planned their response to 'Below the Green Corrie':

- Introduction: the poem focuses on one feature of nature – mountains – and shows that the writer's relationship with them is not simple (5 minutes)
- Explore lines 1 to 4 which suggest threat (5 minutes)
- Explore lines 5 to 10 in which the relationship changes (10 minutes)
- Explore lines 11 to 17 and how the writer's ideas about threat and wonder are reinforced (10 minutes)
- Conclusion: a precise answer to the question in the task (5 minutes)

The timings are not meant to be exact but they give a rough indication of timing which should allow the student to finish the task. By thinking about timings the student can decide which points to include in their response and which to ignore.

The plan approaches the poem in a logical way. To show understanding of structure, the student follows the sequence of ideas in the poem – for example, how the poem opens and ends.

Activity

2 Read Texts C and D, which are extracts from two students' responses to Text A on page 79. The task, remember, was to 'Explore the ways the writers' relationships with nature are developed in a text from the English Literary Heritage.'

Before you read the examiner's response to the two pieces, make up your own mind which is the better of the two and list the qualities which make it better.

Student A

The writer's attitude to nature changes as the poem develops. At the start of the poem he finds nature threatening. He describes the mountains as 'Like bandits'. This idea that nature is threatening is repeated in the next few lines as he writes the mountains are 'full of threats'. However his attitude changes in the fifth line of the poem as he says the mountains 'stood and delivered'. In olden days robbers would say 'Stand and deliver!' to their victims as they demanded their valuables. The writer seems to be saying that the mountains aren't threatening at all, in fact they give things to people. He writes of the wealth he gets from mountains, 'My life was enriched' and says that he soaks something up from them like an 'infusion'. At the end of the poem it is interesting that the darkness and thunder of the opening lines has been replaced by 'a sunshaft'. It seems as though the mountains are shining some light into his life.

Student B

This poem shows how a relationship with nature can change. The opening lines of the poem suggest the person speaking the poem feels intimidated by mountains. This impression comes from the early use of a striking simile, 'The mountains gathered round me like bandits.'

This reminds the reader of kidnappers and violent bandits who prey upon innocent people in remote areas; the writer gives the impression that he feels surrounded and threatened by the mountains. This impression is developed in subsequent lines as the largest mountain is described as a bandit who 'swaggered up' to the person. This suggests a melodramatic, loud villain who is drawing attention to his intimidating stance and this is reinforced by the repetition in 'full of threats, full of thunders'.

The direction of the poem changes however in the fifth line. The change in direction is highlighted by the writer's use of 'But' and then developed through the continuing use of bandit imagery, imagery which is consistently used throughout the poem:

'But it was they who stood and delivered,
They gave me their money and their lives'

The traditional cry of the highwayman is turned on its head: these mountains/bandits don't actually take anything, they give. What exactly they give is never made clear, it's up to the reader to determine that, but whatever it is it is enriching; it makes the life of the person better ...

Teacher's comments

Student A

This is part of the student's response. It is certainly 'clear'. The student provides clear explanations of both the general idea of the poem – the different views of the mountains – and some comment on relevant details. The response begins with a clear focus on the key element of the task. Having made the statement that the writer's relationship with nature changes, the student logically examines the beginning of the poem. The first use of textual detail – 'The mountains gathered round me/like bandits' – is relevant and appropriate although the student needs to extend the comments. The student identifies that the writer is using words which suggest 'threat', a point which is relevant and clear but a little obvious considering that the word 'threatening' is used in the poem.

The student clearly points out the change in the writer's attitude and bases this understanding on an appropriate textual detail, 'stood and delivered' which is well explained by a comment about the cultural context of these words – that they are from an old highwayman expression. This explanation is quite sustained. The comments about the ending of the poem are, however, a little rushed; they could have been further explained.

Student B

The second response may be placed in a higher band mainly because the student's response is 'sustained and developed'. Textual details are explored rather than stated and this student begins to engage in analysis. Meanings are probed and ideas developed in more detailed and subtle ways than in the first response. Like the first response it immediately focuses relevantly on the task. However, this student takes the textual detail, 'like bandits' and spends a little time exploring its meaning and significance. Significantly, this student sustains and develops the idea about bandits, drawing upon another linked textual detail to support their response: the comment on 'swaggered' reveals a student who is interpreting the writer's choice of vocabulary.

When the student explores the change in attitude they pay attention to the writer's continuing use of 'bandit' imagery, providing further evidence of a 'sustained, developed' response.

Activity

3 Read Text E, part of a student's response to 'Storm in the Black Forest'. What advice would you give to the student about how to improve their response? Think about how well they focus on the key words in the task and develop their ideas.

> The writer is describing a storm in the Black Forest one evening, 'Now it is almost night'. In the first five lines he describes the lightning as though someone is pouring it down from the sky, 'Jugfull'. He points out how very white the lightning is because he repeats the word.
>
> In the middle of the poem he changes from describing the lightning as being a liquid. Instead he calls it a 'snake'. This shows that his feelings for nature aren't very good because snakes aren't very nice. He also mentions the thunder and makes it sound like a witch, 'the heavens cackle with uncouth sounds'.
>
> In the end he shows that people think they are wonderful, that they can control anything but in reality they can't control things like the power of lightning because he says 'man is supposed to have mastered' electricity, the phrase 'supposed to' shows that the writer thinks man hasn't been able to control nature, nature is still all powerful.

Check your learning

In this chapter you have:
- learned about how your reading skills are tested in the controlled assessment
- learned more about the ways you can achieve high marks in this part of the course.

Remember when you first started to learn to write? It was all about forming the shapes of letters correctly.

Well, you have come a long way since then and learned that writing is about much more than forming letters on a page. This section of the book will show you how to develop the skills you already have in writing. You will work on improving these skills in two broad areas:

- writing in the daily world
- writing in the world of the imagination.

Spend a few minutes talking with a partner about the differences between these two areas. Use your own experiences of writing to help you define what each area might include.

In this section you will focus on writing fluently and accurately, choosing your content and adapting its form, style and vocabulary to a range of genres, purposes and audiences.

The chapters in this section are designed to help you meet the Assessment Objectives that underpin your GCSE course. These are written for teachers but you might like to read them in full (they are explained in more detail on page 141).

Candidates should demonstrate the ability to:

- Communicate clearly, effectively and imaginatively, using and adapting forms and selecting vocabulary appropriate to task and purpose in ways that engage the reader.

- Organise information and ideas into structured and sequenced sentences, paragraphs and whole texts, using a variety of linguistic and structural features to support cohesion and overall coherence.

- Use a range of sentence structures for clarity, purpose and effect, with accurate punctuation and spelling.

By the end of this section you will have covered all of the skills outlined in the Assessment Objectives. By the end of your GCSE course you will have used these skills to help you write your controlled assessments and to complete Section B of your GCSE English or GCSE English Language exam.

But it doesn't stop there. You don't stop writing once your GCSEs are over. The writers of this book have chosen texts and activities that they hope will interest you and give you a base from which to continue developing your writing skills to meet the demands of the adult world at work, or to make writing itself your chosen career.

13

Getting your message across

Communicating clearly

Communicating is very important, whether you are communicating at home or in school, with friends or in a more formal situation, you need to put your ideas down clearly. Ideas can be communicated in different ways: through speech, in writing and through body language.

Objectives

In this chapter you will:

develop the skills you need to write clearly for the wider world and for your GCSE exams

look at writing and punctuating sentences as well as correcting and editing errors.

Activity

1

a With a partner, make a list of the different ways in which you communicate with others during the course of one week.

b Now highlight all of the ways that depend on written communication.

Next you are going to think about different ways of communicating in writing.

Activity

2

a Look at Text A, a text message.

- Who would be able to follow this message easily?
- Who might find this message hard to understand?
- Who might be the intended audience of this text?
- Why do you think this text was written (its purpose)?

 Ⓐ

> 4getn U is hard 2do 4getn me is up to U 4get me neva but don't 4get we were gr8 2gether!!!!!! mayB coz I waz md just 4U!!

b With a partner, now read Text B, an extract from a book by Bill Gates.

- Does this text communicate clearly to you?
- If not, what made it hard for you to understand?
- Who might be the audience of this text?
- Why do you think it was written (its purpose)?

Ⓑ

> A 'work on behalf feature', which enables a manager to delegate approval responsibilities for any class of personnel requests to other people, has turned out to be the most important HeadTrax function. A vice president might authorize an administrative assistant to approve routine position or personnel changes and authorize senior managers to approve compensation or promotion requests for their teams. 'Work on behalf' gives executives a way to keep the approval process moving.
>
> Bill Gates, *Business @ the Speed of Thought*, 2000

c Decide which text communicated its message more clearly to you. List three reasons why it was easier for you to follow one text rather than the other.

You will probably have worked out that clear communication depends on matching your writing to your audience and your purpose. Both of the texts on page 82 communicate clearly to their intended audiences.

However, people who do not use text messaging would find the first text hard to understand, while the vocabulary in the second text would not be easily understood by a wider audience as it contains specialised technical terms.

If you want a wide range of people to understand your writing you must choose your words, and the way you use them, carefully.

Activity

3 With a partner, list five things you think are important for clear communication in writing.

Then compare your list with two other students and make changes if you wish. Finally put them in the order you think is the most important.

Now compare your order with that of other students in your class and explain the order you have chosen. Is there anything you might now want to change in your order?

Sentence sense

It is not always necessary to write in full sentences (see page 26) – for example, when writing a shopping list or sending a text message. However, when you write Standard English words, must be put together in sentences. A sentence usually needs a **verb** and a **subject** to make complete sense. Look at these examples:

- the car on the icy road
  subject
- skidded on the icy road
  verb
- The car skidded on the icy road.
  subject + verb

In the list above the first two examples are not complete sentences, unlike the third example.

Key terms

Verb: the part of speech that expresses an action (e.g. runs, walks) or explains a state (e.g. is, becomes).

Subject: the person or thing who performs the action of the verb.

Activity

4 The phrases below are not complete sentences. Turn each one into a sentence by adding a subject or a verb.

- collapsed on the hillside
- with great care the man
- the sound of the howling wind
- struggled on through the crowds

Show your sentences to a partner and ask them to underline the subject and the verb in each of your sentences.

Subject–verb agreement

The form of a verb changes according to its subject. This is called **subject–verb agreement**. When writing Standard English the subject and the verb should always agree.

For example:

- The wind blows.
  The winds blow.
- The cloud moves swiftly.
  The clouds move swiftly.

In some sentences working out the subject–verb agreement is not always straightforward; **collective nouns** are regarded as if they are a single subject in a sentence.

For example:

- The crowd was very large. ✓
- The crowd were very large. ✗

Activity

5   Look at the sentences below with a partner. Select the correct verb and check your answers with another student's.

For example:

Question: One of my best friends (is/are) moving to Australia next month.

Answer: is ✓

a   My brother and I (was/were) going on holiday.

b   Our team (was/were) in the lead.

c   Four years (is/are) a long time to spend away from your friends and family.

d   He seems to forget there (is/are) things to be done before he can leave.

e   Fish and chips (is/are) a traditional British dish.

f   James, who (has/have) returned from holiday in France, (intends/intend) to go back as soon as possible.

g   The best programme on TV last night (was/were) EastEnders.

h   Maths (is/are) my favourite subject but my friends all (prefers/prefer) Modern Languages.

Getting the tense right

The **tense** of a verb tells us when an action takes place – the present, past or the future – for example, 'I go', 'I went', 'I will go'. The conditional is used to talk about things that could happen. It is often used with the word 'if' in sentences when one thing depends on another – for example, 'I would go if I could afford it.'

Usually different types of writing are associated with a particular tense – for example, when the writer is recounting something that has already happened, in telling a story or writing a report, they use the past tense. Occasionally writers choose to write a story in the present tense for dramatic effect.

Information texts or advice texts are written in the present tense. Can you think of any more texts that are usually written in the present tense?

Verb tenses change in a piece of writing when there is a change in time. It is important for a writer to keep to the same tense when they are writing about one idea, otherwise they can confuse their readers.

Look at Text C, where tenses have not been used consistently.

> I hear the sound of a car engine speeding towards me. It came closer and closer and I could see the headlights in the fog. It begins to slow down as if the driver had noticed me. The man takes a quick glance at me and then he drove off into the fog.
>
> 'Oh no,' I think to myself. 'He recognised me.'

Activity

6

a   In Text C, work out where the writer has used the present tense and where he or she has used the past.

b   Write out the text using tenses consistently. It does not matter which tense you use as long as you use the same one throughout.

c   Write a short piece of advice for this writer explaining why it is important to use tenses correctly.

Punctuating complex sentences

Commas are a very useful punctuation device because they separate the different parts of the sentence into manageable sections to help the reader understand the meaning. They can be used by writers to control the pace at which the reader receives information; they are used to separate the **main clause** from a **subordinate clause** in a **complex sentence**.

For example:

● The concert was over, but the crowd refused to leave.

● From the top of the building, I could see people walking in all directions, although they looked very small.

● After taking a quick glance around him, the man ran off down the dark street.

Remember commas are used to separate information within a sentence, but they are never used to mark the end of a sentence.

7 Look at the following sentences and decide where you need to put a comma.

- As we all know being a teenager can be very expensive.
- Even though broccoli was a vegetable she detested she ate it out of politeness.
- Fighting my instinct to run I waited until the bear had moved on through the forest.
- The student worked very hard yet his exam results disappointed him.
- If you dare to walk up the path you will find the rotting front door inviting you to open it.

When you have finished, share your responses with a partner and explain your reasons for placing commas where you did.

Using a range of punctuation

As you will know, correct sentence punctuation is very important in clear communication. Without it, meaning is not communicated clearly to the reader and the writing can be difficult to follow. So far you have looked at the use of the comma within a sentence. The best writers use a range of different punctuation to aid their readers' understanding. Look at the text below, which has been annotated to show how this can be done.

Top tip

Remember you will be awarded marks in your exam for using accurate punctuation.

8 Text D is the opening of a letter to a newspaper about young people's concerns about education. Continue the letter by writing two more paragraphs outlining what you consider to be important in the education of students aged 11 to 16. Aim to use a range of punctuation as in the model given.

Dear Sir or Madam,

I am writing to you about what I believe to be the most important things in education up to the age of sixteen. Which are the key years in students' secondary education? Clearly they are Years 10 and 11 because these are the years when they are preparing for or taking their GCSEs, arguably the most important exams in their lives.

Their GCSE results will open or close doors for them in the future; their results will determine whether students get the job they want, an apprenticeship or a college place. In my opinion (and the opinion of many parents and employers) Maths, English and Science are the most important of all the subjects as the skills acquired in them are needed in most jobs.

As a result of this, many teachers in my school are very willing to help students in these subjects in several ways: by giving after school classes, lunchtime classes, individual interviews and by inviting examiners into school to work with us.

Full stop to indicate end of sentence

Question mark to indicate readers are being asked to think about something

Comma separates additional information from rest of sentence

Semi-colon used to separate two main clauses used in a sentence

Brackets present additional information as an aside

Colon indicates a list is to follow

Commas used to separate items or a list

Making your meaning clear

A very important rule of writing is to know exactly what you want to say and to check that your meaning comes across clearly.

Sometimes the meaning of what is written can be ambiguous; it can be interpreted in more than one way.

Activity

9 Look at Text E, a group of newspaper headlines, with a partner and discuss possible meanings for each.

E **Missing Puppy Found by Snowman**

School Railings Replaced by Parents

Children Should be Belted on School Buses

The previous examples were ambiguous because meanings can be interpreted in more than one way. Sometimes using the wrong order in sentences can create confusion for the reader – for example:

- If found guilty, the Football Association could fine the players.

In this example it seems as if the Football Association is guilty, which is not the case. The meaning could be expressed more clearly as:

- The Football Association could fine the players if they were found guilty.

Activities

10 In the following sentences the meaning is unclear because the writers have not thought carefully enough about the word order.

- When he was only five John's father married again.
- After graduating from college his grandparents gave him a new car.
- The only spectators were a woman carrying a small baby and a large policeman.
- We saw the Eiffel Tower flying from London to Paris.

Rewrite each sentence so that the word order helps the readers to understand the meaning's adding extra words if necessary – for example: When John was only five, his father married again.

11 Write a piece of advice for Year 7 students on how to communicate clearly. You should include:

- an explanation of why communicating clearly is important
- how to write clearly in sentences
- how to punctuate sentences
- how to avoid making your meanings ambiguous or confusing
- examples of your own.

Check your learning

In this chapter you have:

- thought about what is needed for clear communication
- revised sentence formation and subject–verb agreement
- practised punctuating sentences
- understood how to avoid writing ambiguous sentences.

<table>
<tr><td>

14

Objectives

In this chapter you will:

explore how you
might adapt your use
of language to suit
audience, purpose and
form

explore non-fiction texts,
including aspects of text
messaging, emails and
letters.

</td></tr>
</table>

Making the right choices

Text messages

The language used in text messages is very different from the standard kinds of language used in, for example, letters. SMS (short message service) language has developed as mobile phones in particular have become widespread. A new kind of language has been developed by users as they have found imaginative ways to abbreviate language so that messages can be conveyed in 160 characters or less.

Activity

 1

There are competitions that challenge people to write poetry as imaginatively as possible in the language of text messages. The maximum length is 160 characters. Look at Text A, an example of text poetry:

> **(A)**
>
> 21st century romance:
> 3a.m. How cn i begin 2 expln 2 u
> in abrev txt
> how im feelin now im alone?
> How cn i get ths text 2 u
> without yr g/frend hearin th beep?

Show that the language of text messages is up to the job of writing poetry. Write your own poem using a maximum of 160 characters. Choose one of the following as your title:

- 21st century romance
- My mobile phone
- Dear Mum.

Text messaging is almost always used with known audiences for informal purposes. Problems can occur when informal text message language is used in more formal situations. In recent years there has been considerable publicity about young people using text message language inappropriately in exams. Read Text B, an extract from an article on the subject.

Chief examiners' reports on pupil performance in history papers taken this summer identified a 'disturbing tendency' among candidates to use abbreviations commonly found when text messaging, such as 'u' for 'you' and 'r' for 'are'. Other candidates resorted to abbreviations such as 'ToV' for the Treaty of Versailles.

The report, by exam board Edexcel, told schools to make it clear that text-speak was 'not appropriate for public examinations' and pupils would lose marks if the quality of written communications is poor.

Adapted from Julie Henry, www.telegraph.co.uk/news/ uknews, 23 August 2008

Despite this criticism, some countries, such as New Zealand and Scotland, have experimented with the idea of allowing students to use text message language in their exam answers.

Activity

2 Think about the points that could be made by those on different sides of the argument and list them. When you have made your lists, join a partner and compare and adapt your lists. Use a table like this:

Why it is wrong to use text message language in exams	Why text message language should be allowed in exams

It is very important that you realise that all Awarding Bodies in the UK require students to use Standard English. They consider public examinations to require formal use of language. Standard English is usually defined as the version of the language that is generally considered to be 'correct' in grammar and vocabulary. It can be spoken in a variety of accents but the words and word order will be the same in whatever part of the country they are spoken.

Emails

Email is an area that can be very formal or informal depending on the audience, purpose and context. Many people communicate informally using email but it is also used quite formally in, for example, schools and businesses. Although both forms of communication use a keyboard, email is very different from instant messaging. Instant messaging – a chat in real time – is very much a medium for informal communication.

Activity

3 Email is often used in informal ways because of the context. Read Text C and Text D before answering the following questions.

a Identify three features of Text C that show its informality.

b Identify three features of Text D that show its formality.

c Why might the two writers have written in such very different styles?

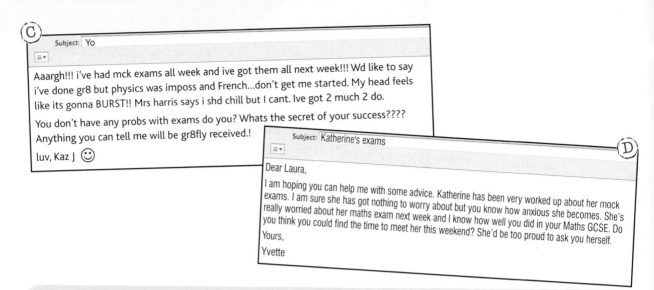

C

Subject: Yo

Aaargh!!! i've had mck exams all week and ive got them all next week!!! Wd like to say i've done gr8 but physics was imposs and French...don't get me started. My head feels like its gonna BURST!! Mrs harris says i shd chill but I cant. Ive got 2 much 2 do.

You don't have any probs with exams do you? Whats the secret of your success????
Anything you can tell me will be gr8fly received.!

luv, Kaz J ☺

D

Subject: Katherine's exams

Dear Laura,

I am hoping you can help me with some advice. Katherine has been very worked up about her mock exams. I am sure she has got nothing to worry about but you know how anxious she becomes. She's really worried about her maths exam next week and I know how well you did in your Maths GCSE. Do you think you could find the time to meet her this weekend? She'd be too proud to ask you herself.

Yours,

Yvette

Email can be used in much more formal contexts. Because it is a fairly recent form of communication the rules concerning its use are not as established as with letter-writing. There are, however, helpful rules or 'conventions' concerning emails that should be used in formal situations.

Conventions of formal emails:

- address the reader appropriately, just as in a letter
- state the purpose of the email concisely at the beginning
- write concisely in proper sentences
- write mostly in Standard English
- use standard forms of punctuation
- sign off the email appropriately as in a letter.

Activities *k!*

4 Different emails might require different levels of formality. Consider the following list of situations in which emails might be written. Put the list in order of formality, with the most formal at the top and the most informal at the bottom.

An email to:

- a small local company to ask about a work experience placement
- your form tutor about a problem concerning your work experience placement
- an adult family friend asking if they could consider giving you a work experience placement at their local shop
- a close friend about your first day at your work experience placement
- the head of the local company – someone you have worked with for two weeks – to express your thanks for the placement
- your local newspaper to give your opinions on whether work experience is worthwhile or not and to be published in the 'Local Opinion' page.

5 Working with a partner, read Text E, a job ad from a local paper, and Texts F to H, three responses to the job ad. Which response would you consider the most appropriate and why? In your answer consider:

- the way the recipient is addressed
- the appropriate use of language or otherwise
- how the email is signed off.

When you have reached a decision share it with another pair and discuss any difference of opinion.

(E) The *Broughton Express* is an award-winning local newspaper. We are looking for an energetic, dependable person to undertake general office duties in our newsroom. The successful applicant will have good communication skills and be familiar with basic ICT applications. If this interests you, get in touch with us.

E-mail responses welcomed.

For further details contact Gareth Turner at …

(F)

To:	Gturner@broughtonexp.co.uk
Cc:	
Subject:	JOB

Hi Gareth,

I'm really interested in the job advertised in your paper for a job working in the office. Sounds great! I've got lots of energy and I'm very reliable. I've got C grades in GCSE English and ICT. I'm interested in finding out more so could you get in touch. My mobile number is …

Lauren Sutcliffe (Loz)

(G)

Subject: General office duties vacancy

Dear Mr Turner,

I am writing about the advertisement for someone to work in the office of the *Broughton Express* which I saw in the newspaper yesterday.

I would be very interested in finding out more about this job. I left school a month ago having achieved eight GCSEs at grade C or above. I achieved a grade C in English and, although I did not take ICT as a subject, I am very familiar with applications such as Microsoft Word and Excel.

Could you please send me further information. My contact details are …

Yours sincerely,

Ms Lauren Sutcliffe

(H)

Subject: BROUGHTON EXP. OPPORTUNITY

To whom it may concern,

I am writing in response to the advertisement placed in yesterday's edition of the *Broughton Express* concerning a position based on undertaking general office duties in the newspaper's office.

Notwithstanding my lack of experience – I have only recently left school – I earnestly believe I have the appropriate skills to fill the position more than satisfactorily.

Were it necessary, I would be available for interview at any time in the next two weeks.

Yours in anticipation,

Miss Lauren Sutcliffe

Letters

With the growth of digital communications and the use of computers, the writing of informal letters between people, especially young people, is becoming quite rare as the use of text messaging and email increases. However, there are still occasions when writing a letter rather than an email can be required. These are usually occasions when formality and therefore use of Standard English is necessary – for example:

- letters of application for jobs
- letters of complaint or praise
- letters asking for information
- letters to institutions such as councils, newspapers.

While it is important to follow the proper conventions of setting out a letter, the most important aspect of letter writing is that the content is focused, concise and the tone is appropriate.

Text I is an example of a letter written to the letters page of a local newspaper and send by post.

19 Acacia Road
Solminster
SM22 8HH

23 April 2010

Dear Sir,

It makes me so cross to see cyclists without lights putting themselves and other road users in danger, as well as giving cyclists a bad name. It has become quite common to see people on bikes without lights riding on the roads in dark conditions.

There is, however, another side to the coin and that is: when will motorists look out for cyclists?

My husband is a keen cyclist who has been riding bikes for many years. Knowing the dangers, he always rides in bright colours and, after dark, in luminous clothes with «bright lights front and back. This didn't stop him being knocked off his bike at a roundabout last week when a driver didn't look properly. Luckily he was not badly injured, just a few cuts and bruises, but the result could have been much worse.

It happens all too often that drivers glance but don't look properly or overtake cyclists so close, putting the rider in danger. Drivers are cocooned safely in their metal boxes and seem unaware of the dangers faced by cyclists. It only takes a moment's impatience or loss of concentration for a driver to knock a cyclist off a bike. How often are drivers twiddling the radio controls, adjusting the satnav or, even, talking on a mobile phone?

Some cyclists may be putting themselves in danger because of their cycling habits but careless driving is a far greater problem. Think bike!

Yours,

Mrs Smith

Activities

6 The writer has adopted a very reasonable, calm tone in Text I. Match the following statements to the appropriate highlighted section of the text.

ⓐ Doesn't personalise the argument, targets bad driving habits rather than personally criticising drivers.

ⓑ Implies a criticism by asking a question rather than directly attacking.

ⓒ Understates any possibly 'dramatic' information.

ⓓ Shows that she has knowledge of the subject.

ⓔ States her feelings in a very measured way.

ⓕ Uses language to stress the importance of her argument without overstating.

ⓖ Recognises there are two sides to the problem.

7 People write letters to newspapers for a variety of purposes – to entertain, inform, complain, argue, etc. What does this writer's use of language tell you about the purpose of the letter and the writer's assumptions about readers?

Tone can be changed by making different vocabulary choices, as you can see from Text J, the start of another letter on the same subject.

(J)

Dear Sir,

It drives me round the bend when I see stupid cyclists without lights putting their pathetic selves and other innocent road users in danger as well as making everybody think cyclists are thick. There are thousands of idiots riding around on bikes in the dark. Stupid or what!

This uses a mixture of Standard and non-Standard English: the use of colloquialisms such as 'drives me round the bend' and 'thick' as well as the rather ungrammatical final sentence show a more informal use of language which suggests greater strength of feeling than the previous letter.

Activities

8 Rewrite the next two paragraphs of Text I to make it angrier and more confrontational.

9 Write your own letter to a newspaper in which you express your opinion about an issue of local importance. You might:

- respond to a letter that has accused young people of making a nuisance of themselves by hanging around in the local area
- complain about the absence of things for young people to do in your area
- respond to something you have seen happen (or have been told about) in your local area
- write a defence of young people using text language in exams.

Make sure that:

- The purposes of your letter are made clear at the start. Most pieces of writing have more than one purpose. For example you may wish to complain about something but you will also be *drawing readers' attention* to an issue and hoping to *influence* people's opinions. The purpose expressed at the start of your letter will simply be the main one.
- You consider tone. You could create a variety of tones: reasonableness, anger, irritation, disbelief, sarcasm, light-heartedness. The tone will depend on the purpose: sarcasm may be effective in showing your strength of opinion but it might not be considered very constructive if your main purpose is to make suggestions.
- Your letter is carefully structured into paragraphs.
- You use the Standard English that might be expected in a newspaper.

Check your learning

In this chapter you have:

- considered how audience and purpose affect your choice of language
- explored language choices in a variety of non-fiction types.

15

Organising writing

Sequencing sentences

Organised writers are organised thinkers who can arrange their sentences in a sequence that will help their reader to understand their ideas easily.

Activity

1 Read Text A, which is taken from an article entitled about 'Things That Can Go Wrong On Holiday'. The sentences have been placed in the wrong sequence. Work with a partner to decide on a sequence that makes sense. Look out for:

- sentences that develop or continue points
- sentences that repeat information
- sentences that contrast with each other.

Begin by ordering the sentences on paper. When you have finished, compare your sequence with those of other students. Did you have the same sequence as them? If not, which sequence is most effective?

(A)

1. Whether it's missing luggage, cockroach-infested hotels or rip-off taxi drivers, we seem to take a perverse delight in regaling our friends and relatives with tales of our holidays from hell.

2. Sadly for most of us this is rarely the reality.

3. Going away on holiday should mean time to kick back, relax and leave the stresses and strains of the daily grind behind you.

4. In fact according to a new study, 80% of British holidaymakers have experienced at least one 'disaster' while on holiday.

5. These holiday horrors understandably impact on our enjoyment of our holidays, with one in eight admitting to being disappointed by their recent holiday.

6. From the moment the taxi pulls up outside your home until the plane touches back down in rain-soaked Blighty, your week, fortnight or month away should be an oasis of calm, tranquillity and happiness.

Activity

2

Here is the opening sentence to a piece of writing entitled 'Things I Love About Holidays':

> 'Being on holiday is a time to relax, catch up with friends and generally have fun.'

Write five more sentences continuing this writing.

Aim to:

- develop or continue points
- repeat information and/or make contrasts.

Organising sentences into paragraphs

Writers use paragraphs to give structure to a text by linking ideas from one paragraph to another. Often ideas referred to in one paragraph are linked and developed in the ones that follow. This gives the text a clear structure. Read Text B, an article about plastic bags, before answering the questions that follow.

(B)

Banish the bags

The 13 billion ways YOU can help

A typical British family heads home laden with plastic bags full of the weekly supermarket shop.

Cut to the haunting image of a sea turtle, thousands of miles away, struggling through the deep ocean waters as discarded plastic bags wrap themselves around its flippers and body.

These majestic animals are dying in alarming numbers because they mistake the flimsy translucent bags – which in theory come from British supermarkets – for jellyfish, a key element of their diet.

Once swallowed by the turtle, the tough plastic becomes lodged in its gut. It is indigestible and wraps itself around the turtle's insides resulting in a slow and agonising death by starvation.

Closer to home, other animals pay the price of our dependence on disposable plastic bags handed out free in their billions to shoppers. In April 2002 a dead minke whale was washed up on the coast of Normandy. When her stomach was cut open 2lb of plastic bags was found. She had mistaken them for food and had died a similarly painful death.

An astonishing 13 billion free single-use plastic bags are dished out by Britain's High Street stores every year. These flimsy bags – a by-product of crude oil – are issued at a rate of more than 800 a year to every family in the land. Typically they are only used for 20 minutes before being thrown out. But they will take up to 1,000 years to rot away. If the Normans had used plastic bags in the 1066 invasion, archaeologists would still be digging them up today.

During their long decay millions linger like urban tumbleweed to pollute our streets, the countryside, parks, rivers and seas. Britain's coast is washed with a toxic 'plastic soup' carried on the tide which threatens our seabirds, turtles, whales and other wildlife.

Gannets off Cornwall suffer a long painful death, unable to feed or fly after getting entangled. Dolphins scoop up plastic bags and carry them around, risking strangulation and suffocation. And some 8 per cent of the world's seal population has reportedly been harmed by plastic bags.

Today the *Daily Mail* launches the Banish the Bags campaign in an effort to rid the country of these single use plastic bags, the most ubiquitous feature of our disposable society.

Sean Poulter and David Derbyshire, *The Daily Mail*, 27 February 2008

3 Answer the following questions to help you understand how the paragraphs are linked in Text B (page 95).

a How does the heading link with the opening paragraph?

b Although the focus of paragraph 2 changes, what are the words that link it with paragraph 1?

c In paragraph 5 to what does the phrase 'a similarly painful death' refer? Which paragraph does this phrase link back to?

d Paragraph 6 refers to the long life of plastic bags. Which words and phrases in paragraph 6 refer to (i) plastic bags and (ii) their long life?

e In paragraph 5 which idea mentioned earlier is developed? Where was this idea first mentioned?

f Which part of the article does the final paragraph refer to?

Linking ideas within a paragraph

Now that you have seen how ideas can be linked throughout a series of paragraphs, you are going to look more closely at how ideas are linked within one paragraph.

4

a Look again at paragraph 5. The main topic and the linking words have been highlighted to show you how the links are made.

- A dead minke whale is used as an example of 'other animals'.

- Her refers back to the minke whale.

- She also refers back to the minke whale. Why has the writer chosen not to repeat the words minke whale?

> Closer to home, other animals pay the price of our dependence on disposable plastic bags handed out free in their billions to shoppers. In April 2002 a dead minke whale was washed up on the coast of Normandy. When her stomach was cut open 2lb of plastic bags was found. She had mistaken them for food and had died a similarly painful death.

b Re-read paragraph 6. What is the topic of this paragraph? Which other words does the writer use to refer to this topic?

5 Write a paragraph of between six and eight sentences explaining your feelings on a topic *you* feel strongly about – for example, litter in the streets or improved facilities in your school. Your title is 'Something I Would Like to Change'.

Follow these steps:

- list ideas you could include
- make a note of words and phrases you could use
- think about how you are going to link your ideas within your paragraph.

Show your work to a partner and ask them to tick the words and phrases you have used to:

- link ideas with the title
- connect and develop ideas throughout your text
- link your final point to the title and the opening paragraph.

Ask your partner to make suggestions about how you could improve the linking of your ideas.

Understanding writers' techniques

The techniques used by writers play an important part in helping readers to connect meanings in a text and within a paragraph.

6 Read Text C, a description of a fire in a forest taken from William Golding's *Lord of the Flies*, and answer the questions around it.

(C)

❶ How does the writer indicate the fire is just beginning?

❷ What effect does the word 'crawled' create for the reader?

❸ Why do you think the writer uses the simile of the spreading fire being like a squirrel? What effects did the writer want to achieve?

Smoke was rising here and there amongst the creepers that festooned the dead or the dying trees. As they watched, a flash of fire appeared at the root of one wisp, and then the smoke thickened. Small flames stirred at the bole of a tree and crawled away through leaves and brushwood, dividing and increasing. One patch touched a tree trunk and scrambled up like a bright squirrel. The smoke increased, sifted, rolled outwards. The squirrel leapt on the wings of the wind and clung to another tree eating downwards. Beneath the dark canopy of leaves and fires the smoke laid hold on the forest and began to gnaw.

William Golding, *Lord of the Flies*, 1954

❹ Why has the writer used the metaphor 'wings of the wind'? What effect does this metaphor convey?

❺ What vocabulary does the writer use to develop the image of the squirrel in the rest of the paragraph?

❻ Why is the use of the word 'gnaw' appropriate? What is the effect of using this as the final word in the paragraph?

Key terms

Metaphor: a description of something as though it were something else.

Activities

7 Write a paragraph in which you develop a description of one of the following: heavy rain, a blizzard, a storm, or extreme heat. Begin by making notes on:

- features of your chosen topic – for example, howling wind
- comparisons you could use to emphasise your description
- vocabulary you could use to develop your ideas.

Write your paragraph and then check you have created the effect you intended. Make any helpful alterations.

8 Read Text D (on page 98), the opening paragraph from 'Children of Strikers', a short story by Fred Chappell.

a Decide what kind of atmosphere is created.

b What mood does the word 'black' create in the opening sentence?

c What other words reflect this mood throughout the paragraph?

d How do the words 'even darker than usual' encourage the reader to read on?

e Rewrite these sentences, replacing the words you have listed with words that create a happy and joyful mood – for example: 'They were walking, the twelve-year-old girl and the younger bronzed-looking boy, by the edge of the glistening gurgling river.'

(D)

They were walking, the twelve-year-old girl and the younger bleached-looking boy, by the edge of the black chemical river. A dreadful stink rose off the waters, but they scarcely noticed it, scuffling along in the hard sawgrass among the stones. It was a dim day, rain threatening and the girl's dun face and dark eyes looked even darker than usual.

Fred Chappell, 'Children of Strikers'

Activity

9

Write the opening three paragraphs of a story in which you create a fearful and tense atmosphere.

Follow these steps:

- Think about the atmosphere you want to create.
- Make a list of your ideas to develop the setting – for example, you could include the place, the time of day and the weather.
- Make a list of vocabulary you will use.
- Decide which characters you will introduce. Decide on appropriate vocabulary to make their appearance and behaviour link with the mood you are creating.

After your first draft, ask a partner to:

- check whether you have developed and linked your ideas throughout the three paragraphs
- check whether your vocabulary helps to continue your chosen mood throughout each paragraph
- make suggestions for improvement.

When you have made any alterations necessary, write the final draft.

Check your learning

In this chapter you have:

- considered how sentences can be organised in a logical sequence
- examined how sentences are organised into paragraphs
- studied how ideas are linked within a paragraph
- worked out how writers use a range of techniques to connect meanings within a paragraph
- explored how words can be used to create atmosphere.

16

Getting the words right

Selecting vocabulary

To do well in English you need to show that you can select particular words for particular purposes.

Writers occasionally set themselves challenges which affect the vocabulary they can choose. There are at least two entire novels in which the writers chose to completely avoid the letter 'e'. One test of your ability to choose vocabulary is to choose a vowel and write a passage in which every word contains that vowel.

Activity

1 Look at Text A, a passage based on the letter 'a':

> Alarmed and afraid, Stuart walked anxiously along a narrow, dark alley. As dark had fallen, cicadas had started a constant wailing.

Choose a vowel and see how far you can get when every word of what you write has to contain that vowel.

Choosing from a variety of words

The English language is rich in synonyms so that in descriptive writing there is a wide variety of vocabulary from which to choose.

Activity

2
a 'Walk' and 'shuffle' are verbs that describe the way people move. Write down as many other verbs of movement that you can think of in two minutes.

b Share your list with a partner and create an even bigger list.

c You now have a list of words that are similar in meaning. Working with your partner, group your words into sub-groups. Which words could be used to describe:

● fast movement

● slow movement

● clumsy movement?

d Assemble other sub-groups of words of movement.

When you have finished you will find that you have created groups of similar words, just as happens in a thesaurus, from which you can choose depending on what kind of movement you are describing. If a writer is trying to create a vivid description, as part of a story for example, they can engage the interest of a reader more successfully if they choose words precisely.

Choosing a word precisely can save the writer having to use more words:

- 'he swaggered' instead of 'he walked in an arrogant fashion'
- 'he ambled' instead of 'he walked in a leisurely way'
- 'he limped' instead of 'he walked unsteadily'.

Each verb describes precisely a different kind of movement. But you can still add descriptive information to verbs like this and introduce the kind of variety in sentence structure that you will look at further in the next chapter. 'He limped' is a very simple declarative sentence. Some complexity could quite easily be added by adding a simile as an additional subordinate clause for example. In the example below, the subordinate clause is put at the front of the sentence; it could, of course, be placed at the end.

- Like a runner at the end of a marathon, he limped down the path.

Or there is a construction in which the sentence begins with a present participle – a verb ending in 'ing':

- Grimacing with pain, he limped down the path.

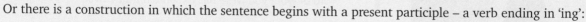

Activity

3 Choose five of your synonyms of movement. For each word write two sentences, one beginning with a simile and one beginning with a verb ending in 'ing'.

Creating tone

Descriptive vocabulary can be chosen to develop a tone. Tone is the writer's attitude towards the subject and reader, and can be serious, comic, sarcastic, formal, bitter, angry, light-hearted and so forth. Text B is written in a light-hearted tone.

Slaloming slowly down the street, waving her stick randomly as if she were swatting a swarm of uncooperative bluebottles, Mrs Jenkins moved her ample, wobbly body towards the Post Office. Nearing the small shop's entrance she came to a hesitant, horrified halt, her eccentric progress impeded by a small car parked half on the road and half on the pavement. Foam flecking her furious face, she screeched at the unoccupied car to move. The sky darkened.

The tone is created by the vocabulary choices and by the ways the words are structured into complex sentences, which have the effect of compressing information together for maximum impact. In the first sentence the main clause is 'Mrs Jenkins moved her ample, wobbly body' but, before the reader reaches that main clause, they have been given vivid detail in subordinate clauses at the start of the complex sentence.

- the use of **alliteration**
- the choice of an unusual simile
- the choice of unusual words (like 'slaloming' – the idea of an elderly lady skiing along a street is unexpected).

A very short, simple sentence then adds contrast and creates some tension.

> **Key terms**
>
> **Alliteration:** the deliberate repetition of consonant sounds at the beginning of words to gain a particular effect.

Activity

4 Write your own short description of someone walking down a street. You should focus on two main features: choosing precise words of movement and adding detail in subordinate clauses to make complex sentences. You might also want to use one very simple, short sentence by way of contrast. Make the tone of the description one of the following:

- sarcastic
- angry
- humorous.

Writing techniques

Text C displays a variety of techniques used by a writer to add interest to a descriptive passage. Read it first before exploring the technique.

If you listen, you can hear it.

The city, it sings.

If you stand quietly, at the foot of a garden, in the middle of a street, on the roof of a house.

5 It's clearest at night, when the sound cuts more sharply across the surface of things, when the song reaches out to a place inside you.

It's a wordless song, for the most, but it's a song all the same, and nobody hearing it could doubt what it sings.

And the song sings the loudest when you pick out each note.

10 The low soothing hum of air-conditioners, fanning out the heat and the smells of shops and cafés and offices across the city, winding up and winding down, long breaths layered upon each other, a lullaby hum for tired streets.

The rush of traffic still cutting across flyovers, even in the dark hours a constant crush of sound, tyres rolling across the tarmac and engines rumbling, loose drains and manhole
15 covers clack-clacking like cast-iron castanets.

Road-menders mending, choosing the hours of least interruption, rupturing the cold night air with drills and jack-hammers and pneumatic pumps, hard-sweating beneath the fizzing

hiss of floodlights, shouting to each other like drummers in
rock bands calling out rhythms, pasting new skin on the veins
20   of the city.

Restless machines in workshops and factories with endless
shifts, turning and pumping and steaming and sparking, pressing
and rolling and weaving and printing, the hard crash and ring
and clatter lifting out of echo-high buildings and sifting into the
25   night, an unaudited product beside the paper and cloth and steel
and bread, the packed and the bound and the made.

Lorries reversing, right round the arc of industrial parks, it
seems every lorry in town is reversing, backing through gateways,
easing up ramps, shrill-calling their presence while forklift trucks
30   gas and prang around them, heaping and stacking and loading.

And all the alarms, calling for help, each district and quarter,
each street and estate, each way you turn has alarms going
off, coming on, going off, coming on, a hammered ring like a
lightning drum-roll, like a mesmeric bell-toll, the false and the
35   real as loud as each other, crying their needs to the night like an
understaffed orphanage, babies waawaa-ing in darkened wards.

Sung sirens, sliding through the streets, streaking blue light
from distress to distress, the slow wail weaving urgency through
the darkest of the dark hours, a lament lifted high, held above the
40   rooftops and fading away, lifted high, flashing past, fading away.

And all these things sing constant, the machines and the
sirens, the cars blurting hey and rumbling all headlong, the hoots
and the shouts and the hums and the crackles, all come together
and rouse like a choir, sinking and rising with the turn of the
45   wind, the counter and solo, the harmony humming expecting
more voices.

So listen.

Jon McGregor, *If Nobody Speaks of Remarkable Things*, 2002

Most descriptive writing focuses on what
can be seen. One thing that makes Text C
interesting is that the writer focuses on what
can be heard.

Activity

5   The writer uses a variety of vocabulary to
describe noises. Re-read Text C and find the
different words used to describe sounds.

The writer does not only use a variety of words to describe sounds, he also chooses words because of
their sound.

Short vowel sounds – such as, 'a' as in bat, 'o' as in pot, – can be selected to suggest short, sharp sounds
especially when 'hard' consonants such as 'c', 'b', 'd' are also used. Lower, gentler sounds might be better
captured with longer vowel sounds such as 'ee', 'i' as in flight especially when accompanied by softer
consonants such as 'f', 's', 'l'.

Activities

6 Write out the following two extracts from Text C. Annotate them to draw attention to the sounds used for effect by the writer.

> … drains and manhole covers clack-clacking like cast-iron castanets.

> Sung sirens, sliding through the streets, streaking blue light …

7 To bring variety to the writing, the writer occasionally uses similes to capture sounds.

  a Find and list the six similes in Text C.

  b Five of the similes are very similar. Which is the odd one out and why?

Another technique that the writer uses to capture sound is through the use of metaphors. The idea that a city can 'sing' is a metaphor – cities can't really sing but the idea of song is transferred into a description of a city and the metaphor is extended over several sentences.

Activity

8 Explain the following examples of the writer's use of metaphor. The first one is done for you.

Metaphor	Explanation
'Lullaby hum'	This is a metaphor because air-conditioning machines don't actually hum lullabies – only humans can do that. The writer uses the metaphor to suggest that there is something very soothing about the sound of air-conditioning units at night; they can lull you into sleep.
'Road menders … pasting new skin on the veins of the city.'	
'And all the alarms … crying their needs to the night.'	
'the cars blurting hey and rumbling all headlong'	

Organising the description

The writer also builds up the effects of noise and the energy of the city through repetition and listing, and by using a variety of sentence structures. The passage begins with fairly simple sentences before a succession of complex sentences – the number of commas and use of 'and' give an indication of how much detail is added to each sentence. Then the writer ends the passage with a very simple sentence which acts as a kind of full stop.

Look again at the following section from Text C:

Restless machines in workshops and factories with endless shifts, turning and pumping and steaming and sparking, pressing and rolling and weaving and printing, the hard crash and ring and clatter lifting out of echo-high buildings and sifting into the night, an unaudited product beside the paper and cloth and steel and bread, the packed and the bound and the made.

In one sentence the writer uses the word 'and' fifteen times. The word 'and' could be replaced with a comma. Why does the writer choose to repeatedly use 'and'?

Activities

9   After line 10 in Text C, each paragraph introduces a separate aspect of the sounds of the city and each paragraph is a single sentence.

   a   What simple technique makes it easy for the reader to identify the focus of each paragraph?

   b   Why do you think the writer decided to use single-sentence paragraphs?

10   Re-read the section above. Experiment with this kind of listing using 'and' to link verbs ending with 'ing'. Choose a noisy scene – something like a school playground, a canteen, a city street – and, using the section above as a model, write your own short passage, no longer than the section above.

11   You are now going to use some of the techniques you have explored to write your own short description. Choose a place that has a wide variety of sounds. It might be something like a school, a house or a park. Begin your piece of writing with 'The school, it sings' or 'The house, it sings'.

Write three paragraphs in which you practise the kind of techniques you have explored in this chapter. Each paragraph should focus on a separate aspect of the place. For example, if you choose a park you might write three paragraphs based on:

- the playground – the sounds of children playing, the sounds of the swings, slides, etc.
- the café – the sounds of people talking, the coffee machine, the sounds of crockery and cutlery
- the animal life – the dogs, ducks, birds.

Concentrate on using the kinds of techniques you have explored:

- words chosen for their sounds
- use of occasional similes
- use of listing
- use of variety of sentence structures.

Check your learning k!

In this chapter you have:

- explored the effects of different vocabulary choices
- experimented with different ways of structuring vocabulary.

Making sense of sentences

Objectives

In this chapter you will:

practise using a range of sentence structures

match your sentence structures to the audience and purpose of your text

express your ideas clearly, emphasise your meaning and create effects for your readers.

Sentence types

When writing sentences, writers make decisions according to their purpose and audience and what they are trying to achieve. They vary the structure and type of their sentences according to the needs of their readers.

Sentences can be divided into four main types:

- **a declaration or a statement:** for example, 'Tigers are found in eastern and southern Asia.'
- **a question:** for example, 'What happened next?'
- **an exclamation:** for example, 'We won the competition!'
- **an imperative or directive:** for example, 'Drink 6 to 8 glasses of water per day.'

> **Key terms**
>
> **Exclamation:** an abrupt, forceful utterance.
> **Imperative:** expressing a command.

Sentence structures

The ways in which sentences can be structured can vary.

There are three main types of sentence structure:

- A simple sentence consisting of one main clause which makes sense on its own. For example:

> Tigers are solitary animals.

A compound sentence consisting of two or more main clauses joined by 'and', or 'but' or 'so'. For example:

> Tigers are solitary animals and do not welcome other animals onto their territory.

- A complex sentence consisting of one main clause and one or more subordinate clauses. For example:

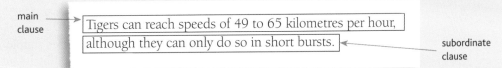

main clause → Tigers can reach speeds of 49 to 65 kilometres per hour, although they can only do so in short bursts. ← subordinate clause

The choice of sentences depends on the needs of the audience or reader – for example, in a text for children simple sentences would be easier for readers to understand. Writers also select sentences to match their purpose for writing.

Activity

1

a Read Texts A to C. For each one write out:

- who the intended reader is
- what the purpose of the text is.

b Then compare your answers with those of a partner. Discuss the reasons for your choices.

A

It was a beautiful summer's day. Sam and Lily were feeling very excited. They were going on holiday to the seaside. 'I want to go on a boat,' said Lily. 'I want to play in the sand,' said Sam.

B

Garlic mushrooms: Serves 1

Delicious, but don't breathe over other people after eating these! Serve with bacon to make a more substantial meal.

You will need: 100 g mushrooms, 1 clove fresh garlic, 1–2 rashers bacon (optional), 25 g butter with 1 tsp cooking oil.

Wash the mushrooms. Peel chop and crush the fresh garlic. Fry the bacon if used and keep hot. Melt the butter and oil in a saucepan over a moderate heat. Add the garlic …

Jan Arkless, *Student Grub*, 1991

C

A heady mix of stunning scenery and the best of contemporary living, Guernsey is the perfect destination. Inspiring walks along the cliff paths, rambles through the rural interior or lazy days on the island's beautiful beaches, Guernsey has it all.

St Peter Port, the island's capital, is a bustling harbour town, a tapestry of architectural styles that tell the story of the region's changing fortunes. Here bistros, restaurants and boutiques jostle for your attention, while in the harbour ferries are readied to take you to the sister islands.

www.visitguernsey.com

Activity

2

Look again at the texts in Activity 1 and your notes on purpose and audience before answering the following questions.

a Which sentence structures are used in Text A? What could be the reason for this?

b What is the main sentence type used in Text B? Can you explain why it is used?

c How does the sentence structure suggest that Text C is for adult readers?

Considering audience and purpose

As you will have noticed, writing for a younger audience uses simple sentence structures so that the text can easily be understood by its readers. However, for older audiences this type of writing can be uninteresting to read. Older audiences can absorb more information presented in longer sentences.

Activity

3 Read Text D which has been written to provide information for younger children and that uses simple sentences in order to get the information across clearly and simply for a younger audience. Rewrite the text for an older audience using a wider range of sentence structures to make the writing more interesting. You will need to consider how to combine sentences and may miss out some words or alter the word order if you wish.

D Carnivorous plants are also known as insectivorous plants. They can trap insects or spiders for food. The plants grow in places with poor soil. These could be bogs or rocky outcrops. The soil does not contain many nutrients (food for the plants).

Different plants have different ways of trapping the insects. Some plants are pitcher plants. The insects fall into the pitcher and cannot escape. Other plants use 'flypaper' traps. These plants can secrete a sticky glue. The insect is trapped on the leaves of the plant by the glue.

Creating emphasis and variety

Writers often use a range of sentence types and structures to provide variety for their readers and to emphasise certain points, as in Text E, an article offering advice to young people on how to survive a family holiday.

E When you hear the words 'family holiday' how do you feel? Many teenagers dread the thought of going away with their parents, yet research shows most parents are reluctant to let their 16 year old go away with their mates. So you really have only two choices – either stick it out with your mum and dad and little brother or sister or make things work in your favour.

Remember you are getting a free holiday! Once your parents start planning that all important summer vacation, it's time for you to show an interest. Put forward some ideas of your own so that you can end up in a resort you really want to go to.

Rhetorical question after feel

Complex sentence offers alternatives to reader using 'or' to link two clauses

Imperative to give clear direction to readers

Activity

4 Continue the article from Text E. Write between 8 and 10 lines and aim to vary the range of sentence structures and sentence types you use.

When you have finished, pass your work to a partner and ask them to annotate it to show the range of sentence structures you have used.

Creating patterns: lists and repetitions

Writers create patterns with their sentences to make an impact on their readers and to draw attention to their key points. Repetition and lists have a powerful impact on readers as they reinforce the writer's ideas. Techniques used include:

- repeating sentence beginnings
- repeating sentence endings
- repeating similar structures within a sentence
- using words or phrases in groups of three.

Read Text F, which is taken from the acceptance speech made by the United States Presidential candidate Barack Obama in August 2008 when he accepted the Presidential nomination for the Democratic Party. You'll see that it uses some of the techniques mentioned.

(F) http://

You have shown what history teaches us, that at defining moments like this one the change we need doesn't come from Washington. Change comes to Washington.

Change happens – change happens because the American people demand it, because they rise up and insist on new ideas and new leadership, a new politics for a new time.

America, this is one of those moments.

I believe that, as hard as it will be, the change we need is coming, because I've seen it, because I've lived it.

Because I've seen it in Illinois, when we provided health care to more children and moved more families from welfare to work.

I've seen it in Washington, where we worked across party lines to open up government and hold lobbyists more accountable, to give better care for our veterans, and keep nuclear weapons out of the hands of terrorists.

And I've seen it in this campaign, in the young people who voted for the first time and the young at heart, those who got involved again after a very long time.

www.nytimes.com

Activity

5 Copy and complete the following table, giving examples of the different sentence pattern types used in Text F and writing down the idea that the speaker wants to emphasise (the first one has been done for you).

Sentence pattern	Example	Idea the writer wants to emphasise
Repetition of sentence beginnings	Change comes to Washington. Change happens …	Change is now inevitable in the United States
Repetition of sentence endings		
Repetition of similar structures in one sentence		
Using words or phrases in groups of three		

Activity

6

a Think of a topic that might engage an audience – for example, animal experimentation or high wages paid to footballers. Write the opening paragraph of a speech entitled 'The Time Has Come'. Aim to use some or all of the techniques on the list at the top of page 108.

b When you have finished pass your work to a partner and ask him or her to annotate your speech to indicate which techniques you have used.

Using sentence structure to create effects

Writers consider how to vary sentence structure to add emphasis to their writing. Longer sentences can work well for incorporating several pieces of information and short sentences can often emphasise crucial points or create a dramatic effect.

Activity

7

Read Text G and then answer the questions around it.

The carter waved his whip towards huge stones looming to the right of us, rearing out of the close cropped grass. I stared, transfixed. This must be the great Temple of the Winds. My grandmother had told me about it. A circle of stones, much, much greater than any other built far to the south of us. Such places are sacred to those who live by the Old Religion. At certain times of the year my grandmother would set off for some stones that lay a day's journey or so from where we lived. She never told me what went on there, or who else attended, and I knew better than to ask her.

Soon the great stones faded. Darkness drew in on either side and there was only the road unwinding like a thread in the moonlight.

Beyond that all was black.

Celia Rees, *Witch Child*, 2000

Who does this sentence focus on? How does it help to draw the reader into the girl's experience?

What has the writer done to build up tension in this sentence?

How does this short sentence prepare the reader for the next section of the text?

This is the final sentence in the chapter. What effect might it have on the reader?

Activity

8

Write 5 to 8 lines of a description of a place which ends with the same sentence as the one above: 'Beyond that all was black.' Aim to vary your sentences, including some that are short as in the extract above. Think about how you will build up to the final sentence.

Punctuating sentences

Punctuation is used to guide readers through a text. It can be seen as a signpost to meaning. Commas are used by writers to control their writing and enable their readers to take in information gradually.

Using commas to separate additional information

Commas can also be used to mark off additional information within a sentence – for example:

- The house, tall and forbidding, stands at the end of the lonely country lane.

Using commas to create pace

A comma can be used to slow down the pace of a sentence and to make your reader pause momentarily – for example:

- If you dare to walk up the path, you will find the crumbling front door tempting you to open it.
- Slowly and cautiously, I stretch out my trembling hand.

Using commas to separate adjectives

When using several adjectives for effect, a comma is used to separate them to ensure that the meaning of each word stands out – for example:

- The dark, gloomy hallway with yellowing, peeling wallpaper …

Activity

9

a Write one paragraph of a story where you aim to create an atmosphere of tension for your readers. This could be a description of a house, a room or a street. Remember to include commas to signpost meaning for your readers.

b Show your work to a partner and explain why you chose to put your commas in the places you did.

Controlling the pace of your writing

Writers can control the pace of their writing by varying their sentence structures and allowing their readers time to pause occasionally to take in what is being said. They know how to balance their sentences. As you have also seen, they use punctuation to emphasise their ideas and control the way in which their readers respond.

Read Text H, a student response written under exam conditions, answering the question:

> School students sometimes say they get bored in the long summer holidays. Write an article for a local newspaper advising students of the different things they could do to prevent boredom.

(H)

List of three phrases — With the summer holidays upon us, the horrors of school banished from our minds and exam stress evaporating daily, you would think that we would all be feeling a sense of relief and joy at the approach of the holidays. But are we? ← Short rhetorical question balances previous complex sentence and allows reader to reflect on it

It seems that feelings of joy and relief are not at the top of our list, rather a sense of gloom at the thought of long days of boredom. A recent survey indicated that 60% of students said that they found holidays too long. We must really love school after all! ← Short exclamation underlines writer's surprise that students are bored during the holidays

Contrasting ideas separated by commas

It is hard to imagine why some students feel this way. After all, there are so many interesting and challenging things for young people to do nowadays, boredom should be the last thing on our minds.

However, if you should feel this way there is no need to worry any longer. Read on to find out how you can have the most exciting summer ever! ← Instruction given to readers in fairly simple compound sentence to encourage them to read on

Use of word 'however' separated by commas prepares reader for suggestions in rest of text on how to avoid boredom

Stretch yourself

Continue Text H, writing two more paragraphs containing advice for students.

You should aim to:

- use commas to control the pace of your writing
- vary the length of your sentences
- use lists and repetition where appropriate
- use sentence structures that emphasise your ideas.

Check your learning *k!*

In this chapter you have:

- revised a range of sentence structures
- chosen sentences to suit your audience and purpose
- used a range of sentences to create an impact on your readers
- used punctuation in sentences to control the pace of your writing.

Getting it together 1: non-fiction writing

Planning your writing

In the exam you will be given brief details of a writing task, which is likely to focus on functional kinds of writing. You will need to quickly organise your thoughts and plan a structure for your response to the task. To achieve high marks you will need to shape your writing in thoughtful and creative ways.

Activity

1 Think about your own approach to planning pieces of writing.

a What kinds of writing and in what circumstances are you most likely to produce a plan before writing?

b What kinds of plans do you tend to use?

c Explain why you do or don't find planning helpful.

There are different ways to plan and structure a piece of writing. Different people plan in different ways, some of which are illustrated below.

Spider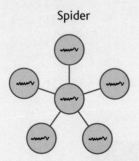

Bulleted list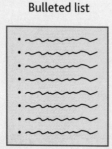

Table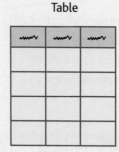

Tree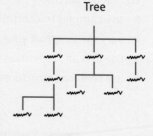

The purpose of a plan is to give structure – a beginning, middle and end – to your writing. How you structure your writing will depend upon purpose, audience and context. Journalists, for example, use a variety of structures for writing their news stories. You might have heard of the 'inverted pyramid' structure. In short paragraphs the journalist is required to sum up the most important news first: the 'who', 'what', 'when', 'why' and 'how'. As the article progresses, less important information is added which an editor can cut out.

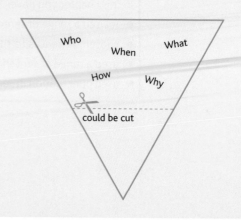

Read Text A, an article about a neglected child.

Russian police find five-year-old 'Mowgli' girl who barks like a dog after parents neglected her

A girl of five has been raised by dogs since she was a baby because her parents neglected her, it was claimed yesterday.

Natasha speaks no words, laps up her food and drinks with her tongue, and walks on all fours.

While she lived in filthy conditions in the same home as her parents in the Siberian city of Chita, child experts say she appears to have been treated as one of the dogs and cats.

'They never let her out, we didn't know she existed,' said one neighbour.

'They walked the dogs – they have three really vicious and angry ones – but we never saw this child.'

The girl, who police said is five but looks more like a two-year-old, was not registered with local doctors or hospitals.

Adapted from www.dailymail.co.uk

Activities

2 Decide at which stage the 'who', 'what', 'when', 'why' and 'how' have been addressed by the writer in Text A, so that the editor could start to cut the story but still leave the reader knowing the important facts.

3
a Why do you think this story is organised into single-sentence paragraphs?

b To make the story coherent, every paragraph focuses on the girl, but to bring variety a different word is used for her each time. In the second paragraph she is 'Natasha'. What words are used in other paragraphs?

For longer news stories journalists sometimes use what is called the 'hourglass' structure. In this structure the first part of the story focuses on facts which are then fleshed out with a narrative version in the second half.

Read Text B, which is an example of an 'hourglass' structure.

Escaped bull on the loose in store

It may not have been a china shop, but shoppers were stunned when an out-of-control young bull charged through a supermarket.

Miraculously, no one was hurt when the animal escaped the clutches of its owner and ran into a Tesco Metro store in the centre of Glaminton.

By the time the bull was eventually recaptured by its owner, a local farmer, the only damage done was to fruit and vegetable stands.

The bull had been at the local mart a few hundred yards away when it made its great escape.

It was being herded out of the cattle ring when it bolted free and ran through an open gate into the street.

Pursued by owner Andy Sutcliffe, it raced down the High Street before careering into the small Tesco store.

Shop owner Bob Elliott said: 'The bull ran down one aisle and into the store area where he had a good look around and came back out again.

'He then charged down another aisle, and out the front door again.

'There were a lot of people in the shop at the time, staff and customers.

'Amazingly, no one came directly in his path or it could have been very bad news. It was a happy ending to a story that could have gone very wrong.

'Some of the staff ran after him when he went into the store, but they got out of the way again when he turned around to come out – and I wouldn't blame them.

'People were joking afterwards that our beef was fresh and fully traceable,' said Mr Elliott. 'He passed the local butcher's to get to us. That tells its own story.'

Adapted from www.belfasttelegraph.co.uk

4 Decide where the essential factual part of Text B ends and the narrative part begins.

5 The story is arranged into mainly single-sentence paragraphs.

a Why do you think this decision was taken? Choose from the following reasons:

- the story was in a tabloid newspaper and the writers aren't as clever as broadsheet journalists
- the writers think their readers can't cope with anything more complicated
- it makes the story easier to cut down if space is required
- it's easier to read the story quickly.

b How could the story be structured into a smaller number of multiple-sentence paragraphs?

6 Use the details in the following table to write your own 'hourglass' article. Begin with a single-sentence paragraph, followed by one or two multiple-sentence paragraphs which summarise the essential facts of the story, before another two or three multiple-sentence paragraphs in which you 'tell the story' of what happened.

	Use this as the basis for your story	Or make up your own
Who?	A 16-year-old girl	
What?	Has won through to the heats of *Britain's Got Talent*	
When?	Last night	
Why?	She wowed the judges	
How?	She gave an amazing performance of 'Simply the Best'	

Structuring your writing

The kinds of writing you will do in the exam require quite simple, clear structures. They will not always be the kinds of writing that allow you to tell a story. Much non-fiction writing is about ideas that need to be organised into paragraphs. A paragraph should be devoted to the development of one main idea.

Activities

7   **a** Read Text C, a piece of non-fiction writing that concerns a description of the sighting of a fox. It consists of four paragraphs, the order of which has been mixed up. Put them into the correct order.

C

1. Not just any fox. A fox of beauty and charm and elegance, apparently freshly groomed, lithe and gleaming red. The white tip of his brush vanished into the lilac and then for a moment I saw him continue his journey along the top of the wall, a creature at home in his world, unstoppably self-confident and positively glowing with health.

2. I went for a pee and had a vision of transcendent beauty. I had managed to get my fair share of prosecco at my sister's house in Mortlake and found it necessary, as my grandfather used to say, to 'make a call'. And a moment of glorious revelation from the bathroom window.

3. It is always a deeply cheering thing to come up against the wild world deep in the haunts of humankind. It is a message that we haven't concreted over every last square inch; that we haven't mucked it all up quite yet; that there is a way in which human beings can live alongside the wild world. Never mind the prosecco, that was a champagne moment.

4. The outlook was wonderfully and suburbanly verdant, my sister's garden playing a full part in the landscape of intricately compartmented green. And there, on the roof of the neat little shed that stood hard against the wall – just before it disappeared behind the branches of a stupendous lilac in full purple bloom – a fox.

Adapted from www.timesonline.co.uk

b Share your answer with a partner and explain how you worked out the original structure of the article.

c What word in the opening paragraph is used in the concluding paragraph to bring the article to an end and express the writer's attitude about the fox?

8 The writer uses a simple structure to express an opinion about urban foxes. Use the same structure to express an opinion about another kind of animal. It does not have to be a positive opinion, as this example shows.

The structure	Your ideas
A brief setting	Looking out of a window into a garden
An important object of attention is introduced	Among the flowers is a cat
More detail about this object	The cat is watching some songbirds at a bird feeder
A significant point is made	How the 'pretty' world of nature is a rough, wild place

Use a table like this to plan your own piece of writing. Include more than one sentence in each paragraph.

Much tabloid writing uses very simple paragraph structures. In any context, it is an important skill to be able to connect and group sentences into paragraphs. Look at Text D, a paragraph from a newspaper article, and read the annotations.

Ⓓ

Why do we treat children as the enemy?

It's very strange. According to the press, the country is awash with yobs, thugs, sick, feral, hoodies, louts and heartless, evil, frightening scum. These words, shown at the WiJ conference, came from one year's pick of the main newspapers. The point was repeated again and again. The vast majority of stories about teenage boys centred on crime and drugs. Sport and entertainment barely got a look-in and, even more depressingly, when they did, the majority of the coverage was neutral or negative.

www.independent.co.uk

A short, snappy sentence to intrigue the reader

An explanation of what is 'strange'

'These words' clearly refers to the list in the preceding sentence

This emphasises the point made in the opening three sentences

This sentence sums up the issue the writer is drawing attention to before …

ending the paragraph by suggesting how things could have been different

Activity

9 Now read Text E, a paragraph from another newspaper article, in which the sentences have got into the wrong order. Write down the correct order of the mixed-up sentences. Then, annotate the paragraph to show how the sentences connect.

Ⓔ

And although, yes, 27 knife murders in London in one year is an appalling statistic, we all know in our hearts that this is a terrible variegation, not the golden rule. None of these are ever reported. In my work I visit hundreds of schools and meet thousands of boys who read, pass exams, live normal lives. I have given out Duke of Edinburgh awards to kids who have shamed me with their energy and generosity. How can this be?

Activities

10 The writer of Text D has responded to the negative ways teenage boys are portrayed in the media. To organise your own response to you will need to think of three or four reasons for agreeing or disagreeing with the media's portrayal. Imagine them as separate slides in a PowerPoint presentation which have the key points but not the details.

a Give three separate reasons why constantly portraying teenagers (boys and/or girls) in negative ways is unfair and unwise. For example, one reason might be:

- teenagers could easily be portrayed in a better light because of all the good things they do.

Produce a rough list of ideas:

- as a straightforward list
- as a spider diagram or mind-map
- as PowerPoint slides.

b Share your ideas with a partner and adapt your own ideas according to what you find.

11 Write a newspaper article with the title 'Why teenagers deserve a better press'.

- Begin with a paragraph in which you describe concisely the issue you are writing about.
- Organise your article into four or five paragraphs, each paragraph being about a different main point.
- End with a short paragraph that clearly sums up your thoughts and feelings.

Check your learning 🄺!

In this chapter you have:

- explored different kinds of planning
- explored different ways of structuring your non-fiction writing.

19

Objectives

In this chapter you will:

explore different ways of structuring and planning your imaginative writing.

Getting it together 2: fiction writing

Imaginative writing

For controlled assessment you will produce more 'imaginative' forms of writing which require structure just as much as non-fiction forms. There are many different ways of structuring imaginative or narrative writing and several ways of getting ideas.

You might have written mini-sagas earlier in your school career; they require you to be very thoughtful in your choice of words. Mini-sagas must be exactly 50 words long. A complete story is condensed into that very small number of words. The challenge in this particular version of the mini-saga is to begin with one word and end with its opposite. Look at Text A, an example of a mini-saga which begins with 'love' and ends with 'hate'.

Love Blues

Love was in the air. He offered the beautiful red rose; on his left hand she saw the blue blur of a tattoo. 'Ouch,' she muttered as a thorn pierced her skin. Using his handkerchief, he dabbed the speck of blood away. She saw, on his right hand knuckles, 'Hate'.

The little story that connects the two words seems to suggest that in relationships you get a mixture of love and hate.

Activity

1. Write your own mini-saga. This exercise will impose a beginning and ending on your writing so that your challenge is to develop the middle section of a very short piece of writing. Choose your own two opposites or select one of the following: love/hate; black/white; winter/summer; bright/dark; hot/cold. Remember your story must have exactly 50 words.

Organising writing chronologically

One of the options in controlled assessment for GCSE English will be to write about your own life. However, whichever topic you choose in your controlled assessment you will need to think about the structure. One way to structure a piece of writing is to arrange your material chronologically in the order it happened.

Your choice of detail will bring interest to the writing. In a piece of writing recalling an encounter with a couple of boys, one writer begins:

The first time I was ambushed by the Baxter Gang, I was ten years old, walking home from choir practice at the local church of St Vincent de Paul.

The opening sentence is a useful model for a way to begin a piece of personal writing:

1 'The first time …' introduces an episode, an event.
2 'I was ten years old …' gives the reader important added information about the main character.
3 '… at the local church …' gives the reader a setting.

Activity

2 Think about some 'first times' from your earlier childhood and use Sentence 1 as a model. Write three opening sequences using Sentences 1–3 which would similarly draw a reader in.

The opening sentence of Text B gives all the important information the reader needs: it establishes characters, a setting and basically what is going to happen. It also sets up expectations in readers who will want to know the details of what happened when the writer was ambushed. It is often a good idea to delay the action by providing further information about the setting and characters.

The writer follows the opening sentence with a passage to set the scene. The story is set in London one very hot afternoon and the writer was eating a frozen lolly. Read the passage below in which some of the writer's main nouns have been highlighted. But instead of simply using a noun, the writer builds up detail by attaching other words to the noun, creating **noun phrases**.

> **Key terms**
>
> **Noun phrases:** a group of words that functions in the same way as a noun in a sentence.

B

The first time I was ambushed by the Baxter Gang, I was ten years old, walking home from choir practice at the local church of St Vincent de Paul. It was a dusty, sun-bleached London Saturday afternoon in high summer, so hot that the granite pavement winked at you until your eyes hurt, your black school brogues felt like twin ovens round your baking feet, and the only solace for your raging thirst was to spend two shillings on a pyramid-shaped lump of frozen orange squash called a Jubbly. It was not an elegant form of water-ice – you had to strip back the slimy, orange-silted bits of cardboard from the apex and plunge your mouth over it, grinding away with all your teeth at once, like a horse, to loosen some icy shards of squash and hold them, melting, in your mouth until you couldn't stand the pain any longer. Satisfying, yes, but strangely head-ache inducing.

Activities

3
a What is the complete noun phrase used by the writer to add interesting detail to each highlighted noun in the paragraph?

b The paragraph is given cohesion by the writer focusing on details that concern heat and summer. List all the words and phrases that focus in some way on the heat.

4 Think about an early childhood experience from your own life. Choose one of your three opening sentences and then follow it with a paragraph in which you describe the setting. Concentrate on selecting details and using noun phrases to add interest.

The structure of a story that begins, 'The first time …' tends to be chronological, but it is a good idea to think about other ways of bringing interest to the structure of a story.

Using flashbacks

Another interesting way of structuring a story is to introduce a flashback, a change in tense. Text C, the opening of a short story called 'Compass and Torch', is in the present tense but the story then moves to the past tense as the writer takes the reader back in time. You can find 'Compass and Torch' in the AQA Anthology.

C

Compass and Torch

The road ends at a gate. The boy waits in the car while the man gets out. Beyond the gate is the open moor, pale in the early evening with bleached end-of-summer grass, bruised here and there with heather and age-old spills of purple granite. The boy, though, is not looking that way, ahead. He is watching the man: the way he strides to the gate, bouncing slightly in his boots, his calf-muscles flexing beneath the wide knee-length shorts, the flop of hair at the front and the close-shaved neck as he bends for the catch.

The boy is intent. Watching Dad. Watching what Dad is. Drinking it in: the essence of Dadness.

The man pushes the gate with one arm, abruptly, too hard – the boy misses a breath – and sure enough, the gate swings violently, bounces off the stone wall and begins to swing back again while the man is already returning to the car. But then it slows, keels out once more, and comes to rest, wide open, against the wall: the man judged correctly after all. The boy is relieved. And, as the man drops into the driving seat something in the boy's chest gives a little hop of joy and he cries excitedly, 'Oh, I brought my torch!'

Coming downstairs after finding his torch, he overheard his mother say what she thought of the expedition.

Mad, she was calling it, as he knew she would. 'Mad! The first time in four months he has his eight-year-old son and what does he plan to do? Take him camping up a mountain!'

Elizabeth Baines, 'Compass and Torch', 2007

Activity

5 Read Text C.

    a Identify the place where the change of tense from present to past occurs.

    b Who is the new character introduced at this change of tense?

    c Comment on the change of tone that occurs when the tense changes.

The story moves forward to the point where the boy mentions his torch and it becomes very clear how important it is to him. But instead of moving the plot further forward the writer uses the word 'torch' to take the reader back to a time before the opening. The reader knows that the flashback will concern the torch in some way.

Activity

6 Use this flashback device as a model for your own writing, autobiographical or imagined:

- the opening of the story is in the present tense and is a very vivid and detailed description of an event
- an object is mentioned at the end of the description which shifts the story back in time
- the events leading up to the opening are described.

For example:

- a crowd of young people, an argument, the start of a fight, the flash of ...
- ...a knife
- a father is giving his son a birthday present, a penknife because the son has found his first job as an apprentice gardener and it will be a useful tool.

Introducing a 'twist'

Changing tense and using a flashback are two ways of bringing interest to the structure of narrative writing. Another way is to leave a surprise at the end for the reader.

Stories with a surprise ending need to be very carefully plotted: there have to be some clues on the way.

Read Text D, another short story. Voodoo is actually a religion, but one thing that has become associated with it (probably wrongly) is the practice of cursing a person by sticking pins in an effigy/doll of them.

Voodoo

Mr Decker's wife had just returned from a trip to Haiti – a trip she had taken alone – to give them a cooling off period before they discussed a divorce.

It hadn't worked. Neither of them had cooled off in the slightest. In fact, they were finding now that they hated one another more than ever.

'Half,' said Mrs Decker firmly. 'I'll not settle for anything less than half the money plus half the property.'

'Ridiculous!' said Mr Decker.

'Is it? I could have it all you know. And quite easily too. I studied voodoo while in Haiti.'

'Rot!' said Mr Decker.

'It isn't. And you should be glad that I'm a good woman for I could kill you quite easily if I wished. I would then have all the money and all the real estate, and without any fear of the consequences. A death accomplished by voodoo cannot be distinguished from death by heart failure.'

'Rubbish!' said Mr Decker.

'You think so? I have wax and a hatpin. Do you want to give me a tiny pinch of your hair or a fingernail clipping or two – that's all I need – and let me show you?'

'Nonsense!' said Mr Decker

'Then why are you afraid to let me try? Since I know it works, I'll make you a proposition. If it doesn't kill you, I'll give you a divorce and ask for nothing. If it does, I'll get it all automatically.'

'Done!' said Mr Decker. 'Get your wax and hatpin.' He glanced at his fingernails. 'Pretty short. I'll give you a bit of hair.'

When he came back with a few short strands of hair in the lid of an aspirin tin, Mrs Decker had already started softening the wax. She kneaded the hair into it, then shaped it into the rough effigy of a human being.

'You'll be sorry,' she said, and thrust the hatpin into the chest of the wax figure.

Mr Decker was surprised, but he was more pleased than sorry. He had not believed in voodoo, but being a cautious man he never took chances.

Besides, it had always irritated him that his wife so seldom cleaned her hairbrush.

Fredric Brown, 'Voodoo'

The main point of interest about that story is the twist at the end but it is worthwhile noticing how the writer structures the dialogue. You will see how the conventions of punctuating speech help the reader:

- the spoken words are enclosed in speech marks
- each time it moves to the next speaker a new paragraph is begun
- having established at the start who is speaking the writer does not have to keep repeating 'said Mrs Decker' because it is obvious she is speaking.

Activities

7 As the dialogue alternates between Mr and Mrs Decker:

a How does the writer make their contributions different?

b Why, when it is not necessary, might the writer keep repeating 'said Mr Decker'?

8 Here are some scenarios for very short stories with a twist at the end:

- Two people argue childishly. At the end of the story the reader discovers that they are actually very old.

- Two people seem to have a conversation. At the end of the story the reader discovers that there is only one person who has been having an 'inner' conversation with him/herself.

- Two teenage girls talk on the phone. One is upset because her boyfriend is seeing someone else. At the end the reader discovers the 'someone else' is the other girl.

Choose one of these or invent your own scenario. Write your story, remembering to:

- begin with a brief setting

- use dialogue and consider how to structure the dialogue and differentiate between the two speakers

- have the twist at the very end.

Stretch yourself

Imaginative writing for controlled assessment might focus on yourself, inviting you to create interesting pieces of writing that focus on your own life and experiences. Read Text E.

The structure of the poem provides a model for a story:

- a setting is described which gives some factual details – a girl, cold and upset, seems to have received some bad news in a telephone call and will have to walk home alone

- in the last four lines the writer draws out the meaning of the little scene – the girl has been rejected and that has made her cry.

Perhaps the most important part of the girl's story – what was said to her on the phone and by whom – is left to the reader's imagination.

- How does the writer use 'ice' and other words of coldness to create an effect on the reader?

The writer doesn't just create a wintry scene and then move into a story. Instead, the idea of ice holds the text together from start to finish.

Write a poem based on the structure of 'First Ice' which is, instead, called 'First Light'.

First Ice
A girl freezes in a telephone booth.
In her draughty overcoat she hides
A face all smeared
In tears and lipstick.
She breathes on her thin palms.
Her fingers are icy. She wears earrings.
She'll have to go home alone, alone
Along the icy street.
First ice. It is the first time.
The first ice of telephone phrases.
Frozen tears glitter on her cheeks –
The first ice of human hurt.

Andrei Voznesensky
'First Ice', 1987

Check your learning

In this chapter you have:

- explored different kinds of planning

- explored different ways of structuring your fiction writing.

Meeting the needs of your readers

Objectives

In this chapter you will:

think about different ways of engaging your audience

use a range of language features to suit audience and purpose.

Thinking about purpose

In this chapter you will consider different purposes for writing. You will also explore different ways of engaging and sustaining the interest of your readers in a variety of texts.

Writers adapt their writing to suit their audience and their purpose. Often a text can have more than one purpose. For example, an advertisement for a holiday resort is intended to persuade readers to go there. However, it will almost certainly inform readers about facilities or local attractions as well.

Activity

1 Look at Texts A to C with a partner. Copy and complete the table below. Identify at least two purposes for each text and support each purpose with evidence taken from the text.

Text	Purpose 1	Evidence	Purpose 2	Evidence
Ⓐ	Inform	Beef from cattle … of Inner Mongolia		
Ⓑ				
Ⓒ				

Ⓐ
The king prawns are almost too good for the sweet and sour. Freshly caught in the Yellow Sea that morning, they sit beautifully on an equally beautiful bone-china plate. Amid the symphony of chopping, chatting and the clattering of pans and woks comes the scent of fresh coriander, toasted chilli and a mixture of ginger, spring onion and garlic. The star anise wafts through from a pot of mouth-watering tender beef from the cattle bred on the lush steppes of Inner Mongolia.

Xiaomei Martell, *Lion's Head, Four Happiness*, 2009

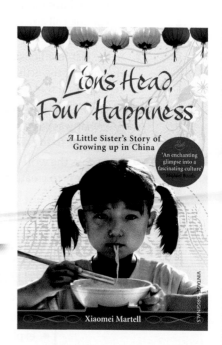

Lion's Head, Four Happiness

A Little Sister's Story of Growing up in China

'An enchanting glimpse into a fascinating culture'
Michael Booth

Xiaomei Martell

VINTAGE ORIGINALS

(B)
Do you have what it takes? It's a question of conviction. A matter of self-confidence. It's about defining your own values. Becoming *Only the Brave* is becoming your own hero. He who takes charge of his own life and destiny. He who knows how to play on his strength and his inner serenity. The Bottle. A symbol of strength.

Price per 100ml: (35ml EDT) £77, (50ml EDT) £69, (75ml EDT) £62, (200ml Gel Douche) £10

(C)
◄ ► | ¢ | + | 🜨 http://www.skcin.org   ↻

There's no getting away from the fact that sunshine makes us feel good. It's essential to enable our bodies to produce vitamin D and it triggers the so-called 'happy' chemical, seratonin, that boosts our mood. Casual exposure of the hands and face is sufficient to give most people adequate vitamin D levels to sustain bone health.

There's no avoiding the fact that skin cancer is on the increase and it's a killer. So, before you strip off and feel the warmth of the sun on your skin this summer whether you're on an idyllic beach abroad or you're enjoying something as simple as a picnic or a bike ride in the country, ask yourself one question: Am I being sun safe or am I dying to get a tan?

www.skcin.org

Engaging the interest of your readers 🙋

Whatever their purpose(s), writers know they must capture their readers' attention by using language effectively. Perhaps the makers of the aftershave (Text B) named their product *Only the Brave* because they knew this short phrase would stand out for readers. Can you explain why?

Activity

2

a Look again at Text A, which is the opening paragraph of an autobiography, and answer these questions:

● Which adjectives does the writer use to make the reader feel the food is appetising and delicious?

● Which of the five senses does the writer use to draw the reader into the experience she is describing?

● Why do you think the writer chose the metaphor of a symphony?

● Which three verbs does the writer use to help the reader appreciate the sounds of cooking? What is the effect of the three verbs together?

b Using Text A as a model, write a short paragraph about food that you remember eating and enjoying when you were young.

You should aim to:

● choose vocabulary that will engage the interest of your readers

● use a range of adjectives to make the food sound as appetising as possible

● include some of the five senses in your description.

(D)

Arena Spectacular has life-size animatronic creatures, brought to life by the Creative Technology Company for the BBC

Dinosaurs are like London buses. Nothing for 65m years, then a load of them turn up all at once. As proof, around the back of the Newcastle Arena is quite the most bizarre bus queue of all time.

Begins by referring to an experience readers will be familiar with

Over there stands an enormous brachiosaurus with a long, elegant neck. Her skin hangs from her spine in enormous brown curtains like an 'after' shot of extreme liposuction. Next to her, much shorter, but still the size of a Transit van, is a torosaurus, with two enormous horns jutting from his forehead and a nasty red gash on his neck. Nearest me is a vicious-looking blighter with evil green eyes and big, stained teeth.

Detailed description draws reader into account quickly

Ending of paragraph makes reader want to read on to find out more

He's an allosaurus, and as I edge closer he rears up and thrashes a long tail. Bending his considerable neck to look me in the eye, he blinks slowly, and a funny thing happens. Even though I can hear the hydraulics hiss and clank inside him, even though I've felt his foam and Lycra skin, and even though … well, I just know he's not real, all of a sudden I'm 10 again, and a little voice inside me says 'Cor!'

Writer makes the experience seem personal by describing his own reaction

Walking with Dinosaurs: the Arena Spectacular features 15 life-size creatures that walk, breathe, blink and roar their way through the Triassic, Jurassic and Cretaceous periods – that's 180m years in 90 minutes. So far they've got as far as Newcastle, where rehearsals are taking place, before the show kicks off in Glasgow on Wednesday.

Withholds specific details about the event until the end

Paul Croughton, 'Walking with Dinosaurs', the Arena Spectacular, *Sunday Times*, 28 June 2009

Activities

3 Answer these questions to help you understand more about how the writer maintains the interest of his readers.

   a Why do you think the writer compares the queue of dinosaurs to a bus queue?

   b To what is the torosaurus compared? How does this comparison help you to imagine the creature?

   c At the end of paragraph 2 the writer introduces a new dinosaur: 'Nearest me is a vicious-looking blighter …'. Why do you think he begins a new paragraph to continue the description?

   d Why does the writer withhold details of the event until he reaches the end of the review?

   e What different feelings does the writer appear to have for the dinosaur show? Give reasons for your answer.

   f How does the writer make the dinosaur models seem like living creatures?

   g Would this review persuade readers to go to the dinosaur show? Give reasons for your answer.

4 Choose an event you have attended, such as a concert or a football match, or a place you have visited such as a theme park. Write a review in which you share your experiences (either positive or negative) with readers. Think about:

- the details you will include in your review
- when you will reveal these details
- how and where to include your own opinion
- how to engage the interest of your readers in the opening paragraph
- how you will end each paragraph to encourage readers to read on
- how you will maintain the interest of your reader through word choices.

Use this checklist to assess your completed review and then pass your work to a partner asking them to comment on how well you maintained the interest of your readers.

Influencing your readers

There are many ways in which writers attract their readers and encourage them to keep reading. One way of doing this is to use a conversational tone to make readers feel as if the writer is talking or chatting to them. Another way is to make the reader feel as if the writer understands their feelings and has shared some of their experiences. Using words and phrases from the reader's everyday speech helps the reader to appreciate the ideas in the text.

Activities

5 **a** Read Text E which follows on page 128. Copy the chart and complete the grid to help you understand how these features work in the text.

Technique	Examples of usage	Effects
Use of personal pronouns e.g. 'we', 'our', 'us', 'you'	We're turning down every invite …	
Use of words and phrases from reader's every day speech		
Humorous examples		Entertain readers and helps them to relate to the text
Short sentences at key points in the text		

   b Now that you have looked closely at some of the features of the text, discuss with a another student whether or not you think the tone of this text would appeal to the target audience.

CAM'S BOY BLOG

THIS MONTH: CAM, 15, ON WHERE BOYS GO IN JANUARY

"Nooo. I don't want to!" shrieks my mate Andy, hiding his face under a pillow, when I ask whether he's coming to Lucy's house party. This is *Andy*: the animal known as party, the guy first in at every gathering and leaping about before the clock chimes six. And *he* doesn't want to come out. It must be January.

Maybe you've noticed we're a bit thin on the ground this month. We're turning down every invite that comes our way and heading straight home after school with a face that makes Chris Martin look chipper.

January is the lamest of all months, for these reasons: All our clothes appear to have shrunk at the waist. Which is weird, 'cause the length is still OK.

We're back to school, facing the prospect of exams without a hint of sudden-onset genius. We're broke, following our over-enthusiastic festive spending. And now we've got to spend our time watching the little bro enjoy the pricey present we got him, which could – in hindsight – have been better spent escorting the new girl to Burger King.

Plus it's still seriously Baltic and we don't have the advantage of make-up to tone down our embarrassingly red noses and cheeks. What's more, we're expected to wear the ridiculous knits our nan fashioned us as presents without complaint.

So this year me and my mates have just one shared New Year's resolution. To bunk down at the bottom of Andy's garden with his hibernating tortoise, Marty – and skip January altogether. See you in February, girls.

> **We're sporting faces that make Chris Martin look positively chipper**

⚠ **WARNING**
CONTAINS BRUTALLY HONEST LOVE ADVICE

This article appeared in *Sugar Ladmag*, February 2009

Activity

6 Choose an experience which is common to many teenagers. Write an article aimed at readers of your own age sharing this experience with them. You might choose to write about catching up with coursework or returning to school after the long summer holidays. Your purpose is to entertain your readers.

In order to engage your readers you should use:

- personal pronouns
- words and phrases from your reader's every day speech
- humorous examples
- short sentences at key points in the text to summarise the main ideas.

Adding details to interest your readers

Writers engage their readers with a range of interesting details that help the reader picture what is being described.

Activities

7 Read Text F, in which the writer describes some of his relatives at Christmas time.

>
> Some few large men sat in the front parlours, without their collars, Uncles almost certainly, trying their new cigars, holding them out judiciously at arm's length, returning them to their mouths, coughing, then holding them out again as though waiting for the explosion; and some few small Aunts, not wanted in the kitchen, nor anywhere else for that matter, sat on the very edges of their chairs, poised and brittle, afraid to break, like faded cups and saucers.
>
> *Dylan Thomas*, 'A Child's Christmas in Wales', *Collected Stories*, 1993

  a Identify where the writer describes:
   - his characters' appearance
   - their actions.
  b What do the uncles' actions reveal about them?
  c What do the aunts' actions tell you about their characters?
  d How are similes used to tell you more about the characters?
  e How do the commas help to build the description?

8 Write a short description (of about 100 words) of a new student arriving in a classroom for the first time. You might choose to make your student very confident or very nervous.

You should aim to:

- refer to one or two details about their appearance
- focus on their actions, ensuring that these portray either confidence or nervousness
- include a simile to help your readers picture your character.

Compare your description with those of other students.

Stretch yourself

1

Read Text G which also describes relatives.

As you read the extract think about how the writer:

- structures the text
- builds up a range of details to maintain the readers' interest.

G

My sister, Mrs Joe Gargery, was more than twenty years older than I, and had established a great reputation with herself and the neighbours because she had brought me up 'by hand'. Having at that time to find out for myself what the expression meant, and knowing her to have a hard and heavy hand, and to be much in the habit of laying it upon her husband as well as upon me, I supposed that Joe Gargery and I were both brought up by hand.

She was not a good-looking woman, my sister; and I had a general impression that she must have made Joe Gargery marry her by hand. Joe was a fair man, with curls of flaxen hair on each side of his smooth face, and with eyes of such a very undecided blue that they seemed to have somehow got mixed with their own whites. He was a mild, good-natured, sweet-tempered, easy-going, foolish, dear fellow – a sort of Hercules in strength, and also in weakness.

My sister, Mrs Joe, with black hair and eyes, had such a prevailing redness of skin that I sometimes used to wonder whether it was possible she washed herself with a nutmeg-grater instead of soap. She was tall and bony, and almost always wore a coarse apron, fastened over her figure behind with two loops, and having a square impregnable bib in front, that was stuck full of pins and needles. She made it a powerful merit in herself, and a strong reproach against Joe, that she wore this apron so much. Though I really see no reason why she should have worn it at all: or why, if she did wear it at all, she should not have taken it off, every day of her life.

Charles Dickens, *Great Expectations*, 1861

2

Write a description of a relative – you can invent some details or exaggerate to interest your readers. Aim to:

- gradually reveal more information about your character's appearance, actions and personality
- reveal your opinion of your character
- sustain the interest of your reader.

Check your learning

In this chapter you have:

- examined the audience and purpose of a range of texts
- examined the way writers use language and purpose to engage their readers
- used language in an interesting way to engage your readers
- selected details to make your writing interesting.

21

Different kinds of writing

Genres

In the world of literature there are three main genres: drama, poetry and prose, but genre is not as simple as that. Drama can be subdivided into different genres such as tragedy and comedy. Prose can be subdivided many times, into, for example, autobiography, novels, short stories and so forth. The genre of the novel can be divided into lots of sub-genres: adventure, thriller, romantic and many more. Different genres can be connected to form sub-genres such as tragicomedy.

Different genres can be recognised by certain characteristics or conventions. Sometimes these characteristics concern plot: certain things tend to happen in the plots of horror stories which are different from the kinds of things that feature in the plots of romantic stories. Other characteristics concern settings: a story set on a spaceship exploring the galaxy is likely to be recognised as a science-fiction story. There are different features of language in different genres: certain kinds of words are associated with different kinds of stories.

Description

All stories need a setting, a place in which the action takes place. But setting is not simply a matter of describing a place, it also involves the creation of atmosphere. A wood, for example, can feature in a children's adventure story and the writer can make it an exciting, unthreatening place or it can feature in a horror story in which it becomes a scary, threatening environment. You are going to read and explore passages of description from four pieces of writing from four different genres.

Activity

1 Read Text A and answer the following questions:

- What genre of story do you think this is?
- What details selected by the writer suggest the strangeness of this setting?
- What is the effect of calling the candelabrum (a large decorative candlestick with several arms) a 'vast' or 'iron' spider?
- A candelabrum could be described as a 'vast jewelled crown' or a 'vast birthday cake'. How would either of those change the atmosphere of the passage?

Ⓐ

Like a vast spider suspended by a metal cord, a candelabrum presided over the room nine feet above the floor boards. From its sweeping arms of iron, long stalactites of wax lowered their pale spilths* drip by drip, drip by drip. A rough table with a drawer half open, which appeared to be full of birdseed, was in such a position below the iron spider that a cone of tallow** was mounting by degrees at one corner into a lambent*** pyramid the size of a hat.

*spilth: an old-fashioned word for anything spilled
**tallow: candle wax
***lambent: softly bright

Mervyn Peake, *Titus Groan*, 1946

Activity

2

Read Text B and answer the following questions.

- What genre of writing do you think this is?
- What details of the passage show that this is a very different genre from the first passage?
- Re-write the last sentence of the passage to convert it into something that might appear in a ghost or horror story. Change 'you' to 'he', 'she' or 'it'. Change 'can take a break' to a different verb phrase and change the tense to past. Change 'very pretty' to something more sinister.

B

The southern part of the 12e arrondissement, which borders on the Bois de Vincennes, is fairly well-to-do, and at the weekend hordes of cyclists and soccer players head for the woods. But walkers can also clear away the cobwebs with a stroll along the Promenade Plantée, a green footpath along the avenue Daumesnil viaduct. At the foot of the arches, shops, art galleries and cafés have opened up one by one. On the other side of the Gare de Lyon, you can take a break in the very pretty parc de Bercy, where an orchard, a vegetable patch and a garden have replaced the old wine market.

Steve Fallon, *Lonely Planet City Guide: Paris*, 2004

Activity

3

Read Text C and answer the following questions:

a This passage focuses on a description of smog. How do you know it is not part of a scientific article about, for example, global warming?

b What is the attitude of the narrator in this passage to the scene being described?

C

The weather was hot and sticky and the acid sting of the smog had crept as far west as Beverly Hills. From the top of Mulholland Drive you could see it levelled out all over the city, a groundlike mist. When you were in it you could taste it and smell it and it made your eyes smart. Everybody was griping about it. In Pasadena where the stuffy millionaires holed up after Beverly Hills was spoiled for them by the movie crowd, the city fathers screamed with rage. Everything was the fault of the smog. If the canary wouldn't sing, if the milkman was late, if the Pekinese had fleas, if an old coot in a starched collar had a heart attack on the way to church, that was the smog. Where I lived it was usually clear in the early morning and nearly always at night. Once in a while a whole day would be clear, nobody quite knew why.

Raymond Chandler, *The Long Goodbye*, 1973

Activities

4 Of Texts A to C, one is from a travel guide, one from an American private eye crime story, and the other is from a mid-twentieth-century Gothic fantasy.

   a Which extract do you think is which?

   b List the conventions you have noticed in each genre – for example, the Gothic fantasy uses old-fashioned vocabulary to describe an old-fashioned setting; the atmosphere is strange and slightly sinister.

5 Choose one of the three passages to rewrite, keeping roughly the same details but converting it into a different genre. Text C, for example, could be converted into travel writing by changing the tense, using second person and adopting a more positive tone than the original:

'The weather can be quite hot and it might take you some time to become accustomed to the smog, which can reach as far west as Beverly Hills …'

The following two descriptive passages are taken from two different genres. The first is an example of travel writing and the second is from a novel which is a ghost story.

Activity

6 Read Texts D and E. The first passage, an example of travel writing, is annotated to indicate features of the description intended to draw attention to the beauty of Antarctica. Using these annotations as an example, identify features in Text E that indicate the writer's intention to create a sinister, unpleasant atmosphere.

(D)

A list of three adjectives intrigues the reader – 'strange' in what way?

A list of variations of the same basic colour. Packing them together emphasises the vividness of the colours

A list of three descriptive terms again, with 'dramatic' linking with 'wonderful' and 'beyond imagining'

Another list of colours, variations this time of red rather than the blue of the ice. This adds contrast

Another list of three colours. The repeated use of lists emphasises the range of colours

So this is Antarctica. Everything is strange and wonderful and unexpected. Despite all I have read about it, the experience is beyond imagining.

I didn't expect so much colour. The ocean is cobalt, sapphire, navy, even brilliant turquoise, turning gunmetal grey when the weather closes in. The mountains are dark rock, sheer and dramatic, crowned by glaciers. The ice isn't simply white: there is old ice, turquoise and navy blue, in the folds of the glaciers; and red algae dusted over the tops. There are lichens, orange and red and gold, sage and brown, in great splashes over the rocks.

The sky goes on forever and is filled with birds following the ship, making kaleidoscopic patterns of white and black and brown through which wandering albatrosses swoop, big as a man.

A statement that emphasises the sense of wonder

A phrase that suggests majesty and wonder

Use of 'great' connects with previous vocabulary choices such as 'crowned'

Jenny Barnes, www.telegraph.co.uk

(E)

The fire, which never drew well in this chimney, was sluggish, black and smoking unpleasantly again, but the chill I felt around me had to do with more than that. The temperature was low and the air felt clammy, damp and stale. And, with the change of air, I felt something else, a presence in the room. I was being watched with hating, hostile eyes. I sat terrified, as I had been that night in the great library at Alton. Here, there was no gallery, and no possibility of anything being hidden behind the lines of bookcases, here I could look around the room and see everything, books on the walls, tables, chairs, oak panelling, stone fireplace, the portrait of some jowly, beady-eyed ancestor with whip and stock that reared above it – the only unattractive picture in the house, and somehow, I had come to think, fittingly placed in this cold, hostile room.

Susan Hill, *Mist in the Mirror*, 1992

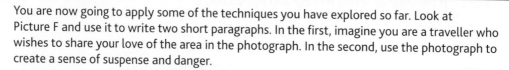

Activity

7 You are now going to apply some of the techniques you have explored so far. Look at Picture F and use it to write two short paragraphs. In the first, imagine you are a traveller who wishes to share your love of the area in the photograph. In the second, use the photograph to create a sense of suspense and danger.

(F)

Think about:

- the details you select to describe
- the vocabulary you use to describe them
- the atmosphere you create.

A different form

Drama

The writer John Steinbeck wrote the same story in two genres. The novel, *Of Mice and Men*, was published and the play of the same name first performed in 1937.

Much of the dialogue in the play and novel is identical. What is different is the way setting is handled by the writer because of the demands of the two different genres: one is intended to be read and the other to be watched and listened to.

Activity

8 Read Text G, the opening three paragraphs of the novel, and Text H, the opening two paragraphs of stage setting from the play.

a   What details feature in the novel that are excluded from the stage setting?

b   Using the details you have identified, explain why they were dropped from the stage setting.

c   Several animals are mentioned in the opening paragraphs of the novel but in the stage setting the writer only mentions two kinds of birds and 'ranch dogs', neither of which is mentioned in the novel's opening paragraphs. Why did the writer change the animals?

(G)

A few miles south of Soledad, the Salinas River drops in close to the hillside bank and runs deep and green. The water is warm too, for it has slipped twinkling over the yellow sands in the sunlight before reaching the narrow pool. On one side of the river the golden foothill slopes curve up to the strong and rocky Gabilan mountains, but on the valley side the water is lined with trees – willows fresh and green with every spring, carrying in their lower leaf junctures the debris of the winter's flooding; and sycamores with mottled, white, recumbent limbs and branches that arch over the pool. On the sandy bank under the trees the leaves lie deep and so crisp that a lizard makes a great skittering if he runs among them. Rabbits come out of the brush to sit on the sand in the evening, and the damp flats are covered with the night tracks of 'coons, and with the spread pads of dogs from the ranches, and with the split-wedge tracks of deer that come to drink in the dark.

There is a path through the willows and among the sycamores, a path beaten hard by boys coming down from the ranches to swim in the deep pool, and beaten hard by tramps who come wearily down from the highway in the evening to jungle-up near water. In front of the low horizontal limb of a giant sycamore there is an ash pile made by many fires; the limb is worn smooth by men who have sat on it.

Evening of a hot day started the little wind to moving among the leaves. The shade climbed up the hills toward the top. On the sand banks the rabbits sat as quietly as little gray, sculptured stones. And then from the direction of the state highway came the sound of footsteps on crisp sycamore leaves. The rabbits hurried noiselessly for cover. A stilted heron labored up into the air and pounded down river. For a moment the place was lifeless, and then two men emerged from the path and came into the opening by the green pool.

Thursday night. A sandy bank of the Salinas River sheltered with willows – one giant sycamore up R. The stage is covered with dry leaves. The feeling is sheltered and quiet. Stage is lit by a setting sun.

Curtain rises on an empty stage. A sparrow is singing. There is a distant sound of ranch dogs barking aimlessly and one clear quail call. The quail call turns to a warning call and there is a beat of the flock's wings. Two figures are seen entering L or R, it makes no difference, in single file, with George, the short man, coming in ahead of Lennie. Both men are carrying blanket rolls. They approach the water. The small man throws down his blanket roll, the large man follows, then falls down and drinks from the river, snorting as he drinks.

In Shakespeare's time there was little scenery on stage so that Shakespeare gave his characters speeches in which they would set the scene for the audience. In these advanced technological days it is less important for characters to have to describe settings for an audience, but in radio drama when an audience cannot see anything, pictures have to be created using sounds and the words spoken by characters.

Activity

9 Imagine that the opening scene to *Of Mice and Men* was going to be dramatised on radio. Anything that is a sound – like the sound of ranch dogs – can be captured in a sound effect. What are the things that can be seen which present a challenge for anyone wishing to adapt the novel/stage play for radio? What suggestions do you have for how the challenges could be overcome?

Activity

10 Write a script for a 60-second radio drama that is spoken by a single character about a place. There are a series of problems to be solved. You will need to think about the following:

- How can a story about a place be developed in only 60 seconds? It will need careful thought about an appropriate kind of story.
- Why might a place be important? Did something important happen there in the past? Is something important going to happen in the future?
- Who is your narrator and what is their connection with the place?
- How can you give your radio audience some idea of the atmosphere and visual appearance of the place in such a short time?

Poetry

Poetry is full of different forms, all of which can be used to create new poems. Some forms, such as ballads, seem quite simple, whereas others, such as sonnets, seem complicated, but they all present a range of opportunities. Read Text I, a poem called 'She Pops Home'.

She Pops Home

She pops home just long enough
    to overload the washing-machine
    to spend a couple of hours on the phone
    to spray the bathroom mirror with lacquer
    to kick the carpet out of line
    to say 'that's new – can I borrow it?'

She pops home just long enough
    to dust the aspidistra with her elbow
    to squeak her hand down the banister
    to use the last of the toilet roll
    to leave her bite in the last apple

She pops home just long enough
    to raid her mother's drawer for tights
    to stock up with next month's pill
    to hug a tenner out of dad

She pops home just long enough
    to horrify them with her lack of responsibility
    to leave them sweating until next time

She pops home just long enough
    to light their pond like a kingfisher

She pops home just long enough

Cal Clothier, 'She Pops Home'

11

a The form of the poem is based on patterns that repeat and change. What patterns can you find?

b On the basis of the first four stanzas, what seems to be the view of the girl presented in the poem?

c How does the image in the fifth stanza change the presentation of the girl?

d The poem ends with the single line that has been repeated throughout the poem. Now that it is on its own, placed at the end of the poem, what meaning does it convey?

12 Write your poem using this form to write affectionately but honestly about someone, using the line: I love her/him even when (s)he …

The poem, even though it seems to be about love for a person, will be a list of a person's shortcomings. The phrase 'I love her/him even when (s)he' will be repeated in your poem, and each time the phrase is used it will be followed by a list of things that are probably little irritations. For example:

> 'I love her even when she
>   tidies my room
>   asks me what time I'm going to be home …'

That example is focused on a mother, but the form could be used to write about famous people or friends. By the end of the poem the reader might be wondering if the voice of the poem really does love the person: the poem could be very sincere or very sarcastic.

Check your learning

In this chapter you have:

- explored some different genres of writing
- experimented with different kinds of writing.

22

Making your writing skills count in the exam

Objectives

In this chapter you will:

learn more about how your writing is tested in the exam

study questions in a sample paper

plan, write and assess an answer

read other students' answers and the examiner's comments on them.

About the exam

In the study of the past nine chapters, you have been developing your skills in writing. These skills will help you to cope with the demands of the exam.

There is one exam paper in GCSE English and GCSE English Language. Its focus is:

● Understanding and producing non-fiction texts.

The paper is divided into two sections:

● **Section A:** Reading (one hour, worth 20% of your final marks)
● **Section B:** Writing (one hour, worth 20% of your final marks)

In this chapter we will deal with Section B. You can find out more about Section A in Chapter 11 which follows the Reading chapters.

In Section B, you will be asked to complete two Writing tasks: one shorter task worth 16 marks and one longer task worth 24 marks.

What you need to know

When you take the exam you have one hour to complete the Writing section. This is not a lot of time in which to demonstrate all the skills you have accumulated in writing since starting your GCSE course. You need to know what to expect and what skills you need to demonstrate to your examiner if you are to gain the most marks you can in that single hour.

We will start with the Assessment Objectives. These are the aims of your GCSE course. They underpin the questions you will be asked in the exam and the marks scheme that examiners use to assess your answers. The Assessment Objectives are written for teachers to help them develop your course of study. It is, however, possible to break them down into more student-friendly language.

On page 141 you will see the three parts of the Assessment Objective for Writing that underpin Section B of your exam. The annotations show you what they mean in terms of the skills you need to show your examiner.

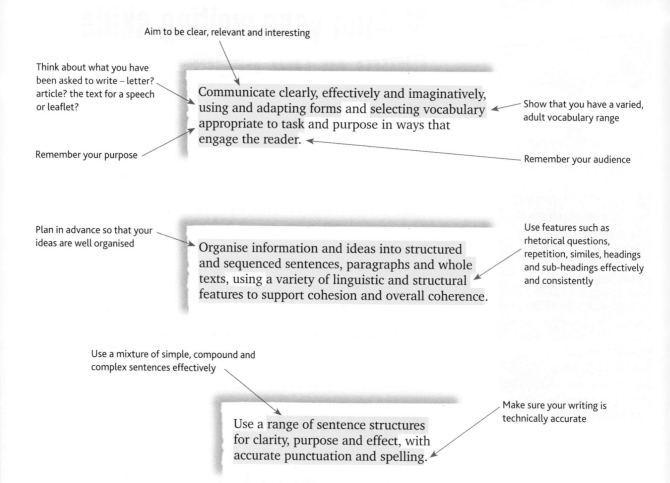

Aim to be clear, relevant and interesting

Think about what you have been asked to write – letter? article? the text for a speech or leaflet?

Remember your purpose

Communicate clearly, effectively and imaginatively, using and adapting forms and selecting vocabulary appropriate to task and purpose in ways that engage the reader.

Show that you have a varied, adult vocabulary range

Remember your audience

Plan in advance so that your ideas are well organised

Organise information and ideas into structured and sequenced sentences, paragraphs and whole texts, using a variety of linguistic and structural features to support cohesion and overall coherence.

Use features such as rhetorical questions, repetition, similes, headings and sub-headings effectively and consistently

Use a mixture of simple, compound and complex sentences effectively

Use a range of sentence structures for clarity, purpose and effect, with accurate punctuation and spelling.

Make sure your writing is technically accurate

Sample questions ⓚ

The questions in the exam are designed to test your skills in the areas covered by the three parts of the Assessment Objective for Writing that you have just considered.

Here are two questions, typical of the exam you will take. Both questions test the full range of skills. The marks awarded for each answer are also indicated.

You should divide your time according to the number of marks awarded to both tasks. As a rough guide, allow 25 minutes for the first task and 35 minutes for the second task.

1   Write a review for a website of something you have seen or read recently. It could be a film, a sports match, a book, a TV programme or something else. You should aim to inform your reader.

(*16 marks*)

2   Some people think that finding treasure, winning the lottery or suddenly coming into money is the key to happiness in life. Write an article for a magazine read by people your age in which you argue for or against this idea.

(*24 marks*)

Before writing you need to analyse the question and plan your answer. Spend about four to five minutes on this. Follow Steps A to E to see what you need to do.

Step A: Analyse the question to work out your subject, purpose, audience and the form your writing needs to take:

> Write a review for a website of something you have seen or read recently. It could be a film, a sports match, a book, a TV programme or something else. You should aim to inform your reader.
>
> Subject: something you have seen or read recently
>
> Purpose: to inform
>
> Audience: readers of the website
>
> Form: a review

Step B: Choose something you know about and jot down a range of things connected to it – for example:

Life on Mars: TV series, set in 1970s, crime, cops and robbers type, main character from present, shows attitudes of past – racism and sexism, set in Manchester, implausible, funny, Sam Tyler, Gene Hunt, coma, radio and TV messages.

Step C: Think about the order in which you are going to place your ideas. Aim to plan three, or at most four, coherent paragraphs. You might think of new things as you do this – for example:

- Para 1: main character – Sam Tyler – from present – lands in 1970s – contrast in attitudes and policing methods
- Para 2: talk about one incident in detail – Manchester/drugs/violence – cops and robbers – Ford Cortina
- Para 3: mystery – coma – voices on radio/TV – unanswered questions – keeps you watching – recommend watching on DVD.

Step D: Remind yourself of the skills you need to demonstrate in your writing. You need to:

- engage and interest your reader
- use Standard English
- use a range of sentence structures
- use a varied, mature vocabulary
- make sure your writing is technically accurate.

Step E: Think of an interesting opening that will engage your readers and start writing, for example:

> Many of us weren't alive in the 1970s. For those who were, Life on Mars will bring back …

Activity

1

a Take Question 2 from the exam paper on page 140. Follow Steps A to E and continue to write your full answer. You have longer for this task – about 35 minutes – and should aim to write four or five coherent paragraphs.

b When you have written your answer, spend two or three minutes reading though and correcting or improving it.

c In groups of three or four, read each other's answers. Use the following assessment statements to help you write a comment on each student's answer.

- You communicate your ideas with some success/clearly/convincingly.
- You engage the reader with some linked arguments/detailed arguments/detailed and persuasive arguments.
- You use an inappropriate/appropriate tone which has little effect/manipulates the reader's response.
- You use devices such as rhetorical questions and repetition rarely/effectively/very effectively.
- Your range of vocabulary is limited/varied/mature and sophisticated.
- You use paragraphs inappropriately/appropriately to enhance your meaning.
- Your use of varied sentence structures is limited/varied/effective.
- You show mostly inaccuracy/accuracy in your spelling and punctuation.

Keep the assessments of your answer to use in Activity 2.

When you receive your assessment, look again at your answer. Consider ways in which you could improve it and make a note of these.

Sample answers

You are now going to look at Texts A and B, two students' answers to Question 2. They have been assessed by an examiner. The annotations show you the examiner's comments on each student's writing.

(A) Student A

Would you like to win the lottery? I know I would. Every week my parents buy a ticket and use our birthdays to choose their numbers. We watch the draw but so far have never won more than £10, still it's worth a try. We already know exactly what we would do with the money if we were lucky enough to win a couple of million.

The very first thing we would do would be to buy a bigger house. Theres five of us living here and it gets pretty crowded especialy when we all want to use the bathroom in the morning. We'd buy a house with at least three bathrooms and everyone would have their own enormous bedroom with wardrobes full of the latest fashions and the biggest plasma TV hanging on the wall.

Then we'd buy a holiday place in Dubai, we went there a few years ago and loved the sunshine and the fabulous hotels and beaches. We even liked the camel races and we all had a go at riding one. If we had a house there we'd be able to go for hollidays all the time and that would make us really happy.

We'd also buy a new car for my Dad, he's been driving the same one for years and he'd really like an Astin Martin or a Jaguar or even a top of the range Land Rover so that we could all pile in and go for visits to different places.

Then we'd buy … Well, I could go on and on as there is a very long list of things we'd like to have. The point is that winning the lottery would make us really happy and there would be enough money to make sure all our freinds and relatives got some as well. When you read about people who spend the money they win on things like drugs and wild parties you just think what a waste. They could have really changed their lives and made themselves much happier. It all depends on who wins the lottery and what they do with the money whether it makes them happy. If they spend it to make themselves happier then that's a good thing but if they just waste it on drugs and things then that's not. I know what I would do. Do you?

142

Examiner's comments

What the student does

The writing is organised into sentences and paragraphs and the student matches the writing to purpose and audience, with an appropriate opening and ending. There is some variety in vocabulary and sentence structure, though this is limited. Commonly used words are usually spelled accurately and there is some range in punctuation though commas are sometimes used where full stops or semi-colons are needed.

What the student needs to do to improve

The student needs to think about the content of each paragraph more carefully before starting to write. This would help him/her to vary the paragraph openings and make them less repetitive. The student should aim to show a wider, more adult vocabulary range and the ability to structure complex sentences using commas correctly.

Student B

Imagine waking up one morning to find all your dreams have come true. You awake in cool linen sheets, freshly laundered, breakfast is served in bed on a silver plate, your wardrobe is bursting with all the latest 'it' bags (or whatever takes your fancy) and, emerging from your sleep slowly and lazily you gaze outside at your tailored lawns, outdoor swimming pool and magnificent private theme park (again, replace with personal preference). You have everything you've ever wanted. You never need to go to school, or work, again. You simply have to enjoy yourself and the luxury of your life. Are you happy? 'Of course,' you answer gleefully.

But wait. Think again. It's very quiet this morning. Where are the terrible twins, those two who have made your life a misery by waking you with their screams, laughter, secret smiles and, more recently, their energetic play, every morning for the last four years, eight months and twenty-two days? Why is your Dad not shouting a grumpy 'Morning' as he heads to the bathroom, his only place of solitude? Why is your Mum not just at this very moment calling you frantically downstairs to 'get your breakfast or you'll be late'? And why, as the clock's hand moves towards 8.30 is your best friend, the one you've had since primary school, not knocking frantically on your front door ready to entertain you with stories of her previous evening's escapades?

And then you remember. You did a deal. You wanted to escape. You won and chose freedom – the freedom that only a huge win on the lottery can bring. Freedom to leave all your past life behind. Freedom to escape from the drudgery of the same old routine. Freedom to do just what you want. But therein lies the problem. What do you want to do? You've left your old life behind; you rarely see your parents or your brother and sister any more and your best friend, quickly feeling your neglect, has found a new 'best' friend to tell her stories to. The ambitions you once had – to be a doctor working to save the lives of others – have long since been abandoned. Who needs to work when they have millions in the bank?

You wander across to the window and gaze at your tailored lawns. The swimming pool reflects the clouds of the morning sky and the theme park sits quiet and empty. Are you happy? The deafening silence is the only answer given.

Examiner's comments

This is an excellent answer. The writing is coherently structured, with a lovely mirroring of the ending of the first paragraph in the final two sentences. The student adopts an imaginative approach to the subject, and successfully engages the reader throughout with the skilful use of the second person (you). Vocabulary is varied and mature and the student demonstrates full control of sentence structure, varying this for maximum effect. Repetition is used effectively and the writing demonstrates a high level of technical accuracy in both spelling and punctuation.

Activity

2 Look back at your own answer to Question 2 and the assessments that were made of it. Using these assessments and what you have learned from studying the examiner's comments on two students' answers to this question, consider how you could improve your own answer. Make a note of the different things you could do in order to gain a higher mark.

Check your learning

In this chapter you have:

- studied how the Assessment Objective for Writing is tested in the exam
- examined questions in a sample paper
- planned and written a sample answer
- studied sample answers and examiner's comments
- considered how to achieve the highest marks you can in your exam.

23

Making your writing skills count in the controlled assessment

Objectives

In this chapter you will:

learn more about how your writing is assessed in controlled assessment

learn more about the tasks in controlled assessment

read other students' answers and the examiner's comments on them.

What is controlled assessment?

During your GCSE course, the writing skills that you have developed during the first nine chapters of this section of the book will be tested by controlled assessment. What this will involve depends on whether you are studying GCSE English or GCSE English language.

GCSE English

Controlled assessment title
Producing creative texts

Mark value
20% = 40 marks

Choice of task
Two of:
- Moving images
- Prompts and re-creations
- Me. Myself. I.

Planning and preparation
You are allowed to spend time preparing for and planning your writing, and you may make brief notes which can be taken into the controlled assessment.

Time for writing
Up to 4 hours

Expected length
About 1600 words over both pieces of writing

GCSE English Language

Controlled assessment title
Creative writing

Mark value
15% = 30 marks

Choice of task
Two of:
- Moving images
- Commissions
- Re-creations

Planning and preparation
You are allowed to spend time preparing for and planning your writing, and you may make brief notes which can be taken into the controlled assessment.

Time for writing
Up to 4 hours

Expected length
About 1200 words over both pieces of writing

You are allowed to take brief notes into the controlled assessment. You are not allowed:
- pre-prepared drafts (you must not write out a 'rough' version of your response and either seek advice about it or take it into the controlled assessment)
- dictionaries, spell-checkers or thesauruses
- to take your writing out of the controlled assessment room between sessions.

Introducing the tasks

There are three options for the controlled assessment task.

GCSE English

- Moving images (writing for or about moving images)
- Prompts and re-creations (using a text or prompt to develop writing)
- Me. Myself. I. (Writing from personal experience)

You will produce two pieces of writing in response to tasks from two of these categories, totalling around 1600 words across both pieces.

GCSE English Language

- Moving images (writing for or about moving images)
- Commissions (responding to a given brief)
- Prompts and re-creations (taking a text and turning it into another)

You will produce two pieces of writing in response to tasks from two of these categories, totalling around 1200 words across both pieces.

One of the most important differences between exams and controlled assessments is that you have quite a lot of time to prepare for the controlled assessment task. You will know the task – unlike those in the exam – and you will be able to discuss and research it in lessons before the controlled assessment.

To do well in the controlled assessment task you will need a good understanding of the Assessment Objectives for Writing. You will find a detailed breakdown of what each of the objectives means in Chapter 22, which focuses on the writing part of the exam.

Sample questions and sample answers

Prompts and re-creations

Here is a sample task based on the Prompts and re-creations topic area, which is common to both GCSE English and GCSE English Language (simply referred to as 'Recreations' in the GCSE English Language specification).

---

1   Look at the poems in the Literary Heritage section of the 'Place' cluster in the *AQA Anthology*. Choose a poem and use it as the starting point for writing about a place.

You need to show your ability to:

- use language to create effects on the reader
- structure your narrative in ways which will engage, help or challenge the reader
- write in a technically controlled, accurate way.

This would be one of two pieces of the controlled assessment and you would have approximately 600–800 words and around 1–2 hours in which to complete it.

Firstly you need to decide on:

- which poem you wish to use
- what kind of writing you intend to produce.

It is important to notice that the poem is to be a 'starting point'. This does not mean you have to pick up the story of the poem from its last line. Rather it means that you can interpret the poem in almost any way you wish. That allows you a great deal of freedom in deciding how you want to proceed.

There are eight poems in the Literary Heritage section of the 'Place' cluster. You would need to read them to make up your mind which might lead to the most interesting writing. Here is an example of how the task could be undertaken, based upon the choice of William Blake's 'London'.

London

I wander through each chartered street,
Near where the chartered Thames does flow,
And mark in every face I meet,
Marks of weakness, marks of woe.

In every cry of every man,
In every infant's cry of fear,
In every voice, in every ban,
The mind-forged manacles I hear:

How the chimney-sweeper's cry
Every blackening church appals,
And the hapless soldier's sigh
Runs in blood down palace-walls.

But most, through midnight streets I hear
How the youthful harlot's curse
Blasts the new-born infant's tear,
And blights with plagues the marriage-hearse.

William Blake, 'London'

The instruction is to simply use the poem as a 'starting point'. There are many possibilities for further writing:

- another general piece about London or any other city
- a response to Blake's criticisms of London – writing in praise of London
- a piece that focuses, like Blake's poem, on the problems/horrors of city life
- a response that focuses on detail from Blake's poem – the 'hapless soldier', for example.

You also have to decide what form of writing to use. Your decision might depend upon whether you are taking GCSE English or GCSE English Language.

The best planning will take the assessment criteria into consideration. To achieve a good mark, you will need to provide evidence of the following:

Assessment criteria	Planning
Ideas • An assured awareness of purpose. • Ideas presented in an appropriately sustained way.	**Ideas** You could list some 'contemporary problems' associated with big city life, for example: • pollution, congestion • crime and violence • self-interest rather than community • the gap between rich and poor.
Form and structure • Confident and skilful use of form. • Using structural devices to navigate readers through the writing.	**Form and structure** You could decide to write poetry in stanzas to provide a structure for the reader to follow and could try to use rhyme to create effects.
Language • Assured control and crafting of language. • Sentence constructions self-consciously crafted for effect.	**Language** Blake's poem gives some ideas for how you could craft language. He uses a lot of repetition and some very vivid vocabulary such as his choice of 'blasts' in the final stanza.

Before the controlled assessment you have three or four lessons and time at home to experiment with different ideas and forms. You are not allowed a dictionary or thesaurus in the controlled assessment so you should use your preparation time to fix some difficult spellings in your mind.

Read Text B, part of a student response to the task, and the teacher's comments that follow.

(B)

London 2009

It would be nice to wander through the streets
Through which the stifled traffic cannot flow,
But the sea of toxic diesel fumes which greets
Me threatens to drown me in its slow,

Suffocating grip. Motorised, metallic creatures
Spew out their oily breath to smother
The ancient city and threaten her future:
The lorries, cars and buses will kill her.

In the dark corners grey shapes huddle,
Shunning the bright lights of shop doorways.
Lost souls living in the world of alley and puddle
Victims of the rich man's ways.

Teacher's comments

There is a confident sense of purpose as the poem focuses consistently on negative aspects of the city. The ideas are fairly obvious; the criticisms of modern urban society could not really be called 'subtle', the descriptor from the highest band.

There is confident control of form so far: some of the use of rhyme is a bit obvious and clumsy (huddle/puddle doesn't seem very good) but some is quite inventive (the connection of smother/kill her). There is some example of use of run-on lines (between the first and second stanzas) which helps move the poem along without a clunking halt at every rhyme. There is enough control of form to say this is confident and assured so far although there is not enough evidence of 'sophistication' to place the writing in the highest band.

Crafting of language may be the most significant feature of the poem so far. There is evidence of conscious use of vividly negative descriptive words ('metallic creatures/Spew out their oily breath'), some alliteration, and the marker might like the way some of Blake's words are recycled for effect in the opening stanza.

Activity

1 Text B was based on writing poetry. If you decided to write prose (a story) in response to the Blake poem, you would need to spend time thinking about possible approaches.

Work with a partner. Make a list of five possible ideas for a story that would arise out of the Blake poem. When you have your list, decide which of the ideas would be best, and why.

Moving Images

This topic area is a feature of both GCSE English and GCSE English Language. You are invited to respond in some way to moving images such as films, documentaries, adverts and a variety of things on TV.

Here is a sample task.

> 2   Choose one short, memorable scene from a film you have seen. Use the scene to write a creative piece in which you concentrate on creating atmosphere.

As with all creative writing tasks this shows that you have choices and decisions to make at the thinking/planning stage – for example:

- which film and scene to choose
- which form of writing to choose.

You will need to take these decisions before you move into planning the structure and style of your writing.

Activities

2

a Make a list of sections of films that remain vividly in your memory. About six or eight will be plenty.

b Next to each jot down a few words to describe the atmosphere developed in the scene. To describe atmosphere you need words such as light, dark, frightening, depressing, comic, tense, dangerous, wild, happy, strange.

c Focus on the writing task: you will need to develop an atmosphere using words rather than the mixture of words, images and sounds used in films. Decide which section of film might provide the most interesting basis for your writing.

3 Read Texts C and D, extracts from two students' responses to this task. Text C has been commented on by the examiner. When you have read Text D discuss it with a partner and decide what advice you would give the student to improve the writing. Think about:

- technical accuracy
- paragraphing
- sentence structures
- punctuation.

Text C is based upon the scene in Baz Luhrman's *Romeo and Juliet* when Mercutio and Benvolio are on the beach. Benvolio is worried: it is hot and there is tension in the air. In this piece of writing the student uses this scene very loosely.

(C)

Ben glanced anxiously down the street. In the heat haze the air shimmered like silver water just above the tarmac; ordinary things seemed different somehow. Different.

The street was empty. Houses were shuttered up as the occupants fought back against the all-conquering, blinding sun. Halfway down, in the speckled shade of a laurel bush, an old Labrador lying flat in the dust gaped and panted, ears flicking at the flies.

A beetle, black and shiny, bustled along the base of the wall in the shade of which Ben and Merc were slouching. Ben prodded it with his toe and wondered if beetles felt heat. It barely altered course, safe in its black armour. He watched it scuttle along the base of the wall and under Merc's heel. Ben didn't hear anything as it was squashed, but he imagined a splintering squelch.

'Merc, let's go home. It's hotter than hell and you know the Caps are around.'

'Go if you want; I'm staying. You scared?'

Ben knew there was no point continuing the conversation and the heat had sapped all his energy. He glanced again down the street. A dark figure had turned the corner.

Teacher's comments

This is an engaging, effective piece of writing. The candidate keeps a good focus on the task and succeeds in creating their own individual interpretation of the scene from the film without slavishly following every detail of it. The writing is thoughtfully paragraphed with each separate paragraph focusing on a separate detail. There is a good opening short paragraph which concludes with an effective one-word sentence. There is some variety of sentence structures: the candidate uses simple sentences such as at the start of the second paragraph; compound sentences, such as in the opening sentence of the final paragraph; and complex sentences, such as the final sentence of the second paragraph. The writing is well controlled and technically very accurate – a quite wide range of punctuation is used correctly.

Although not a complete response this is headed towards a very high grade.

Text D is based upon the scene in the film of *To Kill a Mockingbird* when Scout and Jem are walking home through the woods at night.

(D)

The woods were dark but light from the moon shone on the path so that they could see their way.

A light breeze blew through the woods. The branches waved and made strange shadows on the path. The noise they made sounded like a million little creatures scurrying through the undergrowth. The two children kept their heads down not daring to look right or left at the walls of trees. The path was well known to them.

The breeze died down. The only sound was the crunch of dead leaves under their feet as they trudged on. Home was only three or four minutes away.

The quiet was suddenly broken by a screech. The two children jumped. 'It's just an old owl,' Jem said.

The breeze began again and a leaf blew into Scout's hair. Jem was flicking it out of her hair when he heard it. He froze. Scout turned round. 'What's up?'

'Nothing. Thought I heard something.'

But just then they both heard it.

Check your learning 𝑘!

In this chapter you have:

- learned about how your writing skills are tested in the controlled assessment
- learned more about the ways you can achieve high marks in this part of the course.

Speaking and listening

Did you know that unborn babies can hear clearly at about 20 weeks of pregnancy? It takes a bit longer for speech to develop. Babies will cry from birth but it is only when they are about three months old that they will start to make clear sounds in reply to being spoken to.

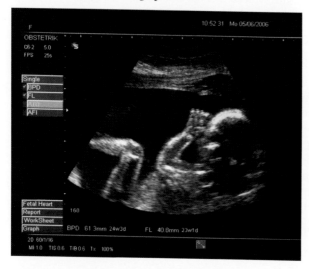

These skills provide the basis for our most fundamental form of communication. People spoke and listened long before they read and wrote. Speaking and listening are very important in both our working and our personal lives. The ability to speak and listen well helps us to deal with new people and unfamiliar situations, and to be clear and effective in the ways we deal with them.

This section of the book will help you to further develop your skills in speaking and listening. You will focus on speaking purposefully and effectively in a range of situations, and on being a perceptive and responsive listener.

The chapters in this section are designed to help you meet the Assessment Objectives that underpin your GCSE course. These are written for teachers but you might like to read them in full (they're explained in more detail on page 177).

Candidates should speak to:

- Communicate clearly and purposefully: structure and sustain talk, adapting it to different situations and audiences; use Standard English and a variety of techniques as appropriate.

- Listen and respond to speakers' ideas and perspectives, and how they construct and express their meanings.

- Interact with others, shaping meanings through suggestions, comments and questions, and drawing ideas together.

- Create and sustain different roles.

By the end of this section you will have covered all of the skills outlined in the Assessment Objectives. By the end of your GCSE course you will have used these skills to help you gain the highest marks you can in your Speaking and listening controlled assessment.

But it does not stop there. You do not stop speaking and listening once your GCSEs are over. The writers of this book have chosen texts, situations and activities that they hope will interest you and give you a base from which to continue developing your speaking and listening skills to meet the demands of the adult world, both at work and at home.

24

Objectives

In this chapter you will:

think about the skills needed to be a good speaker and listener

practise some of these skills

evaluate your performance in speaking and listening tasks.

Building skills in speaking and listening

Getting started

In this chapter you will think about the skills needed to be an effective speaker and listener in a range of situations. You will also reflect on your own skills as a speaker and listener and work out what you need to do to improve.

What makes a good speaker?

When someone speaks, they communicate their ideas to others by the words they use and their tone of voice. Equally important are facial expressions and body language.

Activity

1   With a partner look at the situations below and talk about facial expressions and body language.

There are many qualities that make a good speaker. These qualities are connected to the words a speaker uses, the way they put their ideas across, their body language and the way they interact with their audience.

A good speaker:

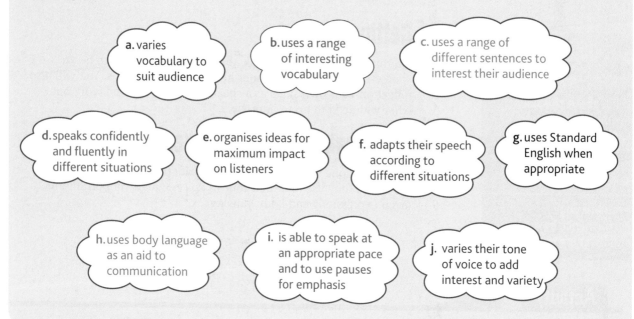

a. varies vocabulary to suit audience

b. uses a range of interesting vocabulary

c. uses a range of different sentences to interest their audience

d. speaks confidently and fluently in different situations

e. organises ideas for maximum impact on listeners

f. adapts their speech according to different situations

g. uses Standard English when appropriate

h. uses body language as an aid to communication

i. is able to speak at an appropriate pace and to use pauses for emphasis

j. varies their tone of voice to add interest and variety

Activities

2 With a partner put the qualities in the list above into order of importance. Number one will be the quality you think is the most important.

3 To practise some of these skills prepare a 60-second talk with the title 'What I'd do with £1,000,000'. You should focus on the following skills:

- using a range of interesting vocabulary
- speaking at an appropriate pace and using pauses for emphasis
- varying tone of voice to add interest and variety.

Learning to be a good listener?

An important part of developing good speaking and listening skills is to focus on being a good listener. Good listeners give support to speakers and show that they understand what a speaker is saying by their body language, such as nodding in agreement or asking an appropriate question during a discussion. They can build on the ideas of others and extend them when contributing to a discussion. They need good concentration skills so they can follow what another speaker is saying.

Activity

4　**a**　Work with a partner. One of you should read Text A, which is the first section of an article that appeared in the *Guardian* on 25 June 2009, while the other listens carefully. At the end of the reading the listener should report back at least three pieces of information from the article.

(A)

Third of ocean species in danger of extinction

Overfishing threatens to drive a third of the world's ocean shark species to extinction, say conservationists. Hammerheads, giant devil rays and porbeagle sharks are among 64 species on the first red list for oceanic sharks produced by the International Union for Conservation of Nature.

Sharks are vulnerable because they can take decades to mature and they produce few young. The scallop hammerhead shark, which has declined by 99% over the last 30 years in some parts of the world, is particularly vulnerable and has been given globally endangered status on the IUCN list, meaning it's nearing extinction. In the Gulf of Mexico, the oceanic whitetip shark has declined by a similar amount.

b　Now the listener becomes the reader. The new listener should be able to report back three pieces of information after hearing Text B, the second section of the article.

(B)

Scientists estimate that all the shark populations in the north-west Atlantic have declined by an average of 50% since the early 1970s.

Announcing the red list of pelagic – open ocean – sharks and rays today, scientists called on governments to set limits for catching the animals on the high seas and to enforce strict bans on 'finning' – the practice of catching sharks, cutting off their fins and throwing their bodies back in the water.

'Despite mounting threats, sharks remain virtually unprotected on the high seas,' said Sonja Fordham, deputy chair of the shark specialist group at the World Conservation Union and policy director for the Shark Alliance.

Evaluating your skills

Have you got what it takes to be a good speaker and listener? Have a look at Text C, a questionnaire, to find out.

(C)

❶ You have been asked to give a presentation to the class. Do you feel:

(a) Terrified? You often find it difficult to organise your ideas and to speak in detail in front of a large group.

(b) Confident? You enjoy the challenge of communicating complex ideas and issues in detail and promoting your points of view to a large group.

(c) Slightly nervous at first? However, you are quite confident you can communicate ideas and issues effectively.

❷ After listening to a presentation in class do you usually:

(a) Have lots of questions to ask because you find it interesting to listen closely to the ideas of other students and enjoy asking for further details or information?

(b) Find it quite easy to follow the main ideas, asking questions which show your understanding?

(c) Find it hard to concentrate sometimes and let other people ask the questions because you can never think of anything to ask? Sometimes it's hard for you to remember the details of a presentation.

❸ When you take part in a group discussion do you:

(a) Enjoy responding to the ideas of others and making contributions to the discussion which move it forward?

(b) Make one or two points, but feel more comfortable agreeing with points made by others?

(c) Enjoy challenging the ideas of others and introducing new points to shape the discussion?

❹ If you are asked to assume the role of a character in a role play do you:

(a) Present the kind of character that is very predictable or stereotypical – for example, a bad-tempered teacher?

(b) Enjoy creating a memorable and individual character by using appropriate language and gesture?

(c) Give some thought to how you will use language and gesture to create your character?

❺ When you are taking part in a speaking and listening task do you:

(a) Consider carefully the audience and purpose for the task and choose a wide range of vocabulary and sentence structures to match these?

(b) Use a range of appropriate vocabulary and sentence structures to match the audience and purpose for the task?

(c) Try to use some variety of vocabulary but often fall back on the vocabulary you normally use?

Activity

5

After answering the questionnaire in Text C, use this table to score points for each question. Add up your points before checking your total against the speaking and listening profiles below.

Questions	(a)	(b)	(c)
1	1	3	2
2	3	2	1
3	2	1	3
4	1	3	2
5	3	2	1

14–15	11–13	8–10	5–7
You are well on the way to becoming a very accomplished speaker and listener. You have a wide range of vocabulary that you can adapt to the needs of your audience and purpose. You are a very good listener who can develop and sustain a discussion. You adapt very well to the demands of different roles, using words and gestures to create convincing characters who have an impact on the audience.	You are a confident speaker and listener. You are successful in adapting your vocabulary to suit your audience and purpose. You adapt your tone of voice and vary your pace to add interest to your speech. You make significant contributions to discussions, building on the contributions of others. In role play you use body language, gesture and speech to create memorable characters.	You are a reasonably confident speaker and listener. You choose your words carefully when communicating with your audience and can make your contributions interesting for your audience by thinking about your vocabulary. You are a careful listener who takes an active part in group discussions, sometimes challenging the ideas of others. In role-play activities you use language and gesture to create characters.	You have some confidence as a speaker and listener. However, you sometimes might find it hard to adapt your vocabulary to the needs of different audiences and purposes for speaking. You are more comfortable as a listener than a speaker in group discussions. You are able to create a simple role successfully and respond in a predictable way.

How can speaking and listening skills be improved?

Read Texts D to F, which are all letters from students explaining some of the problems they have with improving their speaking and listening skills.

Dear Andy,

I really enjoy English lessons, especially the ones where we take part in group discussions. However my friends (and also my teacher) tell me I talk too much and I don't let other people have their say. I think they may be right, but I enjoy putting forward my ideas so much that sometimes it's hard to stop.

What do you think I should do?

A Chatty Year 10 Student

Dear Andy,

I am a very shy student. Although I always get very good marks for written English tasks, I never do very well at the speaking and listening ones. The ones I dread the most are individual presentations to my class. It doesn't matter whether I am with a group saying something on my own or, even worse, standing in front of the class doing a solo presentation, I always do badly.

There are quite a few things that are difficult for me. I find it hard to maintain eye contact with the audience as I feel safer if I read my bit as fast as possible so I can sit down again. I find it hard to prepare the presentation in the first place, as the thought of talking in front of the class makes me so nervous I can never think of good ideas. Although I can use good vocabulary in written work, I can never think of good words for speaking tasks.

I would really like to do something about this so that I can get good marks for Speaking and Listening tasks as well. What can you suggest?

A Shy Year 11 Student

Dear Andy,

I wonder if you can help me. The thing I hate most about speaking and listening tasks is taking part in a role play. I've never been very good at drama and these sort of activities make me feel very uncomfortable as I hate performing. I often let the rest of the group decide the role I will play and whatever role I am given I usually end up standing on the spot and saying my bit as quickly as possible. Most of the time I end up being the character who is cross and shouts a lot like a policeman or a bad-tempered parent. In role-play interview situations I can never think of good questions to ask or answers to give.

I hope you can offer some ideas to help me as I feel I am holding the rest of the group back when I don't do well.

A Self-conscious Student

6

Read Text G, the reply to the first letter.

Discuss the remaining letters with a partner and then write replies giving advice to the writers on how to make improvements.

Dear Chatty Year 10 Student,

I'm sure your friends love you really! However you have to remember that you are not only assessed at GCSE for your speaking skills, but also for your listening skills. Don't worry, it is possible to train yourself to be a good listener.

Perhaps in group discussions you could ask your teacher if you could take the role of chairperson. This would mean that your role would be to encourage other students to speak and this would give you good practice in listening to their ideas.

You could also ask someone in the group to be your 'critical friend' – someone who points out what you are doing well and how you need to improve. They could make a note of the number of times you carry on speaking when other students are trying to express their point of view. Next time there is a group discussion you could try to reduce this number.

Maybe you need to work on the language you use in discussions. For example after you have put your point forward, you could invite other students to comment on your ideas saying something like 'What do the rest of you think?'

I hope you do well at listening in the future.

Take care,

Andy

Review and reflect

Now that you have worked through the activities in this chapter you will have gained an idea of what is expected of a successful speaker and listener in GCSE English.

Write a set of personal targets for yourself identifying your aims for improving your speaking and listening. Here are some of the things you might want to focus on:

- being both an active speaker and listener in group discussions
- making detailed and interesting presentations
- using language and gestures to create a character in role-play activities
- varying your vocabulary and tone of voice to make your speech interesting for your listeners.

Set out your targets like this:

My strengths as a speaker and listener are …

I think this because …

My targets for speaking and listening are …

To help me reach my targets I will …

Check your learning

In this chapter you have:

- thought carefully about the skills needed by good speakers and listeners
- practised your listening skills
- identified your strengths as a speaker and listener
- reflected on ways to improve your speaking and listening
- given advice to others on how to improve.

25

Presenting

Making presentations

Presenting is one of the three contexts for speaking and listening which are necessary for your controlled assessment. In school you will be familiar with different kinds of presentations: assemblies, talks at options evenings, beginnings of lessons when teachers are delivering information, students presenting information to the rest of the class and so on.

Presentations are usually:

- delivered by one person, although it is certainly possible for a small group to deliver one
- delivered without interruption, although there are often question-and-answer sessions at the end.

Activity

1 From your own experience of receiving and delivering presentations in school, what are the factors that:

  a make presentations engaging and effective?

  b make presentations dull and ineffective?

The mark scheme for presentations is headed 'Communicating and adapting language' and that makes it clear that the ability to tailor language for different audiences and situations is very important.

There are three areas that will be the focus for your assessment:

- use of Standard English where appropriate
- using a range of language in ways that engage your audience
- structuring a presentation.

Standard English

One area concerns use of Standard English 'where necessary'. It is actually quite difficult to define exactly what Standard English is but the following might help:

- Standard English does not come from any particular region of the country. If you speak Standard English you do not use local dialect or slang. In different parts of the country people might sound different when they speak Standard English, but that is because of their accent; the vocabulary and grammar of Standard English are the same whichever part of the country you are in.
- Standard English is the form of English that tends to be used by adults such as politicians, Church leaders, broadcasters, lawyers and doctors. Many people consider it to be the 'proper' form of the language, the most 'correct' version.

There are many variations of regional English – Scouse, Yorkshire and Geordie, for example – which you recognise not just because of the accent, but because of regional words and variations in grammar. These could be called non-Standard English.

Activities

2 English can be non-standard for a variety of reasons. Dialect or slang words might be used, subject–verb agreement might be different, word order might be different, such as, in the sentence, 'He wur off down pub':

- 'wur' is 'were' in someone's accent, but in Standard English it would be 'He was'
- 'off' substitutes for a verb. In Standard English it would be 'going'
- 'down pub' in Standard English would be 'to the pub'.

Which aspects of the four examples below are non-standard?

a 'I were wearing t'red 'at and he were wearing t'green un.' (I was wearing the red hat and he was wearing the green one.)

b 'We should put us names int book.' (We should put our names in the book.)

c 'Ar kid.' (Our brother.)

d 'Are yous going out?' (Are you going out?)

3 Give three examples of your own language which you know are non-standard. They might be non-standard because they are associated with teenagers (such as 'innit',) or they might be local to the area you live in. Write them down and put the standard form next to them.

> Nearly everybody uses a mixture of Standard and non-Standard English and most people are able to adapt their language to different situations, using non-standard forms in informal situations and Standard English in a more formal context. The more public the situation, the more likely it is that Standard English should be used.
>
> To achieve high grades you need to be able to demonstrate the ability to use Standard English appropriately.

Activity

4 Look at the following list of possible presentations you could be asked to make. Discuss with a partner to what extent there would be a need for use of Standard English and whether there would also be advantages in using your own non-standard forms:

a You are asked to deliver an assembly to your own year group about the importance of supporting Aids charities.

b You are invited to deliver a talk in a local junior school to Year 6 students. The talk is about moving to secondary school.

c Your English teacher asks you to make a presentation to your class about a poem that you have researched.

d You are invited to make a presentation to camera about your local town or area. The presentation is intended to be shared with young people in other parts of the country.

> For your Speaking and listening controlled assessment you need to consider when it is appropriate to concentrate on Standard usage.
>
> What is appropriate will depend on:
> - who you are talking to
> - the context in which you are speaking.

Using a range of language

The purpose of presentations is to deliver information and opinions to your audience in ways that engage them.

You will need to use a range of vocabulary and language structures in different situations for different purposes. High levels of performance will require a range of 'well-judged' and 'flexible' vocabulary and expression.

Read Texts A and B, annotated versions of two alternative openings to a presentation in which a student was asked to talk about favourite films to the rest of the class.

MATT DAMON
THE
BOURNE ULTIMATUM
THIS SUMMER BOURNE COMES HOME

A

Morning. I'm going to talk about the Bourne films. There are three Bourne films. The first is *The Bourne Identity*. The second is *The Bourne Supremacy* and the last is *The Bourne Ultimatum*. The films are about Jason Bourne who is played by Matt Damon in the three films. *The Bourne Identity* came out in 2002. *The Bourne Supremacy* came out in 2004 and *The Bourne Ultimatum* came out in 2007.

❶ An appropriate concise beginning

❹ Another sentence which begins, boringly, with 'The …'. The student, for the sake of a little variety, could have said: 'Matt Damon stars as the hero, Jason Bourne, in all three'

❷ This is clear but it is another very short sentence. The student could simply have said 'I'm going to talk about the three Bourne films'

❸ This becomes a very boring list. The student could have said, 'In order they are …' or, if the list was to be kept, instead of 'The second is' some variety could have been added by simply saying, 'followed by …'

❺ Another repetition of the film titles in another very dull list. It would have been better to put the date information in the earlier list to avoid this kind of dull repetition

---

B

Good morning. I'm going to talk about the greatest, most spectacular, downright brilliant series of films in the history of movies. It must be Lord of the Rings, you're thinking. Wrong. Well, it must be Harry Potter. Ouch, no! Well, that leaves James Bond. Sorry, they're not fit to lick the boots of … Jason Bourne in the three superb Bourne films.

❸ A one-word sentence used for effect. The student uses a sequence of possible films followed by concise put-downs

❹ Not Standard English, but the slang is perfectly appropriate for the audience and the kind of jokey tone the student is adopting

❶ The student doesn't go for the obvious kind of opening but delays the information. Three adjectives are listed to jokingly build up expectations

❷ The student uses second person to acknowledge the listeners

❺ A simple point, but the student has found a different word from 'great', 'spectacular', 'brilliant'

Structuring your presentation

You need to give careful thought to how you will organise your presentation.

A presentation requires a beginning, a series of points made in the main body of the talk, and an ending.

Beginning

- **Don't state the obvious.** If everyone in your class is making a presentation about work experience, it would not be a good idea to begin with 'Today I am going to talk about work experience'. Think about ways you could attract the attention of your audience. For example, if you are asked to talk about a book you enjoy, you could slightly delay giving them the title.
- **Acknowledge your audience.** The reason you are speaking is to pass information or opinion to a group of listeners, so you need to greet them.
- **Give some indication of the direction of your talk.** The class might know you are going to talk about work experience, but you could give some indication of what you are going to say about your experience.

Activity

5

Imagine your class has been told that over the course of a term each student will make a short presentation to the class about a famous person they admire. The class will not know who you are going to talk about until you tell them.

Work with a partner. Quickly decide which famous person you might be able to talk about. Using your partner as an audience improvise two different ways of starting your talk.

- In one, state right at the start who the person is and outline the main areas about them that you are going to talk about.
- In the other, try to intrigue your listener with some opinion and information before ending your introductory remarks with the name of the person.

When you have each tried this, discuss with each other which of the openings was most effective.

Key points

These are like paragraphs in a piece of writing. Your talk needs to be broken down into sections. For example, if you are invited to talk about a film, you need to think of three or four separate points you will make about the film. Each key point would need to be developed over a few sentences.

You also need to spend a little time thinking about how you will move from one key point to the next. Often a pause, a moment's silence, will be enough to indicate to your audience that you are moving on, but sometimes you might need a form of words along the lines of:

- 'I'd like to move on to ...'
- 'The next point I would like to make ...'
- 'Enough of that ...'

Activity

6 Imagine you have been asked to talk for only two minutes about a favourite film. The purpose of the talk is not to give lots of information about the film; rather, it is to express an opinion. You will either express your enthusiasm for the film or you will criticise it. By the end of your talk your audience will know the reasons you like or dislike the film.

a Prepare the list of four or five key points you would make about your chosen film.

b Using a partner as an audience, present two of your key points. Your partner should listen carefully and give you feedback on:

● how easily they could identify the two key points

● the way you moved from one point to the next.

Ending

A good presentation will have a clear ending which acknowledges the audience and, usually, invites their response, for example, by asking if they have any questions.

Using PowerPoint

PowerPoint, because it is organised into separate slides, can help to bring structure to presentations. Each slide is a separate section, a separate paragraph which will focus on a separate idea or piece of information. It is a helpful tool for the presenter. However, the difference between using PowerPoint as a tool for structuring a talk and simply using notes or cards, is that the audience can also see and read the presentation. PowerPoint therefore should be used to:

● simply highlight the key point or idea of any section of your talk in a concise way

● enhance your words, perhaps with the use of an image or a sound clip. It shouldn't be used to show the audience word-for-word the text of your presentation. The fewer words it shows, the better.

Body language and voice

One issue concerning PowerPoint is that it can distract the audience; instead of watching the presenter, they watch the screen. It is important to have eye contact with your audience. A confident speaker will, in a quite short space of time establish eye contact with virtually everyone in the audience. That is why you should not:

- turn your back on the audience to read slides on a screen
- look down continually at a script and just read it.

You are also more likely to engage your audience if they can hear you clearly, so it is important not to mumble or whisper; you need to speak up.

Activities

7 From your own experience of watching people make presentations, what aspects of body language would you advise students to:

a avoid?

b adopt?

8 Imagine a simple presentation to be called 'Five things I hate about …'. The purpose of the talk is to entertain an audience by explaining, in a light-hearted way, why you hate something. The subject could be anything from vegetables to television programmes to celebrities.

a Choose your subject. Make a list of the five things you hate about it. For each reason suggest an image that could be used on each of five slides, an image that might not be very obvious or might make an audience smile. For example, a photograph of a horribly screwed-up face could be used as an image to represent your feelings about the taste of vegetables. The image will be much more interesting than simply writing the word 'Taste' on a slide.

b In the case of a simple presentation based on five key ideas it would be very easy to become repetitive and dull:

- 'The first thing I hate about …'
- 'The second thing I hate is …'
- 'The next one is …' and so on.

Basing your suggestions on the 'Five things' presentation you selected in a, write the sentences you would use at the start of each of the five ideas. Concentrate on avoiding repetition and, instead, having variety.

It would be a mistake to write the text of a presentation on a series of slides. There would be no reason for your audience to listen to you when they could simply read the words.

c Prepare and deliver a short presentation: 'Five things I hate about …'. The purpose is to entertain your audience – your class. You should make sure that you:

- decide to what extent it is appropriate to use Standard English
- use a variety of language structures
- have a structure to the talk
- consider body language and voice.

To display confidence, you will need to look at your audience rather than at a script, but you will also appear confident if you speak fluently without hesitation. If you need notes to help you, make sure they are very concise so that a quick glance at them will help you make your next point.

Stretch yourself

Prepare a talk for your class on something you feel strongly about.

- Spend some time thinking about a subject.
- Think about a story or anecdote that you can use to bring your talk to life.
- Think about a recurring phrase you can use to help structure your talk.

For example, you could prepare a talk about how the environment is being damaged. Your anecdote might be something you have seen on the internet or in the news about what is happening to a species of animal. Your repeated phrase might be 'If we don't do anything …'.

Check your learning

In this chapter you have:

- thought about appropriate kinds of language to use in presentations
- explored ways of organising and delivering presentations
- delivered a presentation.

26

Discussing and listening

Working together

Working in groups is an important part of learning. Often the saying 'two heads are better than one' is very true. When you are working a group you need to consider:

- the needs of the task
- how to listen and respond to others
- how to build on everyone's good ideas
- how to complete the task in the time allowed.

A good listener can give support to others in a group and help them to make their thoughts clearer by asking relevant questions. Supportive listeners can:

Listen carefully and ask good questions.	Challenge and respond thoughtfully.	Show some interest.	Respond positively and make helpful requests.	Listen sensitively and show empathy (understanding of the feelings of others).

Activities

1 Put the listening skills listed above in order, starting with the most important as number 1. Then discuss your answers with a partner, explaining the reasons for your order.

2 Good listeners are supportive. They concentrate carefully on what others are saying. This activity will help you to practise your listening skills when working with a partner.

You are each going to talk for 30 seconds on the topic 'Things that get on my nerves'. There is no need to plan your talk – just get going! This is a chance not just to have a good moan, but also to entertain your listener.

One person should talk and the other should listen carefully. Do not take notes; rely on your skills of concentration.

When you have both spoken for 30 seconds, work with another pair of students. Take it in turns to report back on your partner's talk. Summarise two or three things that get on your partner's nerves together with the reasons for this.

Developing questioning skills

Knowing how to ask the right questions is an important part of developing your speaking and listening skills. A good questioner can help a speaker to develop their ideas in more detail by asking questions that will prompt the speaker to give more information – for example:

- 'Your holiday sounds really interesting. What else can you tell me about the time you learned to water ski?'

A question like this, which encourages the speaker to carry on talking, is known as an open question. A closed question is one that can be answered very briefly – for example:

- the question 'Did you enjoy your holiday?' could be answered by the words 'yes' or 'no'. Closed questions are not helpful in encouraging speakers to extend their ideas.

You can prompt the speaker into developing their ideas by following one question with another.

- 'Did you enjoy your holiday? If so, could you explain why?'

Activities

3 Here are some questions you could ask to someone who said their little brother gets on their nerves.

- That must be so annoying – but maybe it's entertaining as well? Can you tell us about any funny things he has done?
- Has he stopped doing this now?
- Could you give me any more examples of naughty things he has done?
- When you are older what will you remember most about your little brother and why?

Which of these questions do you think would be most useful in helping the speaker to extend his or her ideas? Give reasons for your choice.

4 Continuing to work in your group of four, you are going to extend your listening skills further. Take it in turns to ask each other questions about the things they have just revealed which get on their nerves. Your aim is to help the speaker give more details.

When you have finished you should think about:

- how helpful the questions were in helping you to expand your ideas
- how easy or difficult it was for you to find questions to ask.

Working with a partner

Sharing ideas with others is an important part of paired work. When you are working with a partner on a shared task you need to:

- have the confidence to put forward your own ideas in some detail
- explain the reasons for the points you make
- listen carefully to your partner's views, noting the main points
- make comments which sometimes challenge their ideas in a positive way
- ask them questions to help them clarify their ideas (express them more clearly or in more detail)
- offer an alternative for your partner to consider
- sometimes reach a shared decision.

Activity

5 Imagine you are a member of the charity committee for your year group. You have been asked to select one charity for fundraising activities for the next year from the three charities shown.

Study Texts A to C with a partner, focusing particularly on the images. With your partner discuss each image in turn focusing on:

- your own response to the images – what they make you think and feel
- how students in your year group might respond to them
- which advert would have the most impact

Once you have discussed the adverts, decide which charity you would select as your charity of the year with reasons for your choice. Next explain your choice and your reasons to another pair of students.

A

Address: ⟩ go

A smile can cheer you up all day. Especially the smile of a child. Today you have the chance to make one of the poorest children in the world happy – by sponsoring them for just 50p a day.

And through sponsorship you'll really see the difference you're making – which we hope will make you smile too.

A Simple Fact: Child sponsorship could change Amenata's life.

Across Africa, Asia and The Americas there are children like six year old Amenata whose smiles are full of hope, but whose dreams may never be realised due to the grinding poverty they live in.

Amenata is lucky, unlike 115 million other children of primary school age, she attends school. However, her family struggles to earn an income and they often go to bed hungry. Unless things change for her family Amenata may not be able to continue her education, and her dream of becoming a nurse may never be possible.

There are many children with stories like Amenata's, some of which you can read here, and all of them share one thing – the hope that you'll sponsor them and help them realise their dreams.

ActionAid child sponsorship gives hope to thousands of children around the world. As a child sponsor, you'll have the chance to help a whole community take control of their lives and end their poverty. Become an ActionAid child sponsor today and find out how you can bring positive change to a child like Amenata.

B

Address: ⟩ go

The number of tigers in the wild is rapidly declining. These are the problems they face:

- Tigers habitat is reducing and becoming more fragmented due to logging, land conversion to agriculture, and infrastructure development, such as roads and railways.
- Tigers are killed by poachers for their skins.
- They're also killed to supply bones and body parts for traditional Asian medicine.
- Their prey is poached.
- They increasingly come into conflict with humans as they stray into areas close to villages, resulting in them being killed, as they try to survive within a shared habitat.

How you can make a real difference

Experts fear that there may now be as few as 3,200 wild tigers left. Please help save them. Adopt a tiger and this is how you'll help:

- Space and protection are imperative to the tiger's survival. When you adopt, you help provide both.
- WWF works with the governments, partner organisations and local people in critical habitats where tigers struggle to survive.
- We will continue to work with governments to strengthen existing legislation that protects the tiger, and help to integrate tiger conservation needs into land-use planning.
- We help increase and connect the habitat where tigers can roam, and put in place measures that reduce conflict with humans.
- We also help to increase protection from poachers and to reduce illegal wildlife trade.

Make a real difference. Adopt a tiger.

Remember

Think about your performance in the Activity 5 and make a record of your score for each skill below.

- 1 = I think I did very well
- 2 = I did well, but I need to do some more work on this skill
- 3 = I tried hard, but I need to do a lot more work on this skill

A. Expressing my opinion clearly and in detail.

B. Giving reasons to justify my opinion.

C. Asking questions to help my partner express an idea more clearly.

D. Think carefully about my partner's points before asking them to defend their point of view.

E. Explaining politely if I didn't agree and offering an alternative.

He told his parents to f**k off. He told his foster parents to f**k off. He told fourteen social workers to f**k off. He told us to f**k off. But we didn't. And we still haven't.

The UK is full of vulnerable children. Many of them with stories that would break your heart. Some of them capable of terrible things. But if you believe that no child is born bad, then you can't watch someone get filed away as a problem. You can't let society play pass the parcel with a young person's life. If a child is referred to Barnardo's we stick by that child. We listen. We look for potential. We give practical support. And if we don't give up on the troubled, young boy, it's not because we enjoy being sworn at, it's because we believe in him.

Believe in children
Barnardo's

© Kiran Masters

Reg. Charity No. 216250 and SC037605.You must be over 18. Standard text message costs apply. Because of the sensitive subject matter we have used an actor.

Working in a group

The challenges of working in a group are different from those of working with a partner. In a group you have to take into account and respond to the ideas of several people. Sometimes it can be difficult to get your point across and to reach an agreement within a group.

One way to get around some of these difficulties is to appoint a chairperson who will:

- ensure the group is kept on task and keeps to time limits
- enable discussion of each suggestion
- make sure everyone in the group has their say
- summarise the different ideas put forward by the group
- make sure a decision is reached.

Working in a group is a collaborative activity. This means that you all have to work together. Here are some useful guidelines to follow:

- everyone must have a chance to speak
- respect the right of others to speak whether you agree with them or not
- ask helpful questions to assist others to develop and clarify their ideas.

6

a Work in groups of three for four. You have been put in charge of selecting activities for a Year 7 events week in your school. Spend 15 minutes discussing suitable activities. You must take into account the differing needs of Year 7 students – remember not all students like sporting activities.

Here are some suggestions:

- a morning at a local watersports centre
- a visit to an Italian restaurant to have lessons in pizza-making
- learning new skills, such as juggling
- inviting a poet into school to work with the students.

Make other suggestions of your own. Consider the advantages and disadvantages of each. At the end of 15 minutes decide on three or four activities. Give reasons for your choices.

b Prepare a report on your decisions for the rest of the class. The rest of the group should spend 10 minutes on this. Your report should include:

- the activities you have decided on
- the reasons for your choice
- suggestions you considered but did not accept.

Review and reflect

Consider this list of features of good discussion skills:

- ▪ Make sensible suggestions.
- ▪ Introduce new ideas to a discussion to move it forward.
- ▪ Question others on the points they make, helping them to review their ideas.
- ▪ Listen to the ideas of other students.
- ▪ Refer in detail to points others make.

1. Write an assessment of your own performance in the group activity. Use the points above to help you.

2. As a group, talk about the good and bad points of your group interaction? Are there any ways in which you could improve? Make a note of them.

Check your learning

In this chapter you have:

- developed your questioning skills
- practised listening with concentration
- expressed and developed your own opinions in partner and group tasks
- responded to the ideas of a partner, challenging them where necessary
- worked collaboratively with others to discuss ideas and reach a conclusion.

27

Creating and sustaining roles

Creating a role

This chapter will focus on the skills needed to create and develop a variety of roles in different situations.

You can either develop a role by interacting with other students who are also creating roles or you can work independently.

It is important to understand what is meant by 'role'. For the purposes of assessment in this part of Speaking and listening, 'role' is usually connected with 'character'. That means you become someone other than yourself. That might mean you become:

● a different age
● a different gender
● someone with a very different personality from your usual self.

It could also mean you become something other than a student; you might become a teacher, a police officer, a parent. It might also mean you remain as yourself but assume the role of chairperson in a discussion.

Character

Character is created through use of voice, gesture and vocabulary. As this is a Speaking and listening chapter, it will be voice and vocabulary that are most important, but it is difficult to create a character without thinking about gestures. If you were going to adopt the role of a parent you might want to build up a background for them:

● **What the character is like?** For example, age, gender, occupation, social class.
● **How you would create the character?** You would need to think carefully about voice, gesture and vocabulary.

Voice

We use tone of voice to give meaning to our words. The same word can be expressed in a range of tones to express a range of emotions: sarcasm, anger, despair, fear, concern, shock, amazement, challenge, etc.

Activity

In a group of three or four, take it in turns to express a single word like 'Yes' or 'No'. Each time you express it try to give it a different meaning or tone. You could think about making the word:

● a challenge
● a query
● an insult
● an expression of amazement, and so forth.

Activity

2

a In your group, improvise a phone call in which you only use one word like 'Yes', 'No', 'OK', and use it several times to express a range of different emotions. The members of your group might be able to work out what you are responding to. Each of you should take a different word.

b When you have all taken a turn, reflect on what kinds of things you have done with your voices to express the range of emotions. You could consider:

- the volume: when do you raise your voice or quieten it?
- the pitch: when do you adopt a more shrill voice and when do you deepen it?
- the speed: how does saying a word quickly change the tone from a drawn-out speaking of the word?

> Of course, most speech consists of more than single words but you need to consider similar ways of using your voice when you string words together. Sentences can be expressed in very different ways, for example, by placing the emphasis on different words.
>
> - '**I'm** not going to wear that hat' suggests that it is unthinkable for the person to wear the hat, or there might be a suggestion that someone else will have to wear it.
> - 'I'm **not** going to wear that hat' suggests a really firm expression, perhaps anger.
> - 'I'm not going to wear **that** hat' could suggest that there might be another hat that could be worn.

Activity

3

In a small group take it in turns to read the following sentences in different ways by:

a emphasising different words

b speaking the sentence in different tones.

- 'There were three of them in that car.'
- 'Please don't touch that book.'
- 'How can you possibly say that about me?'
- 'Say that again.'

Gesture

Just as tone of voice and emphasising particular words reinforces meaning, so do body language, facial expression and gesture. Body language, as the word 'language' suggests, can convey meaning without words.

Activity

4

Work in a small group. Take it in turns to pretend you are having a conversation using a mobile phone. You will not speak, you are to imagine you are listening and reacting, using only body language and gesture.

As you act, the others in the group will watch you and then give you feedback about what they were able to interpret about the telephone call from your expressions, body language and gestures.

Activity

5

a What attitude is suggested by each of the images?

b What other forms of body language are you aware of?

c Working in a small group, take it in turns to adopt the stance and facial expression of the following:

- a sulky teenager
- an authoritative headteacher addressing an assembly
- someone receiving very bad news
- someone who's just found out they've won the lottery
- someone telling a lie
- someone who is protesting their innocence.

d What advice about body language would you give to a character who was:

- at an interview?
- teaching a lesson?
- trying to chat up a girl/boy at a party?

Vocabulary

So far you have been focusing on gestures and attitudes to help create character. You also need to consider vocabulary and ways of speaking. Adults use different kinds of words from young people; bankers use different kinds of language from builders; people from different areas of the country use different words.

Activity

6

a What different words can be used to express the following?

- Sorry.
- I don't understand.
- That's great.

b Work with a partner. One of you – character A – should adopt one of the following roles:

- a teenager (a very stereotypical teenager who uses lots of teen slang)
- someone who talks in a dialect (easy in some parts of the country)
- a young child.

The other – character B – should adopt the role of 'translator'.

Character A should speak a sentence immediately followed by Character B who will provide a translation into Standard English, or what might be considered 'posh' English.

The purpose is to show the distinction between the two people by the way they talk.

You could develop a character through improvisation but it is worthwhile sketching out some features of a character rather than just hoping something will happen when you start to act out a situation.

Activity

7

a Work with a partner. Imagine a situation in which one of you is going to interview the other in a chat show called *The Memory Bank*. In the show the interviewee is invited to recall important memories. Between you, you will need to:

- invent a character and their memories
- decide on what kinds of mannerisms, gestures and words this character will use
- consider how different emotions or moods can be expressed.

Although the focus will be on the role of the character being interviewed, you should also develop a character for the interviewer using the same bullet points above. The interviewer could be gentle, confrontational, sarcastic, sympathetic, obnoxious, thoughtful, curious, or have many other characteristics.

Show your drama to the rest of the class.

b Each performance should be briefly reviewed by the audience:

- How effectively did each student create and develop their character?
- How well did they use voice and body language?
- How could the performances have been improved?

Working in a small group

If you decide to work in a small group it is important to create an interesting blend of characters. Good drama usually is based on contrast or conflict – to have too many similar characters is boring for an audience. It is a good idea to sit down and discuss a blend of characters before trying to act out a situation.

Somewhere between two and four characters is ideal. Any more than that makes it harder for each individual to achieve the highest marks.

Activity

8

In a group of two, three or four discuss a situation that might develop at a kitchen table at breakfast time. For example: might there be tension because it is an important day – a family moving house, the breakfast before a wedding? Or could something have happened the night before – someone came in late?

Decide the three or four different characters. You will need to think about gender, age and background, as well as deciding the relationship between them. Not all the characters need to be at the table – there can be entrances and exits.

To create a 'complex' character you will need to decide how you can show different sides to a character, show some subtlety in the characterisation.

Remember that to reveal and develop a character you will need to consider:

- voice and vocabulary
- gesture
- facial expression
- the expression of different moods.
- When you have discussed the situation and characterisation, present your breakfast table drama to the rest of the class.

Each performance should be briefly reviewed by the audience:

- How effectively did each student create and develop their character?
- How well did they use voice and body language?
- How could the performances have been improved?

Using literary texts 🔑

Although you cannot use the script of a published play in your role play, you can either develop an existing character or use a situation from a literary text you have studied.

Hot-seating is usually used as a technique to tease out your understanding of a character in a text. Romeo, for example, could be asked why he killed Tybalt, or George could be asked why he shot Lennie. But it is possible to act in character as well as simply answering questions. A monologue or interview is one way of approaching this.

Activities

9 Choose a character from a text you have read or studied. Jot down a list of characteristics you noticed as you read the text and also the kinds of situations that led to the display of the different characteristics. For example, if you have read *Of Mice and Men* by John Steinbeck you might suggest that George is at different times:

- irritable
- angry
- friendly
- trusting
- suspicious.

When you have a list of characteristics you could decide to prepare a monologue in which you 'think aloud' about the different events in the text. Alternatively you could prepare a list of questions that would allow you to display different characteristics.

10 Instead of becoming an already known character, you could decide to use the situation of a text to create roles. You could:

- create a 'missing' scene from the text
- modernise a scene from an older text
- dramatise the situation in a poem, especially in the case of poems from 'Characters and Voices' in which characterisation is at the heart of the text.

Check your learning

In this chapter you have:

- considered what a 'role' is
- explored how voice, vocabulary and body language can help shape a role
- created different roles in different situations.

28

Making your speaking and listening skills count in the controlled assessment

What is controlled assessment?

During your GCSE course, whether you are taking GCSE English or GCSE English Language, you will participate in a range of activities designed to develop and improve your speaking and listening skills. This type of work will probably be familiar to you as you will have been working on your speaking and listening skills in your English lessons all through school. However, as part of your GCSE course, you are formally assessed on a regular basis for speaking and listening. You will be formally assessed by your teacher at least three times during the course, and these three activities will each carry 15 marks (you will be able to prepare and plan your work before the assessment). Together, the Speaking and listening controlled assessment mark counts for 20 per cent of your overall grade.

Introducing the tasks

The three activities you will be assessed on come under the following headings:

- Presenting
- Discussing and listening
- Role-playing

AQA will provide broad guidance for your teachers as to the types of task you undertake for each of these activities, allowing for some flexible approaches. There are some examples of the types of task you might undertake later in this chapter. Twenty per cent of your grade is a very significant amount and it is important that you consider the ways in which you can achieve highly in this section of your GCSE course. In fact, you will probably be assessed more than three times in order for your teacher to give you plenty of opportunity to achieve the best possible marks.

Effective speaking and listening skills demand the same kind of rigour and attention to the Assessment Objectives as other parts of your GCSE course. Speaking and listening activities can be used to support and develop your study of other aspects of the course.

What do we mean by speaking and listening?

- **A good speaker:** communicates effectively to others in a range of situations, using their words, their tone of voice and their body language. An effective speaker will be able to adapt the form, style, content and tone of speaking they use to suit the needs of the purpose and their audience.
- **A good listener:** is an active listener, using their body language to encourage the speaker. A good listener will concentrate on the ideas they are listening to and be able to expand and develop these ideas if required.

There are four parts to the Assessment Objective for speaking and listening. Assessment Objectives are written for your teachers and examiners. They are the descriptors of the ways in which you will achieve your grade and are used by your teachers to plan your learning, and by your examiners when your work is assessed. For Speaking and listening, these are:

Speaking and listening is about effective communicating. At a higher level this is about communicating your ideas, feelings and attitudes to your audience

Having a clear sense of purpose is important for higher levels of achievement, demonstrating confidence and clarity in your communication

We use different styles of speaking and listening depending on the purpose and the audience, and being able to change not only what you say but the way in which you say it depending on your audience and purpose is very important

Speak to communicate clearly and purposefully; structure and sustain talk, adapting it to different situations and audiences; use Standard English and a variety of techniques as appropriate.

Structuring and organising what you say is just as important with Speaking and listening as with Writing. Sustaining means being able to maintain your focus and concentration for as long as required by the task

Remember that Speaking and listening is about effective communication. Tone of voice, facial expressions and use of resources can all aid effective communication

This is about using the recognised 'correct' grammar and English when appropriate rather than slang and/or dialect

Careful listening to others, paying close attention and being able to demonstrate real engagement with the ideas being heard is very important

Listen and respond to speakers' ideas and perspectives and how they construct and express their meanings.

Paying attention to what others say, not only their words but also the ways in which they are communicating; their structure, the techniques they use, their tone of voice and register perhaps

When in a pair or a group, playing an active role, listening and responding to ideas, being supportive and helping others to develop their ideas as well as to listen to yours, asking thoughtful questions and encouraging the discussion are all aspects of effective interaction

Interact with others, shaping meanings through suggestions, comments and questions, and drawing ideas together.

Being an effective group member means sorting through the ideas to develop and clarify them, identifying the best ideas and maintaining a strong sense of direction for the talk

This is about having a strong sense of direction and purpose as well as being an active listener. Drawing ideas together means you can sort and sift, identifying the best ideas and developing these, keeping your focus on the overall purpose of your task

Behaving and speaking the way another person would do: whether this is a role given by your teacher or a character from one of the texts you are studying. Staying in that role for the required length of time, even when you are not required to speak yourself

Create and sustain different roles.

A role is a 'persona' or 'acting'. You do not have to be a stunning actor to achieve highly however! For this part of the course you are being assessed on your ability to think and speak like another person, responding as you think that person would do rather than how you yourself would. It is about using your imagination to explore how another person might speak, think, act or behave

Sample tasks and sample answers

Presenting

For this assessment, you are being assessed on your ability to 'communicate and adapt your language'. The types of skills you will be required to demonstrate include:

- **Confidently** communicating information, ideas and feelings, emphasising significant points.
- **Adapting** and **shaping** your talk and non-verbal features (body language, use of resources) to meet the demands of different situations, contexts and purposes.
- Making **appropriate**, **controlled**, **effective** use of Standard English vocabulary and grammar.

There is a very wide range of activities that you might undertake to fulfil your presenting assessment. Some examples of the types of task include:

- Watch an episode of the popular comedy chat programme *Room 101* where guest speakers are invited to select the things that they find most irritating. Present your own *Room 101* speech to the class using persuasive techniques, asking the class to vote for whether your chosen subject should go into *Room 101*.

- Research news stories for a week: local and/or national TV, local and/or national BBC websites. Choose a news story that has particularly affected you. Present a talk to your class in which you explain the context of your chosen news story and give your views on this subject.

- In a pair or small group, prepare a presentation using resources on a topic that your pair/group share an interest in. This might be a band, a hobby, or a particular sport or sporting club. The resources you might consider could include digital resources such as PowerPoint, or some 'show and tell' items, or some sound or video resources.

These types of features in a presenting task would achieve a very sound grade; consider the key words 'confidently', 'adapting', 'shaping', 'appropriate', 'controlled' and 'effective'.

If you wanted to achieve the highest marks, you would need to consider key terms such as 'complex and demanding subjects', 'sophisticated strategies', 'challenging contexts' and 'assured and flexible'.

Activity

1 Look at Texts A and B, two descriptions of student responses to the first task. Use the skills outlined on page 178 to see if you can decide which is the better response and why.

Student A

This student is very confident orally and often makes good contributions in class. They make a lot of eye-contact with the class throughout their five-minute presentation. They have prepared note cards which help them remember what to say. They have chosen three items to go into Room 101, all of which get lots of laughs and nods from the class; they have clearly made choices the class can relate to. They have prepared a PowerPoint with photographs to give some visual support to their presentation. They use Standard English throughout and do not hesitate or seem lost for words.

Student B

This student has chosen one item to go into Room 101. It is a band that the rest of the class have not heard of. The student clearly knows a great deal about this band and also has prepared for the fact that the class might not have heard of them, because the presentation starts with a question to the audience establishing this, followed by a brief overview/summary of who the band are, along with a short video clip. This contextualises the subject of the talk for the audience. What follows is a deliberate series of reasons for why this band should be sent to Room 101. The student uses a range of rhetorical techniques including repetition of key phrases and some extreme exaggeration of negative points (which the audience respond to with a lot of laughter). At the end of the presentation, which lasts for three minutes, all of the class vote to send the band to Room 101.

Top tip

You might be giving a speech to another audience outside your English class; perhaps in assembly or to your student council. Ask your teacher to be present if they can to observe and assess you in this context, as any formal speaking and listening activities can be assessed as part of your GCSE course if your teacher feels it is appropriate to the Assessment Objective.

Discussing and listening

For this assessment, you are being marked on your ability to 'interact and respond'. The types of skills you will be required to demonstrate include:

- **Challenging**, **developing** and responding to what you hear in **thoughtful** and **considerate** ways, seeking clarification through **appropriate questions**.
- **Analysing** and **reflecting** on others' ideas to clarify issues and assumptions and develop the discussion.
- Identifying useful outcomes and helping to structure discussion through **purposeful contributions**.

There is a very wide range of activities that you might undertake to fulfil your discussing and listening assessment. Some examples of the types of activity include:

- Your group has been given the brief of designing the next Year 7 sports day. You have 30 minutes to discuss as a group the type and range of activities, bearing in mind the parameters your teacher will provide. Your group then has to present your ideas to the rest of the class. There will be a vote to decide on the best group's work.
- Watch a programme selected by your teacher in which a variety of people give their views on a given subject. Some examples might include Newsnight or Top Gear. Your task is to outline and summarise the opinion of at least one of the people in this programme.
- Working in a pair, you each have two minutes to talk about your most recent holiday. You are not to spend lots of time planning – the aim is just to talk. If your partner gets stuck, prompt them as you feel is appropriate to get them talking again. When you have both given your two-minute accounts, it is then your task to recount as much as possible of what you heard. You can even both score this activity with one 'point' for each correct aspect remembered.

These types of features in a discussing and listening task would achieve a very sound grade; consider the key words 'challenging and developing', 'appropriate questions', 'thoughtful and considerate' and 'purposeful contributions'.

If you wanted to achieve the highest marks, you would need to consider key terms such as 'concentrated listening', 'interrogating', 'flexibility', 'challenge assumptions', 'initiate, develop and sustain discussion'.

Activity

2 Look at Texts C and D, two descriptions of student responses to the first task. Use the skills outlined above to see if you can decide which is the better reponse and why.

Student A

This student appears comfortable in the group. They lean forward when listening to other people's ideas and smile and nod encouragingly. There is someone in the group who finds working with new people very difficult; Student A deliberately sits next to them and, when establishing the roles for the members of the group, suggests that the less-confident person be the note-taker at the start. The group are rather quiet at the start because they have not worked together before. Student A responds to this by starting the discussion off, asking the others questions to draw them out. As the conversation develops and the ideas start to come, the student challenges lots of the ideas, asking questions such as 'have you thought about what might happen if ...?' and 'yes, I see your point but have you considered ...?' This draws out lots of very useful ideas and ensures the group are heading in a useful direction.

Student B

This student is working with a group who know each other very well. There is a clear sense of purpose to the talk from the start; this group are organised and easily fall into their roles. This student has a clear sense of where the discussion should go as they have discussed these ideas before as part of their GCSE PE project. The other group members are happy for this student to lead the discussion. The group finish quickly, their task being accomplished due to this student contributing most of the ideas which are not challenged by the other group members.

Role-playing

For this assessment, you are being assessed on your ability to 'create and sustain a role'. The types of skills you will be required to demonstrate include:

- Creating **convincing** characters and roles using a range of **carefully selected** verbal and non-verbal techniques.
- Responding **skilfully and sensitively** in different situations and scenarios, to explore ideas and issues and relationships.

There is a very wide range of activities that you might undertake to fulfil your role-playing assessment. Some examples of the types of activity include:

- As part of your study of a text for English Literature or extended reading, undertake a hot-seating activity where you respond in role as one of the characters from the text. Your teacher and/or members of the class will ask the character questions, to which you respond as if you are that person.
- Interview the author: as part of your poetry study, choose one of the poems you particularly like. Working in a pair, one of you will take the role of the poet and the other will be an interviewer. The aim is to respond in role to a series of questions designed to explore the writer's intention, so this task would be very useful preparation for other aspects of your course.

- You are a group of parents working on a governors' sub-committee. Your meeting is to discuss the new plans for 'wider curriculum' that the school is committed to. There are three possible new courses to be offered to GCSE students. Students will take the extra lesson for one hour per week. Your task is to argue the case for or against each one of the following and reach a decision as to which one your school is going to offer, with clear reasons why. Your choices are:
  – driving theory lessons
  – self-defence classes
  – body image and nutrition.

These types of features in a role-playing task would achieve a very sound grade; consider the key words 'convincing', 'carefully selected', 'skilfully and sensitively' and 'explore'.

If you wanted to achieve the highest marks, you would need to consider key terms such as 'complex characters', 'challenging roles' and 'insightful choices'.

Activity

3 Look at Texts E and F, two descriptions of student responses to the first task. Use the skills outlined on page 178 to see if you can decide which is the better response and why.

Student A

The class are working on role play in order to explore the character of Macbeth. They have free choice of the character they choose for their hot-seating task. Student A has chosen to play Banquo. When hot-seated, they clearly answer 'as if they are' Banquo by using first person. They answer some quite interesting questions about the friendship between Macbeth and Banquo, showing Banquo's understanding of Macbeth's character and his concerns that the encounter with the witches may have led Macbeth to have some dark thoughts. They stay in role throughout the hot-seating and use appropriate body language such as head-shaking and sighing to signal Banquo's state of mind. They have used Banquo's soliloquies as a basis for their answers in role, which demonstrates clear understanding of what he says in the play.

Student B

Student B has chosen Lady Macbeth. When hot-seated, all the answers are given as if to an imaginary Macbeth standing at her side, using 'you' rather than 'he' when referring to her husband. The student employs body language in a subtle way – there are long pauses as if she is listening to something the rest of the class cannot hear and on several occasions she rubs at her hands, appearing distracted and lost in thought. When questioned about her relationship with Macbeth she raises her tone as if angry and defensive of her husband, even though the hot-seating scenario is taken from the time in the play when the relationship has broken down between the two characters. There are references to her life before the play started including some subtle references to her father and her desperation for a family life. She has clearly taken inferences from the play and developed them using her imagination.

Activity

4 The key words below are scattered around the page. Spend two minutes looking at them, then turn the page over and on a separate piece of paper, quickly write down as many as you can remember.

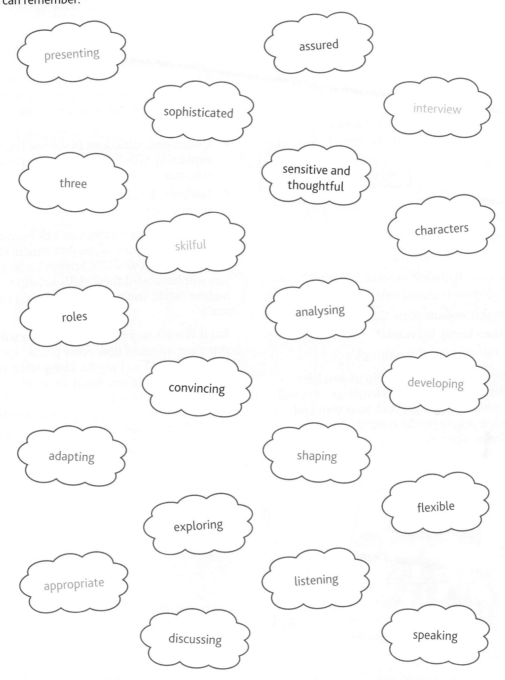

presenting

assured

sophisticated

interview

three

sensitive and thoughtful

characters

skilful

roles

analysing

convincing

developing

adapting

shaping

flexible

exploring

appropriate

listening

discussing

speaking

Section
D Spoken language

Sometimes the lines between speaking, listening, reading and writing are not clearly drawn. The different **modes** overlap. The study of spoken language is an investigative approach to the way oral communication works. It gives you the opportunity to think about and find answers to the following questions:

Key terms

Mode: usually used to mean whether a text is written or spoken.

- Is this written English or spoken English?
- Is he reading or listening?
- Is she waiting for answers?
- Is this written English or spoken English?
- Why are these students talking in dialect?
- Why is this student using Standard English?
- How does he say his words?
- What rules govern this writing?

This section of the book will help to develop your understanding of spoken language. You will consider spoken language, both your own and that of other people, in the context of purpose and audience, and you will investigate the ways in which new technologies have fostered a bridge between speaking and writing.

The chapters in this section are designed to help you meet the Assessment Objectives that underpin your GCSE English Language course. These are written for teachers but you might like to read them in full (they are explained in more detail on page 200).

- Understand variations in spoken language, explaining why language changes in relation to contexts.
- Evaluate the impact of spoken language choices in their own and others' use.

By the end of this section you will have covered all of the skills outlined in the Assessment Objectives. By the end of your GCSE English Language course you will have used these skills to help you gain the highest marks you can in your Spoken language study.

But it doesn't stop there. This section will make you more aware of how other people speak and why they speak as they do. Using what you learn will not only help you listen more carefully to what people say and how they say it, it will also enable you to respond more appropriately and become a more effective user of language.

29 Choosing and using language

Objectives

In this chapter you will:

consider how purpose and audience affect how we speak

examine how your own speech is influenced by external factors

develop skills in analysis of public speech.

Purpose and audience

As with written English, all forms of spoken English are determined by purpose and audience:

- **Purpose:** why you are speaking and what you hope to achieve through speech
- **Audience:** the person or people to whom you are speaking.

You would not speak in the same way when talking with a police officer as you would when talking with a friend. We all adapt our words, tone, body language and even our appearance to match the degree of formality required in each situation. Often we do this automatically.

Activities

1 You are going to have an interview for a part-time job in a shop. Select items from the following list that would be important in having a successful interview.

clear pronunciation   dialect   slouching position   eye contact   appropriate clothing

Standard English   sit up straight   arrive late   smart appearance

casual clothes   bored expression   slang   yawn

smile   friendly manner   punctuality   knowledge about the shop

2 Check your selection with another student's and together place the items in order of importance.

a Work in groups of three. One of you is A, one B and the other C.

- A should observe and make notes on the speech and body language of Student B.
- B and C should role-play the following situations:

(i) Student B talks with a friend C about a car accident B had witnessed on the way to school that morning.

(ii) Student B talks with a police officer C about the same car accident.

b Student A should report back on what he or she observed about:

- the differences in the language used by Student B
- the differences in the tone adopted by Student B
- the differences in the body language of Student B.

c Together, list at least three reasons that would explain the differences noted by Student A.

Activity

3

a Think about a range of situations in which you have spoken recently. These could include face-to-face conversations or telephone conversations with:

- friends
- elderly relatives such as grandparents
- adults such as teachers
- adults you have not met before, e.g. shop assistants.

Choose three different situations, involving different audiences. For each one, describe the situation, and identify the purpose for speaking and the audience. Replay the situation in your mind and write a short extract that shows part of what you said on that occasion. For example:

Situation	Purpose	Audience	What I said
Talking with friends in playground	Telling them about something that happened a while ago	Friends, most of whom I've known since Year 9	Well like it was errm like there was no-one else there an it was all spooky like an I couldn't really see nothin well there was a bit of light like but not so's you could see

b Choose two of the situations in which you used speech differently. Identify the differences and explain the reasons for them.

How speech is recorded

Key terms

Filler: a sound, word or phrase used to fill a gap (e.g. 'er', 'like', 'you know').

Transcript: a written record of a speech or conversation.

You might have experienced difficulty in Activity 1 in working out how to record what you said. The conventions for recording speech are different from those normally used in writing. This is partly because we don't always talk in sentences; we pause to gather our thoughts or to bring the right word to mind or for emphasis, as well as to make sense of what we are saying. We also give emphasis to particular words through the way we say them. And, on top of that, we use sounds to fill gaps in the conversation such as 'mmm' and 'errm'. These are often referred to as **fillers**.

In Text A, a **transcript** of a conversation, you can see some of the main conventions of recording speech. Use the key to help you read the transcript. Try to 'hear' it in your mind as you read.

(A)

Key:
(.) Micropause (less than a second)
(2) Longer pause (number of seconds indicated)
[ ] Simultaneous speech – where two or more people speak at the same time
Bold Emphatic stress

Speaker A	well (.) a job would be the best thing for him (.) wouldn't it?
Speaker B	mmmm well it would be if he gets it
Speaker A	b (.) but what can she write [about him]
Speaker C	[she can lie]
Speaker A	**yeah** (2) no (1) twist the truth (.) **you** write about him (.) she's known him a long time (1) he knows the family (.) he doesn't [steal]
Speaker B	[that we know of]
Speaker A	that we know of (.) he's very bright
Speaker B	he'll probably grow out of it when he gets a bit older
Speaker A	yeah

Activity

4

You could be asked to write a transcript of a conversation in preparation for your Spoken language study. This activity gives you the opportunity to practise what you have learned about writing transcripts.

a Take two of your examples of what you said from Activity 3. Rewrite them using the appropriate conventions of transcript, for example:

> well (.) like (.) it was errm (1) like there was no-one else there (.) an it was all spooky like an I couldn't really see **anything** (1) well (2) there was a bit of light like (.) but not enough to see

b Now try to recall how the conversation went in more detail, including what the other person said. Aim to write 10 lines of transcript based on what you can recall. Remember to use the appropriate conventions of transcript.

Investigating your speech

In Activity 1 you considered whether it was appropriate to use dialect in a formal interview for a job. As you may remember from Chapters 5 and 25 many people across the world speak a variety of regional English, depending on where they come from. This is called dialect.

The place where you are from is, however, only one of many influences on the way you speak or your **idiolect**. There are many others. Read Text B, a description of some of the factors that have influenced Jacob's idiolect. The factors are annotated for you.

Key terms

Idiolect: the term used to describe an individual's distinct language features.

❶ gender

❷ geographical region

❸ parents

❹ social class

❺ siblings

❻ extended family

❼ education

(B) Jacob was born and grew up in Nottingham where his mother had also grown up. His father was from Liverpool and had moved to Nottingham in his early twenties. His mother was a teaching assistant and his father ran a successful local car hire business. When he was little he and his two older sisters spent a lot of time with his maternal grandparents who were both originally from Wales. Jacob went to nursery when he was three and then moved on to the local primary school before attending the local comprehensive.

5

a Think carefully about the way you speak. Suggest ways in which each of the following might have influenced this, and give examples where appropriate:

- where you grew up
- your gender
- your parents
- your social class

- your siblings
- your extended family (i.e. aunts, uncles, grandparents, etc.)
- your education.

b Compare your findings with another student's. Talk about the differences and the reasons for these.

Social groups, made up of individuals, might also have a distinct language style. The group may be small, such as friends at school, or large, such as Goths and Emos. The use of language specific to such a group, be it small or large, is called a **sociolect**. Membership of such a group often depends on the individual's ability to adapt his or her language accordingly. This is clearly seen in the following advice taken from a website article on 'How to Have a Skater Attitude':

Key terms

Sociolect: a particular use of language specific to a social group.

Ⓒ

How to have a skater attitude

Walk the walk and talk the talk. Make sure that you are decked out in your skater attire and that you keep a cool, calm attitude. Know your skater language and use it properly. If you are unsure about some of the vocab, don't use it until you know for sure.

Adapted from www.ehow.com

6

Identify and list the different social groups that you know about and/or belong to. They can be small or large. For each group, identify words or phrases that are commonly used by the individuals in that group.

Share your findings with another group.

It is not just home and social groups that influence the way we speak. You might be interested in a specific subject or follow a particular sport. If you do, it is likely that it will have its own specialist vocabulary – for example:

- **ICT**: burn, rip, text, game, cookie, cyber crime, file sharing, instant message, search engine, navigation bar, blog, podcast, Wikipedia, MP3, WiMAX, dotcom, CD, DVD, Skype, podcast, PC, memory, hard drive, software, server, broadband, wireless

- **Golf**: eagle, birdie, albatross, tee, putt, driver, irons, green, fairway, rough, mashie niblick, spoon, woods, club, putter, par, stableford, greensome, bunker, divot, spikes, feathery, slice, hook, pitch, caddie, bogie

If you want to pursue the interest either for work or play, or participate in the sport, you need to know the vocabulary associated with it.

Activities

7

a Work in pairs. The following words are used in two sports: football and tennis. Sort them correctly into two groups.

groundstroke   umpire   league   crosscourt   defender   penalty   doubles

yellow card   match point   offside   substitute   racquet   line judge

tiebreaker   goalkeeper   striker   serve   Grand Slam   draw   backhand

touchline   Wimbledon   shoot   deuce   forehand   advantage   dive

let   corner kick   foul   return   ace   red card   fault

referee   tackle   hand ball   pitch   goal   volley

set   own goal   double   rally   wall   net   break point

lob   fault   extra time

b Think of an area of work or play that you know about. It could be a particular subject at school, a career that you want to follow, or a sport or hobby that you have. List between five and ten words that distinguish the specialist vocabulary of your chosen area.

8 The language we choose is very much a product of the society within which we use it. Look again at the work you did in Activity 5. Think about other areas that have influenced the way you speak. These may be to do with:

- social groupings
- political/religious and/or other strong beliefs
- reading/music preferences
- specific subject/sporting interests.

For each area you identify, explain how it has influenced your idiolect.

Public speaking (k!)

Just as we adapt our speech in day-to-day situations, so too do politicians. When meeting people on the streets they speak informally. Their aim is to be understood by a small audience and they adapt their language to match this purpose. When speaking publicly, they know they have to reach a wide audience that will include people from very varied social groups. In these situations they tend to use Standard English and features of rhetoric to achieve maximum impact.

You need to develop your skills in analysis of public speech. This involves close examination of:

- the way ideas are developed
- the words that are used to express those ideas
- the intended effect on the audience.

Read Text D, a transcript of part of American President Obama's inaugural speech in January 2009, and study the notes below.

(D)

Today I say to you that the challenges we face are real. They are serious and they are many. They will not be met easily or in a short span of time. But know this, America: They will be met.

On this day, we gather because we have chosen hope over fear, unity of purpose over conflict and discord.

On this day, we come to proclaim an end to the petty grievances and false promises, the recriminations and worn-out dogmas, that for far too long have strangled our politics.

We remain a young nation, but in the words of Scripture, the time has come to set aside childish things. The time has come to reaffirm our enduring spirit; to choose our better history; to carry forward that precious gift, that noble idea, passed on from generation to generation: the God-given promise that all are equal, all are free, and all deserve a chance to pursue their full measure of happiness.

1st paragraph: He moves from the first-person singular (I) to the first-person plural (we). This aligns him with his audience and puts him and them on the same side, working together. The opening sentence introduces 'the challenges we face'. The next three sentences sustain the focus: 'They are', 'They are', 'They will not be', 'They will be'. There is also a shift in tense from the present to the future and the positive assertion at the end ('They will be met') is there to reassure the audience that the problems can be overcome. He addresses his audience as a nation, rather than as a group of individuals: 'know this, America'.

2nd paragraph: Opening 'On this day' reinforces the opening 'Today' of the previous paragraph – emphasising the importance of this occasion. Sustains first-person plural and the use of 'we have chosen' suggests empowerment. The phrase 'hope over fear' is mirrored and expanded in the following phrase: 'unity of purpose over conflict and discord'.

3rd paragraph: Repeats opening of 2nd paragraph to maintain focus on importance of occasion. Uses language emotively with words such as 'petty', 'false', 'worn-out' and 'strangled' to create a negative picture of what has gone before.

4th paragraph: Refers to 'Scripture' and to 'God', suggesting this is the right path to follow. Uses language emotively with phrases such as 'enduring spirit', 'precious gift' and 'noble idea' to create a positive picture of what lies ahead. Repeats 'all' three times to emphasise that everyone in his audience counts.

Now read Text E, the next part of President Obama's inaugural speech.

(E) In reaffirming the greatness of our nation, we understand that greatness is never a given. It must be earned. Our journey has never been one of shortcuts or settling for less. It has not been the path for the fainthearted – for those who prefer leisure over work, or seek only the pleasures of riches and fame. Rather, it has been the risk-takers, the doers, the makers of things – some celebrated, but more often men and women obscure in their labor – who have carried us up the long, rugged path toward prosperity and freedom.

For us, they packed up their few worldly possessions and traveled across oceans in search of a new life. For us, they toiled in sweatshops and settled the West; endured the lash of the whip and plowed the hard earth.

For us, they fought and died, in places like Concord* and Gettysburg*; Normandy* and Khe Sahn*. Time and again, these men and women struggled and sacrificed and worked till their hands were raw so that we might live a better life. They saw America as bigger than the sum of our individual ambitions; greater than all the differences of birth or wealth or faction.

This is the journey we continue today. We remain the most prosperous, powerful nation on Earth. Our workers are no less productive than when this crisis began. Our minds are no less inventive, our goods and services no less needed than they were last week or last month or last year. Our capacity remains undiminished. But our time of standing pat,** of protecting narrow interests and putting off unpleasant decisions – that time has surely passed. Starting today, we must pick ourselves up, dust ourselves off, and begin again the work of remaking America.

* All battles in which American troops fought.

** Being satisfied with things as they are.

Adapted from news.bbc.co.uk

Activities

9 In pairs or small groups, study Text E closely and analyse the use of language in the speech. Remember to work out the effects of the features you identify. Make notes on your findings. Here are a few things to look for, to get you started:

third-person plural   short sentences   *ideas being developed*   shifts in tenses

reference to traditional values   groups of three   historical reference   emotive use of language   repetition

10 Share your findings with another pair or small group. Add to your notes if appropriate.

Stretch yourself

1 a Investigate the idiolect of an elderly person you know, such as a grandparent.

  b Watch President Obama's delivery of his inaugural speech. Make notes on how he delivers his speech. You should focus on:

- when and where he pauses for effect
- his body language
- changes in tone for emphasis.

Check your learning

In this chapter you have:

- considered how purpose and audience affect how we speak
- examined the influences on your own idiolect
- considered the language of different groups
- developed your skills in analysis of public speech.

Multi-modal talk

How we experience language

In an average day we experience language in many different ways:

- we read it
- we speak it
- we hear it
- we write it.

Sometimes we do a combination of these.

Activity

1

a Think back over the last 24 hours. List all the things you have done in that time in which language played a part.

b Use three colours. In the first colour highlight those things that involved spoken language (i.e. things you said or heard). In the second colour, highlight those things that involved written language (i.e. things you read or wrote). In the third colour, highlight those things that involved both spoken and written language.

c Compare your list with that of another student. If you have missed anything out, add it to your list.

Differences between written and spoken language

There are several differences between typical written and typical spoken language. If one example of each – an encyclopaedia and a telephone conversation – is considered it is easy to identify those differences.

Activity

2 The main features of typical written language and typical spoken language are listed in pairs below. Match the correct features to the encyclopaedia entry and the telephone conversation.

An encyclopaedia entry (typical written language)

A telephone conversation (typical spoken language)

Activity

a   It is received through the ears/It is received through the eyes.

b   It is permanent in that it can be checked again and again/It is temporary in that it can only be retained in the memory.

c   It is personal in that it is directed to a specific audience/It is impersonal in that the audience is not known.

d   It is immediate in that it is restricted to the here and now/It is distant in that it can be accessed at any time.

This division, however, is not always clear-cut, though there are some features that are more typical of one mode than the other.

For example, writing is often permanent but sometimes, as with a shopping list, it is only temporary. Speech is usually temporary but if it is a radio broadcast that is archived, it becomes permanent. Furthermore, if we are listening to someone speak we might also be interpreting what they say through our eyes as we watch their body language.

So, at one extreme, there is written language that is permanent, impersonal, distant and received entirely with the eyes, such as an encyclopaedia entry. At the other extreme there is spoken language that is temporary, personal, immediate and received entirely through the ears, such as a telephone call from a friend. There are many stages between these extremes.

Activity k!

3   a   Imagine a continuum from A to Z where A is the extreme of written language and Z is the extreme of spoken language. At which points on this continuum would you place the situations listed below?

A		Z
Written		**Spoken**
e.g. encyclopaedia entry		e.g. phone call from friend
Features:		Features:
received through the eyes		received through the ears
permanent		temporary
impersonal		personal
distant		immediate

Situations:

- text message to a friend
- an internet chat room
- the Bible
- play by Shakespeare
- TV news broadcast
- reality TV programme
- church sermon
- text message from a mobile phone company
- telephone directory
- political speech
- a shopping list
- radio news broadcast
- a poem
- a class group discussion

b   Compare your ranking with another student's and discuss the reasons for any differences you have.

Mixed modes

You have seen how some areas of written and spoken language contain features of both modes. These are known as mixed or blended modes. This is particularly true of some of the new forms of electronic communication, such as texting, also known as text messaging.

Texting

Texting, as a form of communication, has been around for a very short time. Your parents would not have used text (and probably would not have heard of it) when they were your age. It is an area of communication in which, in practical terms, the young are the experts.

4   Work in groups of three or four. In this activity you are going to work out what you know about texting. Follow these steps:

a   Talk about when you text, how often you text and the reasons why you text. List at least four points that would explain why texting has become so popular so quickly.

b   On paper each member of the group should write a text typical of what they would send to a friend. These will provide the material for you to work out some of the conventions of texting.

c   Spread the 'texts' in front of you. Think about each of the following features. Can you find examples of them in your texts? Make a table with the feature in the first column and examples of it taken from your texts in the second column.

- Letters missed out of words (for example, thght)
- Letters missed off ends of words (for example, goin)
- Single letters that sound like a word (for example, r – are)
- Numbers that sound like a word (for example, 2 – two, to, too)
- Words spelt the way they sound (for example, cud – could)
- Words spelt using a combination of letters and numbers (for example, l8r – later)
- Initial letters used (for example, lol – laugh out loud)
- Emoticons used to express feelings (for example, ☹)

d   Look for other features not mentioned above. These may be to do with forms of punctuation and spelling that do not belong with conventional writing. Add them to your table.

e   Compare your table with that of another group. Add any features to your table that you use but had not recorded.

Language changes and develops over time. The language of Chaucer and Shakespeare is not immediately familiar to us today, but those changes have taken many hundreds of years to develop. Texting is developing and changing so quickly that there are websites being produced to help people decipher the language of texting. Read Text A, an example of this.

?4U	I have a question for you	GRL	Girl
4COL	For crying out loud	H8	Hate
ATB	All the best	HAK	Hugs and kisses
AYSOS	Are you stupid or something	ILY	I love you
B4N	Bye for now	IYSS	If you say so
BFF	Best friends forever	JIC	Just in case
CU	See you	JK	Just kidding
CUL	See you later	KK	Knock knock
DM	Doesn't matter	KOTL	Kiss on the lips
DV8	Deviate	LOL	Laughing out loud
E123	Easy as one, two, three	LMK	Let me know
EOM	End of message	M8	Mate
F2F	Face to face	MIRL	Meet in real life
FTBOMH	From the bottom of my heart	N1	Nice one
		NBD	No big deal
G2CU	Great to see you		

Activity

5

Given the rapid development in recent years, it is likely that the language of text will change dramatically over the next 50 years. Write a guide for a student in 50 years' time who is trying to understand the text messaging of today. Start your guide with an explanation of why texting became so popular in the early years of the 21st century. Then explain the conventions of texting and give examples to help them in their study.

While texting is used regularly by young people, it is still a new form of communication and there are concerns about its use and potential dangers.

Activity k!

6

Read Text B, the article 'Texting may be taking a toll', below and overleaf.

a Identify and list the concerns given about texting.

b Add to this list any further concerns you have about texting and concerns that you know others (such as parents and teachers) have.

c Which of these concerns do you consider to be most and least serious? Number them in order of priority, with 1 being the most serious.

B

Texting may be taking a toll

They do it late at night when their parents are asleep. They do it in restaurants and while crossing busy streets. They do it in the classroom with their hands behind their back. They do it so much their thumbs hurt.

The phenomenon is beginning to worry physicians and psychologists who say texting is leading to anxiety, distraction in school, falling grades, repetitive stress injury and sleep deprivation.

Dr Martin Joffe, a pediatrician in California, recently surveyed students at two local high schools and found that many were routinely sending hundreds of texts every day.

'That's one every few minutes,' he said. 'Then you hear that these kids are responding to texts late at night. That's going to cause sleep issues in an age group that's already plagued with sleep issues.'

The rise in texting is too recent to have produced any conclusive data on health effects. But psychologist, Sherry Turkle, said it might be causing a shift in the way adolescents develop.

'Among the jobs of adolescence are to separate from your parents, and to find the peace and quiet to become the person you decide you want to be. If technology makes something like staying in touch very, very easy, these things become harder to do; now you have adolescents who are texting their mothers 15 times a day, asking things like, "Should I get the red shoes or the blue shoes?".' As for peace and quiet, she said, 'If you're being deluged by constant communication, the pressure to answer immediately is quite high. So if you're in the middle of a thought, forget it.'

Michael Hausauer, a psychotherapist in Oakland, Calif., said teenagers had a 'terrific interest in knowing what's going on in the lives of their peers, coupled with a terrific anxiety about being out of the loop.' For that reason, he said, the rapid rise in texting has potential for great benefit and great harm.

'Texting can be an enormous tool,' he said. 'It offers companionship and the promise of connectedness. At the same time, texting can make a youngster feel frightened and overly exposed.'

Texting may also be taking a toll on teenagers' thumbs. Peter W Johnson, an associate professor at the University of Washington, said it was too early to tell whether this kind of stress is damaging. But he added, 'Based on our experiences with computer users, we know intensive repetitive use of the upper extremities can lead to musculoskeletal disorders, so we have some reason to be concerned that too much texting could lead to temporary or permanent damage to the thumbs.'

Although most schools forbid cellphone use in class, it still happens. Teachers are often oblivious. Deborah Yager, a high school chemistry teacher, recently gave an anonymous survey to 50 of her students; most said they texted during class. 'I can't tell when it's happening, and there's nothing we can do about it,' she said.

Dr Joffe says parents tend to be far less aware of texting than of video game playing or general computer use, and the unlimited plans often mean that parents stop paying attention to billing details. 'I talk to parents in the office now,' he said. 'I'm quizzing them, and no one is thinking about this.'

Adapted from Katie Hafner, 'Texting may be taking a toll', *New York Times*, 25 May 2009

Instant messaging

When you send a text message you do not necessarily get an immediate reply. It is not interactive in the way that a conversation is. You complete what you want to say without interruption. The recipient might or might not reply straight away. This is very different from instant messaging as used on the internet. Instant messaging allows the possibility of online communication between two or more participants in 'real time'.

Activities

7 Read Text C, a 'conversation' on an internet messenger. Look back to the work you did in the Activity 4 on page 196 where you identified the features of text language. Read through the following 'conversation' and identify the ways in which the language is similar to that used to text on a mobile phone. Talk about any differences you notice.

8 Now work in pairs.

a Remember the features of typical written language and spoken language texts:

Written	Spoken
received through the eyes	received through the ears
permanent	temporary
impersonal	personal
distant	immediate

Which of these features most closely reflect instant messaging?

b Read Text C and track the threads of the conversation by:

- identifying the different things talked about
- tracking where the shifts in topic occur and how each shift is introduced.

c Think about why the three participants don't take turns and why the responses are not always directly linked to what has come immediately before them. List reasons that would help to explain why this happens.

d The writers regularly aim to help the readers 'hear' how the words would be said, either through spelling or through their use of punctuation. For example, daleo writes: im bacckkkk. List other examples of this.

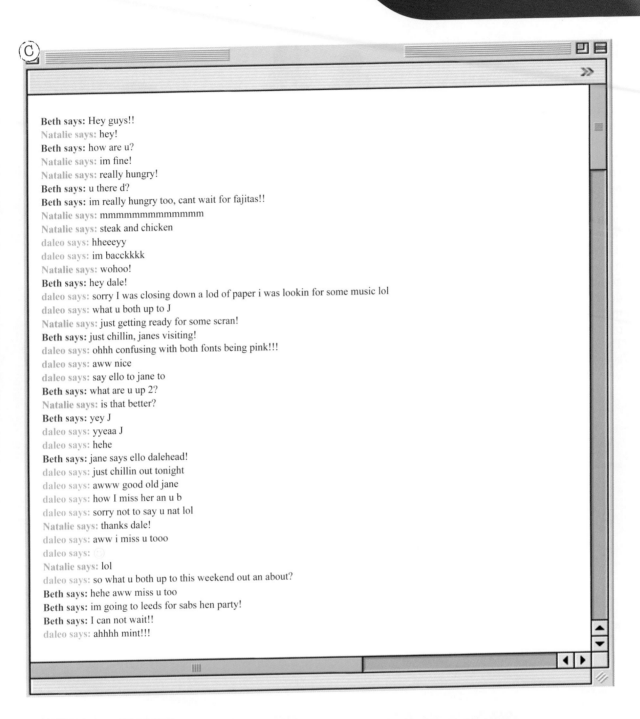

Beth says: Hey guys!!
Natalie says: hey!
Beth says: how are u?
Natalie says: im fine!
Natalie says: really hungry!
Beth says: u there d?
Beth says: im really hungry too, cant wait for fajitas!!
Natalie says: mmmmmmmmmmmmm
Natalie says: steak and chicken
daleo says: hheeeyy
daleo says: im bacckkkk
Natalie says: wohoo!
Beth says: hey dale!
daleo says: sorry I was closing down a lod of paper i was lookin for some music lol
daleo says: what u both up to J
Natalie says: just getting ready for some scran!
Beth says: just chillin, janes visiting!
daleo says: ohhh confusing with both fonts being pink!!!
daleo says: aww nice
daleo says: say ello to jane to
Beth says: what are u up 2?
Natalie says: is that better?
Beth says: yey J
daleo says: yyeaa J
daleo says: hehe
Beth says: jane says ello dalehead!
daleo says: just chillin out tonight
daleo says: awww good old jane
daleo says: how I miss her an u b
daleo says: sorry not to say u nat lol
Natalie says: thanks dale!
daleo says: aww i miss u tooo
daleo says: ☺
Natalie says: lol
daleo says: so what u both up to this weekend out an about?
Beth says: hehe aww miss u too
Beth says: im going to leeds for sabs hen party!
Beth says: I can not wait!!
daleo says: ahhhh mint!!!

Adults who are not used to messaging are sometimes confused when young people say they are having a 'chat' with their friends when they are sitting typing in front of a PC. This is perhaps because messaging has crossed new, and to them unfamiliar, boundaries.

The rules

As you will have gathered by now, there are no fixed rules to govern either texting or messaging. It doesn't matter whether you use capitals or don't use capitals, whether you abbreviate 'are' to 'r' or not, or whether you choose to replace your words entirely with emoticons and other images. What matters is that you communicate with your recipients in a way that is acceptable to them. The rapid development of texting and messaging makes it difficult to predict what will happen next. The only way to find out is to keep doing it!

Stretch yourself

Much is written about the dangers of internet chat rooms:

- 'The most dangerous place for a child to go on line is a chat room.'
- 'Parents are being warned of hidden dangers in internet chat rooms after a teenage girl was duped into meeting a 47-year-old man.'
- 'Sexual predators, cyber bullies, online scams and obscene websites all lurk on the internet chat rooms.'
- 'The government today launched a £1.5m advertising campaign to help parents explain the potential dangers of internet chat rooms to their children.'

Research both the disadvantages and the advantages of internet chat rooms. Write an article for a newspaper in which you argue that chat rooms can be beneficial as long as participants are careful.

Check your learning

In this chapter you have:

- learned about the main features of written and spoken language
- identified and written about the features of texting
- examined an extract of instant messaging
- considered different concerns about texting and messaging.

31

Objectives

In this chapter you will:

learn about how the spoken language study fits into your GCSE English Language course

explore the Assessment Objectives for the Spoken language study

look at the types of task you might undertake.

Making your spoken language study skills count in the controlled assessment

What is controlled assessment?

If you are doing GCSE English Language, you will need to undertake a Spoken language study as part of your course. This is a really exciting opportunity to explore language in a way that is relevant to how it is used in modern society: it's not a study of language that is far out of reach and hidden in the past, it's the study of language that is modern and changing.

GCSE English Language

Controlled assessment title
Studying spoken language

Mark value
10% = 20 marks

Choice of task
One of:
- Social attitudes to spoken language
- Spoken genres
- Multi-modal talk.

Planning and preparation
You are allowed to spend time discussing the texts and task, and you may make brief notes which can be taken into the controlled assessment.

Time for writing
2–3 hours

Expected length
800–1000 words

You will be allowed time to prepare for this task by gathering data in the form of transcripts or clips that you have thought about and discussed. Suggestions for these are provided later in this chapter. You will be able to bring your transcripts with you when you complete the controlled assessment, but you will not be able to bring notes, drafts or essay outlines.

Introducing the tasks

There are three choices of topic area for the Spoken language study:
- Social attitudes to spoken language
- Spoken genres
- Multi-modal talk

There will be two task options for each topic. You will complete one of these. The Assessment Objectives for the Spoken language study areas are as follows:

Be able to analyse differences

Show skills such as inference, deduction, exploration and interpretation

Giving reasons for something

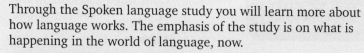

Understand variations in spoken language, explaining why language changes in relation to contexts.

Words that are used when we speak

This is how language changes depending on why, when and how it is being used

Write about the effects of this and how successful you think they are

Evaluate the impact of spoken language choices in their own and others' use.

The effect the spoken language has on the audience

Through the Spoken language study you will learn more about how language works. The emphasis of the study is on what is happening in the world of language, now.

Areas you could study include:

- a younger brother or sister's speech development
- language as used in a soap opera
- language as used in a TV news programme
- a study of your own idiolect
- different modes of language used in different genres of TV programmes
- a study of jargonised, work-specific language
- an exploration of the English language that a non-native speaker uses.

When you are preparing your material, remember the Assessment Objectives. You need to:

- show that you know why people speak in different ways at different times and in different places
- comment the effects of the language that people choose to use.

To do well you need to think deeply about the words people use and how they use them. When working with data you will need to note different things – for example:

- word use – how and why different words are used
- frequency of words
- jargonised words
- word deviations in text- or MSN-speak.

Sample tasks and sample answers

In your written assessment you need to be able to:

- explain, analyse and evaluate your area of study
- show your understanding of the data.

To gain high marks, you will need to do more than simply describe your research and give an account of your data. You must give your teacher evidence that you can explain and evaluate what you have studied. The more **selective** you are about this the better – don't simply quote chunks of text or data; the best essays select certain words to **illustrate** their points and embed them in sentences.

When planning your response, you should bear the following basic structure in mind.

- **Introduction:** a brief outline of the background to the task
- **Key points:** these should be linked and explored.
- **Conclusion:** a few sentences that bring together the main points you have made.

Social attitudes to spoken language

We all tend to speak differently in different situations. There are words that you use when you are with your friends that you might not use with parents or grandparents.

You will be asked to choose a topic and complete one task from this area. The key words for this topic will be 'reflect' or 'investigate'.

- **Reflect** means that you will need to think about why certain language is used in certain situations and share this in your written work.
- **Investigate** means that you will need to explore and examine the spoken language area you choose and share this in your written work.

Here is a sample task from this topic area. Remember, your teacher will be looking for your understanding of the work and your ability to analyse, explore and explain what you have discovered.

---

1   Record a conversation with someone from an older generation about their memories of summer holidays. Investigate the way that they express their views.

1

a Read Text A, an example of **part of** a student response to Question 1, a task in the topic area of Social attitudes to spoken language.

b With a partner identify examples of the following in the response:

- a brief outline of the background
- selection of detail to illustrate the points
- identification of the origin of words
- exploration of why words are used in certain situations
- reflection on the use of languages.

c Now read the teacher's comments on this student response Identify and list what the student needs to do to improve.

Introduction

Great uncle Trevor has worked hard for all of his life and has recently bought a house in France. He is seventy-five years old and I interviewed him to find out how he used to holiday when he was a child. I was very interested in the language which he used to describe his holidays as Great-uncle Trevor is a Cockney and I remember being very interested in the way he spoke when I was little.

Example paragraph

He mentioned money a few times when he spoke. He talked about 'savings'. This interested me because it seemed to be very natural to him. You only seem to hear this sort of thing in the news now, most people talk about spending. He also said that the first holiday they had was to Butlins at Clacton when it opened in 1938. He seemed very excited when talking about this and kept mentioning that his Dad had had to save up a 'beehive' for the family to go for a week. This put a funny picture in my head and I thought how many pictures words can make. He went on to explain that a 'beehive' was a fiver – Cockney rhyming slang for 'five'. There were lots of comments about 'bees' and I thought that the words must have something to do with being busy and working hard. He also talked a lot about 'saving the coppers' and his 'Post Office savings book'. All of this really interested me because his language was colourful and showed very clearly how much people were focused on saving when he was a boy.

Conclusion

Uncle Trevor focused on main areas which make his speech interesting and particular to his age and the time which he was talking about. Many of the words were very colourful and some are rarely heard now, even though they were common when he was younger. This shows how spoken language changes very quickly, especially now when there are so many more things like television and the internet to interest people. It was particularly interesting that his language really focused on the points which were interesting to him and this is when he became very lively and started using a more imaginative vocabulary. This shows how powerful our language actually is.

Teacher's comments

There are many positive qualities: noticing the focus on certain topics of words; commenting on changes over time; commenting on the effects of the chosen language and being able to place the memories in the context of when Great-uncle Trevor was young.

This piece shows understanding of the use of language and the context.

It is beginning to explore. More could be made of this by looking in detail at the origins of some of the words and how they have changed over time in spoken language – for example, the phrase 'saving the coppers' could have been explored in more depth.

There is very little analysis of language use. The focus tends to be on the use of specific words or phrases rather then on the context in which these were used.

Spoken genres

This topic area focuses on how language works in different situations and for different reasons.

You will be asked to choose a topic and complete one task from this area. The key words for this topic will be 'how' is something 'represented', and 'investigate'.

- **How** encourages you to explore what the writers are doing to make something real to an audience. This is why it is linked with **represent** – this means that the language stands for something. It might represent the people of suburban Manchester (*Coronation Street*). What you are being asked to show your teacher is 'how' this is done.

- **Investigate** means that you will need to explore and examine the topic area you choose and share this in your written work.

Here is a sample task from this topic area. Remember, your teacher will be looking for your understanding of the work and your ability to analyse, explore and explain what you have discovered.

> 2   By viewing the same event on different television programmes, investigate ways in which spoken language can change the meaning and power of a news story.

Activity

2

a Read Text B, an example of **part of** a student response to Question 2, a task in the topic area of spoken genres, and the teacher's comments that follow.

b Take the words and phrases that are quoted in this exemplar and listed opposite.

For each one, analyse its meaning and its likely effect on the viewer:

- hero
- cult figure
- violent gang
- vicious pre-meditated attack.

Introduction

The news has recently been full of the great train robbery and its most famous robber, Ronnie Biggs. Different television news programmes have presented him in different ways, reflecting how he is seen by members of the public. In this case he is seen either as a hero or a baddie, even after so much time. It is interesting how the selected detail and the language used can make such a difference to the final story and the impression the viewer is given.

Example paragraphs

Ronnie Biggs has been famous for years as the great train robber. Using the word 'great' has more links with wonderful and brilliant than it does with big. This also comes out when he is spoken about on the news. Some people seem to really admire him and use words such as 'hero' and 'cult figure' to describe him. He is seen as being 'greatly admired'. These are strongly positive words and seem to say that he is some form of super hero who we should look up to and respect. Words like this are normally used to describe a film or pop star and therefore open up a wholly different area of thought in the viewers' minds.

He is not, however, presented in the same way on all television programmes; some have been describing him as part of a 'violent gang' and talking about a 'vicious, pre-meditated attack'. They speak about him showing 'no remorse'. Description such as these show very negative view of him. The differences in these words show that there is no middle area; people feel very strongly one way or another about what he has done and about him being let out.

This shows the power of the television media and how they can use words to manipulate their viewers' thoughts. This can also be seen in different styles of newspapers, the tabloids and broadsheets, but seems somehow more powerful when it is spoken. It is almost as though the power of the spoken word is greater because it is there and does not really require any effort to absorb it; even if you are not really concentrating, and the news is on, the words are forming in your mind.

Conclusion

These points show that television news programmes use language to almost tell us how to think. By changing words and the focus of the words, they are able to make us think and see things in completely different ways. Collections of words can be used to change how we think and then our reactions to things which are happening in the world. It is also necessary to conclude that because of the more invasive nature of spoken language entering our worlds more easily, the spoken word is much more powerful than the written word.

Teacher's comments

The student has chosen distinct differences between the two news reports and explained them well.

Good understanding is shown.

The student is very aware of the power of language and the key differences and effects between spoken and written language. The illustration of the differences between the television news and the printed news of newspapers is used to very good effect. There is evidence of a confident analysis and reflection and a growing awareness of the way in which language is adapted and used for specific purposes.

There are some really clever observations in here which the student explores well. There is, however, a need to analyse language use (and its associations) in more detail.

Multi-modal talk

This topic allows you to explore and explain things such as instant messaging and text-speak. It is an area that is fast-moving and literally evolving as it is used.

You will be asked to choose a topic and complete only one task from this area. The key words for this topic will be 'how', relating to the 'practicalities' of the actual 'communication'.

- **How** relates to exactly what is done in this language to allow people to chat with one another.
- **Practicalities** are the actual facts about how people communicate when it is not face to face.
- **Communication** is what we do when we share information with each other.

Here is a sample task from this topic area. Remember, your teacher will be looking for your understanding of the work and your ability to analyse, explore and explain what you have discovered.

---

3   What are the differences between messaging/texting and normal written communication? How do these differences make messaging/texting closer to spoken rather than written language?

Activity

3

a Read Text C, an example of **part of** a student response to Question 3, a task in the topic area of Multi-modal talk, and the teacher's comments that follow.

b Take one or two others' text-speak terms. Write a paragraph that shows your understanding of the terminology and its effects.

Ⓒ

Introduction

Differences in why messaging or texting are used means that there are differences in words used and how those words are spelt. There is also no need for punctuation in messaging or texting. Messaging or texting is normally used between friends and not for more formal communications. This means that there is more room for a relaxed style. Multi-modal talk is exciting in that it is a fast evolving method of communication which, by its very nature of immediate communication, is adaptable and open to adaptation by multiple users. There is no rule book for this method of communication and, as a result, it is 'owned' and operated by a community which is unafraid of frequent adaptation to meet ever-changing needs.

Example paragraphs

One of the main differences between messaging or texting and normal written communication is that it can be quite short and almost 'rude', not only in terms of content, but also in terms of structure. This is something which is not really considered in other areas of study in this unit. There is no use of formal address and no specific control of punctuation. In removing these controls, elements of social control which assure the etiquette of 'normal' written language are removed; this method of communication, whilst written, moves even closer to its origins in youth speak, alternative language cultures and slang.

SH (stuff happens), PONA (person of no account) and NMP (not my problem) are three examples of the apparent 'rudeness' and shortness of this mode of communication. They are short and snappy, something which you might find in a general conversation moving quickly through many different subjects as young people chat. The sharpness is also something which would be unusual in a normal, polite conversation. This removal of formalities and structure is probably one of the many reasons why some adults are reluctant to involve themselves in the worlds of messaging and texting.

Conclusion

Messaging and texting are communications which are best described as somewhere between writing and speech. They have many points in common with speech, including the speed of communication; but can be confusing and certainly not as clear as speech. The lack of punctuation and alternative speech ordering brings messaging and texting much closer to a spoken rather than written language. It is the existence of these differences which enables the language to evolve more quickly, and also to remove it ever further from the ownership of society as a whole, and into the hands of select age groups and categories. The jargon of texting and messaging is removed from the mainstream precisely because of its almost risqué and unpredictable nature which is constantly being reinvented.

Teacher's comments

There is a great deal of detail in this answer. Interesting areas are covered and the student shows a sustained and at times perceptive analysis.

There is evidence of a sophisticated analysis and evaluation of key issues. The student is not afraid to theorise and explore.

The depth of analysis demonstrates perception. In these paragraphs the student has chosen to explore a little in detail rather than covering a large number of points with little detail.

This is a clear, detailed and controlled response.

Check your learning

In this chapter you have:

- learned about how spoken language fits into your GCSE English Language course
- learned more about the ways you can achieve high marks in this part of the course.

Punctuation

Capital letters

Capital letters are used:

- At the start of each sentence.

  He asked her where the nearest shop was. She told him it was about two miles further on.

- For the personal pronoun 'I'.

  If I arrive early I'll get the caretaker to unlock the door.

- For the first letter of proper nouns (people's names, place names, names of days and months).

  On tuesday Karen went to Newcastle but found out the shop she wanted didn't open until September.

- For the first letter of titles of people and organisations.

  They asked the Head Teacher, Mrs Clasper, to attend the meeting with Social Services.

- For people's initials and abbreviations.

  Here are Dr and Mrs Husain from the USA.

- At the beginning of a new piece of direct speech.

  Sadly, he replied, 'They didn't tell us where they were going'.

- For the main words in titles of books, plays, games, films, etc.

  He thought that The Lord of the Rings was still the best film he'd seen.

Full stops

- The main use of a full stop is to mark the end of a sentence.

  The street was dark and silent. No one spoke a word.

- They are also sometimes used to show abbreviations.

  etc.

Question marks

- The main use of the question mark is to show questions in normal prose writing and in direct speech.

  'Who knows what this is?' the teacher asked.

Exclamation marks

- These are used mainly to mark shouts or exclamations, or to show that something is entertaining or worthy of special note.

  'Stop!' shouted the woman.

Activity

1 Decide which of the following sentences should end in a full stop, a question mark or an exclamation mark. Explain your choices to another student.

Have you ever read a book you just couldn't put down_ Well, if not, you need to try *Smokescreen_* It's the action book with everything needed to keep you on the edge of your seat until the very last page_ Like all the other books in this series, this one's a winner_ Read it now_

Commas

Commas make it easier for the reader to make sense of a sentence. They can be used in different ways:

- Commas separate items in a list.

  If you explore this area you will discover that you can go swimming, play football in the sports centre, visit a range of shops and take advantage of the multiplex cinema.

- Commas mark off extra information.

  Alf Johnson, 32, claimed he had bought the car the day before. Mr Johnson, a father of four, was unable to show a receipt and Judge Christine Carr, sitting at Lincoln County Court, found him guilty of theft.

- Commas separate parts of a sentence.

  Although the bus was late, he still got to school on time.

  Commas mark off the spoken words in direct speech.

  'Come with me,' she whispered quietly to the crying child.

- Commas mark the clauses in a sentence.

  Having been to the shops, Pat decided that, while she still had time, she would get some studying done before the children got home.

Learning how to use commas is the first step. Using them well requires effort. To help you to achieve this:

- Take note, when reading, of how other writers use them.
- Read your own writing aloud to help you work out where you need to pause to make sense of it. Decide whether you need to place a comma at this spot.

Activity

2 The following extract is taken from a computer manual. Read the extract and decide where you need to place capital letters, full stops and commas to help the reader. Copy the extract and punctuate it appropriately.

your computer can catch a virus from disks a local network or the internet just as a cold virus attaches itself to a human host a computer virus attaches itself to a program and just like a cold it is contagious like viruses worms replicate themselves however instead of spreading from file to file they spread from computer to computer infecting an entire system

Compare your copy of the extract with a partner's. Make any changes which you think are helpful in conveying the meaning effectively.

Colons

The colon has three main uses:

- It introduces a list.

> She packed a bag with the few items she owned: an old pair of jeans, two school shirts and the precious photograph of her sister.

- It introduces a lengthy piece of direct speech or a quotation.

> He looked at her and said: 'This isn't easy for either of us. But we knew, when we started, there would be difficulties ahead. Well, this is one of those difficulties.'

- It introduces an idea for which the first part of the sentence has prepared the reader.

> The sermon contained only one message: do as I say, not as I do.

Semi-colon

The semi-colon has two main uses:

- It separates items in a list, when the items are too long to be separated by commas.

> The class raised the grand total by staging a wide range of events: a night-time sponsored walk in the Brecon Beacons; daily cake stalls throughout November; abseiling down the city centre multi-storey car park; and, to the great delight of their parents, silent weekend sleepovers.

- It takes the place of a full stop between sentences which are closely linked in meaning.

> The first book was more interesting with tales of mystery and adventure; the second one was just plain boring.

If used well, the semi-colon can be very effective but you should avoid using it too much. When reading, note how professional writers use the semi-colon and learn from their example.

Apostrophes

The apostrophe has two main uses:

- To show when one or more letters have been missed out (omission). The apostrophe is placed in the exact spot where the letter or letters that have been missed out would have been.
- To show that something belongs to someone or something (possession). We rarely say 'the house of my friend'. We would say 'my friend's house'. The apostrophe is used to show that the house belongs to the friend. The 'friend' is the possessor.
  - When the possessor is singular, as in the case of 'friend', place the apostrophe after the word and add an 's'.
    the toys of the child → the child's toys

Activity

3 The bullet points above explain and exemplify the use of the colon and the semi-colon. For each bullet point, create your own example.

we are → we're	is not → isn't
they have → they've	he is → he's
Susan is → Susan's	I would → I'd

Make a note

Note and learn the following:

won't means will not

shan't means shall not

- When the possessor is plural and already ends in an 's' add an apostrophe.
  the bags of the boys → the boys' bags
- When the possessor is plural but does not end in an 's' add an apostrophe and an 's'.
  the homes of the women → the women's homes.

Make a note

The possessive words **yours**, **his**, **hers**, **its**, **ours**, **whose** and **theirs** are *not* written with an apostrophe.

Activities

4   Use the apostrophe to shorten the underlined words in the following message:

> <u>I would</u> really like to join you on your birthday. Unfortunately, <u>I have</u> a meeting planned for the same date. <u>I will</u> try to leave early so I <u>should not</u> be too late. <u>It will</u> be good to see you again. Hope <u>you are</u> keeping well and <u>have not</u> had too many problems with work.

5   Rewrite the following passage placing apostrophes correctly to show possession:

> Johns mother told him not to go to Peters house during the weeks holiday. However, he borrowed his brothers bike and went straight there. There was no one in, though the younger childrens toys were out on the lawn. Peters window was open and John climbed through it to wait for him. Unfortunately, he was spotted by the neighbours dog and then by the neighbour.

Inverted commas

Inverted commas are also sometimes referred to as speech marks or quotation marks. Most punctuation marks sit on the line of the page. Inverted commas hang in the air. They can be single, or double.

'single inverted commas'

"double inverted commas"

There are two main uses for inverted commas.

- When a writer uses a speaker's actual words. This is known as direct speech.
- When a writer is quoting from another text.

Activity

6   Examine the extract from a story below. Match these rules for the use of inverted commas to examples in the extract:

- The spoken words are contained within inverted commas.
- Each new piece of speech starts with a capital letter.
- Each piece of speech ends with a punctuation mark.
- A new line is started each time there is a new speaker.

> Anna and a group of friends arrived late for the monthly meeting.
>
> 'I'm sorry,' said the receptionist, 'but the meeting has started. I can't let you in.'
>
> 'There really shouldn't be a problem,' Anna said. 'We're only five minutes late.'
>
> 'Rules are rules,' the receptionist replied frostily.

7

The student below is writing about Philip Larkin's poem 'Born Yesterday' in the AQA Anthology. Study the student's writing and the annotations that surround it.

Larkin wrote this poem for a newborn girl who he refers to as a 'tightly-folded bud'. This image reminds us that her life has yet to unfold. He wants to wish something for her but wants to avoid the 'usual stuff' that 'they will all wish you'. His wish is an unusual one. He wishes that she should be 'ordinary'. In doing so he believes he is wishing for:

'Nothing uncustomary
To pull you off your balance'.

Quotation marks are placed before and after the words taken from the poem

More than one quotation can be used in the same sentence

A quotation can be used to give emphasis to a particular word or phrase

A colon can be used to introduce a longer quotation

8

Read the next few lines of the same student's writing. The quotations have been underlined. Copy the lines, adding inverted commas and a colon where needed.

It is as though Larkin believes that <u>being beautiful</u> can be <u>unworkable</u>. In contrast being <u>not ugly, not good-looking</u> can bring greater happiness, perhaps because you put more effort into being happy. It is for this reason that he wishes she should

<u>Have, like other women,</u>
<u>An average of talents.</u>

Spelling

Syllables

A syllable is a unit of sound. A word might contain:

- one syllable

  ❶
  mud

- many syllables

  ❶ ❷ ❸ ❹
  en/ter/tain/ment

  ❶ ❷ ❸ ❹
  po/li/ti/cal

Breaking a word into syllables and sounding each syllable aloud will help you spell the word correctly. For example, saying the word diff/i/cult aloud reminds you of the letter i in the middle.

Activity

9 Copy the words in the box on the right. Break them into syllables, using a forward slash (/) and numbers as shown above. Say them aloud to make sure you have identified the syllables correctly.

Ask a partner to test you on spelling the six words, without looking at them.

extraordinary	parliament
environment	reminiscent
conscientiously	necessarily

Suffixes

A suffix is a letter or group of letters added to the end of a root word, which changes the meaning of the word, for example:

-ly   -able   -ed   -ful   -ing   -ment   -ness   -ity

In most cases you simply add the suffix to the root word, for example:

spend → spending   care → careful   appoint → appointment

Make a note

There are some exceptions you need to learn:

If the word ends in a *c*, add *k* when you add a suffix beginning with *e*, *i* or *y*

For example: picnic → picni**ck**ed

When adding the suffix *-ful* or *-ly* to words that end in a consonant followed by *y*, change the *y* to *i*.

For example: plenty → plent**i**ful   happy → happ**i**ly

When a suffix begins with a *vowel* or a *y* and the root word ends in *e*, drop the *e*.

For example: writ**e** → writing   eas**e** → easy   fam**e** → famous

But when the root word ends in *ee*, *oe* or *ye*, you keep the final *e*.

For example: agr**ee** → agr**ee**able   can**oe** → can**oe**ing

When you add the suffix *able* to a root word that ends in *ce* or *ge* you keep the final *e*.

For example: noti**ce** → noti**ce**able   chan**ge** → chan**ge**able

Consonants are sometimes doubled when you add *-ar*, *-er*, *-ed* or *-ing* to a word that has one syllable and ends with a short vowel and any consonant except *y* or *x*.

For example: run → ru**nn**ing   hit → hi**tt**ing   beg → be**gg**ar   rob → ro**bb**er

If the word ends in *y* or *x* do not double the consonant.

For example: play → playing   tax → taxed

Activity

10 Look again at the list of commonly used suffixes at the top of this page. What new words can you make from these words by adding one or more suffixes to them?

wonder	panic	reason	make
play	dread	tan	challenge
debate	favour	beauty	guarantee
slice	astonish	fax	tap

Prefixes

A prefix is a group of letters that can be added to the beginning of a word to change its meaning.

spell → misspell   appear → disappear   happy → unhappy

Activity

11 Some of the most common prefixes are listed in the first column below. Match them to the base words in the second column to make new words. Some base words work with more than one prefix, for example, disappear, reappear. The base words are in groups of ten. Work through one group before moving on to the next. See how many new words you can form in five minutes.

Prefix	Base word				
re mis in sub im anti ir dis un	1	behave like	place organise	trust obedient	order responsible	honest kind
	2	social healthy	clockwise fortunate	aware form	able insure	conscious produce
	3	effective polite	equality possible	secure rational	proper regular	material standard

Combining prefixes and suffixes

Knowing how to use prefixes and suffixes correctly will help you to spell a wide range of words accurately. Study the examples in this list.

success	honest	satisfy
successful	honesty	satisfied
successfully	honestly	satisfying
unsuccessful	dishonest	satisfiable
unsuccessfully	dishonesty	satisfaction
	dishonestly	satisfactory
		satisfyingly
		unsatisfied
		dissatisfy
		unsatisfactory

Activity

12 Use the chart below to help you make as many words as you can using the root words, a prefix and one or more suffixes.

Prefix	Root word	Suffix
re	agree	able
mis	fair	ment
in	reverse	ly
sub	sense	ed
im	perfect	ful
anti	skill	ing
ir		ion
dis		ible
un		less

Plurals

Plural means more than one.

For most plural forms you simply add 's' to the singular forms.

book → books   computer → computers

Make a note

There are some exceptions you need to learn:

■ When the singular form ends in -s, -x, -ch or -sh, add -es.
For example: bus → buses   tax → taxes   church → churches   flash → flashes

■ If a word ends in -y and has a **consonant** before the last letter change the y to an i and add es.
For example: party → parties   fly → flies

■ If a word ends in -o you usually just add s. However, there are a few commonly used words that need es to make them plural:

tomato → tomatoes   potato → potatoes   hero → heroes

■ If a word ends in -f or -fe you usually change the -f or -fe to -ves.
For example: wolf → wolves   knife → knives

But there are a few exceptions:

roof → roofs   chief → chiefs   reef → reefs

There are some irregular plurals:

child → children	man → men	formula → formulae
sheep → sheep	mouse → mice	crisis → crises
tooth → teeth	person → people	stimulus → stimuli

Activity

13   Using the above rules, write the plurals of the following words.
There are a few exceptions included in the list.

branch   holiday   Christmas
beach   radius   lady   atlas   inch   woman
blush   comedy   cactus   takeaway
hoax   witch   berry   bonus   plus
essay   gas   arch

Homonyms

Homonyms are words that have the same spelling or pronunciation as another, but a different meaning or origin.

There are two kinds of homonym:

- Words that have the same *spelling* as another but a different meaning. The pronunciation may be:

  - the same

    > calf (as in lower part of leg)
    > calf (as in offspring of cow)

  - different

    > lead (as in the metal)
    > lead (as in directing)

- Words that have the same *sound* as another but different meaning and different spelling. This is the most common type.

  > read/reed   pair/pear

Take extra care when using a computer spellchecker. It will only tell you if you have an incorrect spelling, not if you have chosen the wrong word.

Activities

14 The words below are all homonyms. Copy them and next to each one write one word that sounds the same but is spelt differently.

sea	pour	great	rowed	way	piece	profit
soul	lone	pair	hole	hare	hymn	ate

15 There are hundreds of homonyms. Make your own list of at least ten more examples.

Using a dictionary

A dictionary is a very useful tool. It helps you to:

- find the meaning of a word you do not know
- pronounce the word correctly
- spell the word correctly.

For example:

pronunciation   *meaning*

community (say **k'mew**ni-tee) *noun*
Any group living in one place or having common interests.

Heinemann English Dictionary (annotated)

correct spelling

The more you use a dictionary, the quicker you become in finding words.

How a dictionary is organised

A dictionary is organised in alphabetical order. All the words that start with the letter 'a' are grouped together, followed by all the words that start with the letter 'b', and so on through the alphabet.

It is not just the first letter of the word that counts. When you have several words starting with the same two, three or even more letters, then you have to go further into each word to find its alphabetical order.

When you want to find a particular word you should look at the words in bold at the top of the pages. These are the first and last words on that page. They are called guide words. If the word you are looking for comes between these two words alphabetically, then you are on the correct page.

If you are not sure how the word is spelt, use what you know about words and letter combinations to make an intelligent guess. You may not know how to spell the word 'poltergeist', but by saying the word aloud you would be able to work out the first three or four letters – enough to enable you to find it in the dictionary.

Activities

16   Place the following words in each group in alphabetical order.

> drastic   icing   best   public   free   money   risk   envelope   trial   silver
> ready   rush   rattle   reason   ring   robot   range   roller   rider   red
> grief   grind   grit   grill   grime   grid   grizzly   grin   grip   grievance

17   Here are four words and below them the guide words from four pages in a dictionary. Which page would you turn to in order to find each word?

> skull   skate   skyscraper   skill

| Page 966   **sixteen | sketch** | Page 968   **skin-tight | skylark** |
| Page 967   **skew | skint** | Page 969   **skylight | slap** |

18   Find six words in your dictionary that are new to you. Write the words replacing some of the letters with blank spaces. Swap words with another student. See who is quickest at working out the missing letters and finding the meanings of the words.

Glossary

Alliteration: the deliberate repetition of consonant sounds at the beginning of words to gain a particular effect.

Audience: the intended audience of a text is the reader for whom the text is written.

Bias: a tendency towards a particular belief that can exclude other opinions.

Chronological order: the order in which things happen.

Collective noun: a single word for a group of people or things.

Complex sentence: a sentence made up of a main clause and subordinate clauses.

Deduce: draw conclusions based on details given.

Dialect: a variety of a language used in a particular area or region.

Emotive use of language: this is used to make the reader react in a particular way (e.g. feel surprised or shocked).

Evaluate: when you evaluate something you make a series of judgements on it based on evidence.

Exclamation: an abrupt, forceful utterance.

Fact: something that can be proved to be true.

Filler: a sound, word or phrase used to fill a gap (e.g. 'er', 'like', 'you know').

First person: a narrator uses the first person when referring to him- or herself. Words such as 'I', 'me' and 'mine' indicate the first person singular and 'we', 'us' and 'our' indicate the first person plural.

Format: the way a text is arranged or presented, e.g. as a leaflet, letter, poster. Sometimes also referred to as form.

Idiolect: the term used to describe an individual's distinct language features.

Imperative: expressing a command.

Infer: work out things based on details given.

Interpret: work out the meaning or significance of a text.

Irony: the humorous or mildly sarcastic use of words to imply the opposite of what is being said.

Main clause: a clause that contains a subject and a verb and makes complete sense on its own.

Metaphor: a description of something as though it were something else.

Mode: usually used to mean whether a text is written or spoken.

Opinion: a point of view that cannot be proved to be true or untrue.

Perspective: the writer's point of view.

Presentational features: features such as colour, illustrations, font types and sizes which are used to enhance the visual appearance of a text.

Purpose: the intended purpose of a text is the reason for which it is being produced.

Rhetorical question: a question that is asked to draw attention to a particular point.

Scanning: if you are looking for a particular piece of information, your eyes move quickly over the whole text until they focus on the key words that locate the detail you are looking for. This type of reading is called scanning.

Simile: a direct comparison of one thing with another.

Sociolect: a particular use of language specific to a social group.

Standard English: the variety of English most used in public communication, particularly in writing.

Subject: the person or thing who performs the action of the verb.

Subject–verb agreement: where the correct form of the verb is used to match the subject.

Subordinate clause: a clause that does not make complete sense on its own and is always used with a main clause.

Tense: the form of the verb that indicates time.

Third person: when telling a story about someone or something else, a writer uses the third person. Words such as 'he', 'she', 'it', 'his', 'hers', 'its', indicate the third-person singular and 'they', 'them', 'theirs', indicate the third-person plural.

Tone: the mood or atmosphere created.

Transcript: a written record of a speech or conversation.

Verb: the part of speech that expresses an action (e.g. runs, walks) or explains a state (e.g. is, becomes).